Therefore, Choose

Governors'
AWARD
presented to

Alison Sanderson

SAINT MICHAEL'S
CHURCH OF ENGLAND SCHOOL
CHORLEY
LANCASHIRE

October 1986

Success in Commerce

Success Studybooks

Accounting and Costing
Accounting and Costing: Problems and Projects
Biology
Book-keeping and Accounts
British History 1760–1914
British History since 1914
Business Calculations
Chemistry
Commerce
Commerce: West African Edition
Economic Geography
Economics
Economics: West African Edition
Electronics
Elements of Banking
European History 1815–1941
Financial Accounting
Financial Accounting: Questions and Answers
Geography: Human and Regional
Geography: Physical and Mapwork
Insurance
Investment
Law
Management: Personnel
Mathematics
Nutrition
Office Practice
Organic Chemistry
Principles of Accounting
Principles of Accounting: Answer Book
Statistics
Twentieth Century World Affairs

Success in
COMMERCE

Second Edition

Derek Lobley, B.A.
Department of Business and Management Studies
Barking College of Technology

John Murray

To David and John

First published 1975
Reprinted (revised) 1977
Reprinted (revised) 1978
Reprinted (revised) 1980
Second edition 1982
Reprinted (revised) 1983
Reprinted (revised) 1984
Reprinted (revised) 1985

Typeset by Inforum Ltd, Portsmouth
Printed in Hong Kong
by Wing King Tong Co. Ltd.

ISBN 0 7195 3962 5

Foreword

This book is intended for anyone who wants a basic course in commerce. It has been written with students working for 16+ examinations particularly in mind. The commerce aspects of courses such as BTEC General 'World of Work', RSA 'Background to Business' (Stage I) and LCC 'Structure of Business' and 'Background to Business' are also covered.

Each Unit is followed by a number of exercises. First, a series of short questions which can be used for self-testing; they can also be useful as a basis for class discussion. Second, there are questions which need essay-style answers such as those which are required by the majority of public examinations in commerce. Third, there are, where appropriate, some suggestions for projects and assignments.

While *Success in Commerce* provides a self-contained course in itself, it is likely that some students will wish to investigate certain topics in more detail. To help them, a brief Suggested Further Reading list is included at the end of the book.

Commerce is a fast-moving subject and the student should try to keep up to date with new developments, such as changing legislation and Acts of Parliament. Newspapers, especially those concerned with finance, economics and business, are probably the best source of information, and it is a good idea to keep a scrapbook, or files of press cuttings, remembering to write the date and the name of the newspaper on any cutting taken. These press cuttings are invaluable when preparing work or compiling a project or assignment.

For this new edition the text has been thoroughly revised and updated. Tables and diagrams have been compiled from the most recently available data, for example, while changes in the law as it affects various aspects of commerce have been incorporated. Any textbook covering topics which may fluctuate daily as a result of current events can become out of date on the details of some points. However, the broad patterns of commerce remain the same, as do the principles and procedures which we study in this book.

D.L.

Acknowledgments

In writing this book I have been grateful for the assistance of a number of organizations and people.

All tables are based on publications of Her Majesty's Stationery Office and are taken from the following sources: Department of Employment, 1981 (Table 10.1); *Financial Statistics, 1981* (Tables 10.2, 11.1, 12.1, 12.2); *Annual Abstract of Statistics, 1981* (Table 17.1); *UK Balance of Payments Yearbook, 1981* (Tables 21.1, 21.2, 21.3); *National Income and Expenditure, 1981* (Tables 22.1, 22.2).

Photographs are reproduced by courtesy of The Post Office (Figs. 15.1, 15.2); The National Freight Corporation (Figs. 17.1, 17.2); Shell Photographic Service (Fig. 17.3); National Westminster Bank PLC (Figs. 11.2, 11.3, 11.4, 11.5, 11.6, 11.7, 11.12); Lloyds Bank Plc (Figs. 11.1, 11.11, 11.14); Bank Education Service (Figs. 11.9, 11.10).

I am grateful to Trefor McElroy and Stephen Green who read and criticized the book in its early stages. My wife undertook the arduous task of typing the manuscript, for which she deserves especial thanks.

D.L.

Contents

viii Contents

x Contents

Contents xi

xii Contents

Unit One

The Commercial World

1.1 Introduction

Did you buy a newspaper today? If so, did you stop to think how it reached you? Like so many of the things we use, the newspaper is taken for granted. We read it and cast it aside perhaps within an hour, with scarcely a thought for the complex network of industry and enterprise needed to bring it to us punctually and regularly. Hundreds of people working in different occupations combine, often unknowingly, in producing a newspaper. For this reason, the production of a newspaper is a good illustration of the complexities of *commerce*.

The first requirement for producing a newspaper is the paper. This may be manufactured in Britain or overseas, but in either case it will mean a large number of workers undertaking different specialized jobs. Next, this paper must be delivered to the site where the newspaper is produced. A large number of commercial functions are already involved: *transport* must be arranged to deliver the goods; they must be *insured* while in transit; financial transactions take place (the newsprint manufacturer may have to deliver the goods before he is paid or the purchaser may have to pay in advance), and the *banks* may be called upon to make loans; *marketing* facilities including *advertising* will probably be used; and the newsprint will certainly have been held in a *warehouse* pending its dispatch for use.

Meanwhile, other workers produce the other physical components of a newspaper – the ink and the presses, for example. This means more commercial activity, like financing the purchase of machinery which may cost hundreds of thousands of pounds.

Leaving aside these physical components, we now think about the way the news itself is gathered. Journalists all over the world have contributions to make to a single edition of a newspaper, so we can immediately see that means of *communication* are vital. Without these communication facilities news might be weeks or even months out of date before being published. More contributions arrive from photographers, advertisers and many other sources. When all these individual contributions have been received, teams of editors and sub-editors have to prepare copy to be set, while designers plan the layout of the paper. Then the printers and their staff – some highly skilled, others less skilled – get to work. When the papers roll off the presses they have to be packed before they can be delivered by road, rail and air transport to local centres. There, wholesalers, retailers and street corner newsvendors provide the final links in the chain.

Before this stage is reached the skills of advertising agencies and of radio and television broadcasting may have been used to attract our attention to the forthcoming edition. And by the time we come to read it, production of tomorrow's edition will be well under way.

The whole process of the production of goods, from the extraction of raw materials from the earth to the sale of the finished product to the consumer, constitutes the broad study of *economics*. *Commerce* is concerned with one section of this study: it is the system by which raw materials are distributed to industry, and the finished products to consumers. We must look briefly at the economic system as a whole, in order to see exactly where commerce fits into the economic picture.

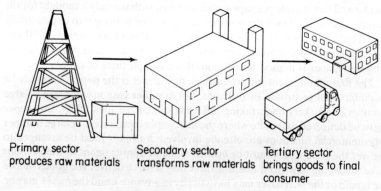

Primary sector
produces raw materials

Secondary sector
transforms raw materials

Tertiary sector
brings goods to final
consumer

Fig. 1.1 The economic system

1.2 The Economic System

Every day in Britain approximately 23 million people go to work. What is the object of their being at work? The obvious answer is that they want to earn an income, but this is not an end in itself. They need the income to buy *goods* and *services* of all kinds, and this is their real reason for working. The combined efforts of these millions of workers convert raw materials into forms that are useful and valuable to the whole population. In this way they are helping to produce the goods and services which ensure a high standard of living for the community in general. As a rule production consists of three main stages, as Fig. 1.1 shows.

(a) Primary Production

This is the first stage of production and includes workers employed in mining, quarrying, forestry and farming – the *extractive* industries. The output of such workers, especially those in mines and quarries, is likely to be in the wrong place or the wrong condition to meet the needs of the final consumer. (There are a few exceptions, of course, such as the fruit grower or poultry keeper, who can sell his products – eggs, apples, strawberries – to the final consumer at the farm gate.) However, most of the output of primary production is in a raw unusable state and has to be moved on to the *secondary sector*.

(b) Secondary Production
In this secondary stage of production people working in all kinds of manufacturing processes transform raw materials into the thousands of goods and products that we need. *Manufacturing* once meant literally *making by hand*, but today a great deal of the work is performed by machinery, as a visit to almost any local factory will show you. It is unlikely, however, that raw materials will go in at one end of the factory and come out as finished products at the other. It is much more probable that they will be turned into semi-manufactured goods in one factory, then sent on to another to be finished off or incorporated into a larger or more complex product. While this is happening the value of the materials is increasing as they are being converted into more useful forms.

(c) Tertiary Production
The process of production may still be incomplete, even when the goods have passed through the secondary stage, for they will almost certainly be in the wrong place for the majority of consumers. A factory in the north of England, for instance, produces goods which are destined to reach consumers all over the country – north, south, east and west. This is where the activities of the *tertiary sector*, the third stage of production, are needed, when the goods are transferred from the factory to the consumer.

It is the tertiary sector that we mean when we speak of *commerce*. Workers in transport, finance, insurance and advertising, as well as wholesaling, retailing and the Post Office, are all commercial workers, involved in getting the goods to the final consumer.

1.3 Commercial Occupations

The main purpose of commercial activity is to facilitate the trading or exchange of goods. This trading may be on an international scale – importing and exporting – or a domestic one. With domestic trade the pattern is always changing, but the basic framework is shown in Fig. 1.2. From producers, goods find their way to wholesalers, whose principal function is to buy in large quantities and resell to retailers in smaller quantities. Many of our groceries reach us in this way. In many cases, however, the traditional framework is loosening and the functions of wholesalers and retailers are now less clearly separated. We shall examine them in more detail in Units 2–5.

However efficient producers, wholesalers and retailers may be individually, they can do nothing without the following *aids to trade* provided by the *service industries*, which we shall be considering in more detail later in this book.

4 Success in Commerce

(a) Transport

The importance of transport in getting goods to the right place at the right time is self-evident. When large quantities of goods are produced in one place everything depends on the suppliers of transport – by land, air and sea – getting them safely transferred to the consumer (see Unit 17).

(b) Finance

The machinery that helps to produce and distribute the goods has to be bought in the first place. The goods themselves are often sold on credit (where the purchaser receives the goods now and pays later); in any case, there may be a long interval between the purchase of the raw materials and the sale of the finished product at a profit. Therefore the producer or purchaser will almost certainly need to borrow money. This is where the *banks* play an important part in providing the necessary finance, and making it possible for trading to take place. In Units 6, 11 and 12 we examine the ways in which money can be borrowed for different purposes and for different periods of time.

The need for cash to pay for everyday items such as food, fares and clothes is even more fundamental, and we shall look at the way in which money has developed, and is made available to the customer through the banks, in Units 10 and 11.

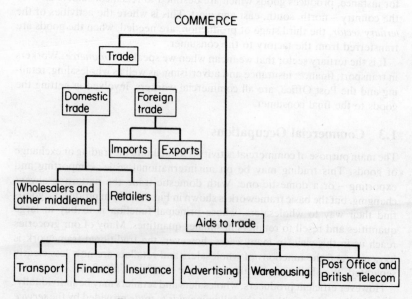

Fig. 1.2 Commercial occupations

(c) Insurance

There is always a danger that goods will be accidentally destroyed or damaged, either during their production or in transit to the consumer. Such accidents could be extremely expensive to producers, but in many cases the insurance companies are prepared to offer compensation in return for the regular payment of relatively small sums of money, known as *premiums*. The number of businessmen prepared to send their goods by air or sea would be much reduced if the goods were not covered by insurance. Thus insurance helps to overcome another obstacle to trade (see Unit 18).

(d) Advertising

More goods are sold if potential customers are told about them by *advertising*. Many people feel that advertising adds to the cost of goods and is an unjustifiable expense but, as we shall see in Unit 16, it has a very important, even a cost-reducing, role to play in commercial life. (So too do many other forms of communication.)

(e) Warehousing

At various stages of their journey to the consumer, goods need to be stored, either because transport is not immediately available, or because the demand for them is uneven or seasonal. Here warehousing is necessary, and this is yet another essential function of commerce.

(f) The Post Office and British Telecom

Businessmen have to communicate with each other at all these stages. The Post Office enables them to do this through the mail services and British Telecommunications (which trades under the name British Telecom) through various forms of telecommunications, as we shall see in Unit 15.

1.4   Direct Services

In most of the occupations we mentioned above, the workers all co-operate to provide the final consumer with a finished product. But in some occupations the object is not to provide consumers with goods but to offer them a direct service. Teachers and doctors are examples of this. They contribute to production by providing a better educated and healthier work force than would otherwise exist. Other kinds of direct services include entertainment, provided by actors and professional sportsmen, and security, provided by the police.

1.5   Division of Labour

A large number of different activities or industries exist within each of the three sectors we have discussed. In the tertiary sector, for example, we might speak of the banking industry or the insurance industry. But within each industry there is further specialization, as different firms concentrate on different aspects of the work of the industry. Thus in the banking industry we find not only the familiar banks such as Barclays and National Westminster, offering a large number of facilities to other industries and to consumers, but also the less widely known merchant banks, offering technical services to industry in general (see Units 11 and 12).

There are also further subdivisions, for each firm is divided into departments, and within the departments individual workers have their own specialized jobs. This is the principle of the *division of labour* or specialization, which is the basis of our modern economy. The alternative to this division of labour would be for each family to produce its own goods, not relying at all on the efforts of outsiders. Adam Smith, the great eighteenth-century British economist, first explained the advantages of this principle in his book *The Wealth of Nations*, published in 1776. We summarize the advantages below.

(a) Advantages

(i) Individual workers can concentrate on those jobs to which they are most suited. Thus the accountant can develop his skill without needing to worry about producing food or clothes. These jobs are done by others, who themselves do not have to worry about the intricacies of accountancy.

(ii) Practice makes perfect: once a man has learned a job his skill at it increases. For example, at bicycle factories a skilled man is able to fit and inflate a tyre in 10 seconds.

(iii) Division of labour normally allows a great saving on tools and equipment. Instead of each worker having a complete set of tools, which would be necessary if there were no division of labour, one set can be shared out among the team.

(iv) As the work is broken down into individual tasks it is likely that new and more efficient techniques will be developed.

The result of all these advantages, and the real purpose of the division of labour, is increased efficiency and hence increased output.

(b) Disadvantages

We should not, however, lose sight of the disadvantages that accompany this kind of specialization.

(i) Each part of a factory or an industry depends on the performance of the others. This interdependence means that if there is a breakdown in one section it can quickly spread to other sections, causing delays and sometimes unemployment. A strike by typists processing orders might soon lead to a whole factory temporarily closing down.

(ii) There is a danger of boredom when a worker is performing a simple continuous routine, often hundreds of times a day.

(iii) As machinery becomes more sophisticated it replaces labour, causing unemployment.

(iv) The spread of division of labour normally leads to a decline in craftsmanship. As machinery takes over, output is standardized, and the choice of goods available to consumers is reduced.

1.6 Production

We can now summarize what we mean by production. It is the process by which raw materials are transformed into finished goods to satisfy the requirements of consumers. In addition to being in the right *form*, the goods must be in the right *place* at the right *time* before the process of production is complete. It is wrong, therefore, to think that producers are only those who *make* goods, and that those who do not make anything are unproductive. Without the people who provide essential services, the flow of goods to consumers would be very much reduced.

As economies become more specialized, a larger proportion of workers are employed in the tertiary sector, producing services. This tendency is illustrated in Fig. 1.3, where you can see the relative increase in employment in the service or tertiary sector. Much of this employment is in commercial services, and we shall examine the role of commerce in more detail in following Units.

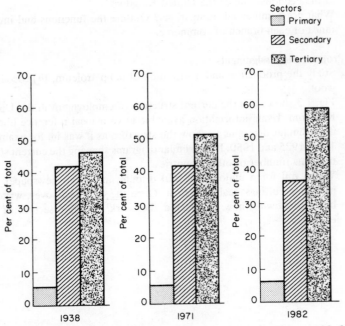

Fig. 1.3   Structure of employment in the United Kingdom, 1938–82

1.7   Questions and Exercises

(a) **Short Answers**
1. Name five occupations found in each of the three sectors of the economy.
2. What is the main purpose of economic and commercial activity?
3. What are the main branches of trade?
4. What are the main aids to trade?
5. What is the main advantage of a system of division of labour?
6. Explain in one sentence what is meant by *direct services*.
7. What is meant by the phrase *division of labour*?
8. Make a list of the disadvantages associated with division of labour.
9. What is meant by *production* in commerce?
10. In what ways are (a) a coal miner, (b) a nurse productive?

(b) **Essay Answers**
1. Select a commodity and show how the division of labour assists its production.
2. What is meant by production? How do commercial occupations contribute to production?
3. Banking and insurance are two branches of commerce. What difficulties would arise for manufacturers and traders if these services did not exist?
4. Compare the importance of manufacturing and commercial occupations in the economic life of the United Kingdom.
5. What are commercial occupations? Outline the functions and importance of each branch of commerce.

(c) **Projects and Assignments**
1. Study the production and distribution of (a) petroleum, (b) cocoa, (c) wool.
2. Fig. 1.3 shows you the current structure of employment in the United Kingdom. Using information available in your local reference library, draw similar diagrams to show the structure as it was in, for example, 1910, 1925 and 1950. Draw similar diagrams showing the current structure in a number of other countries.
3. Watch out for a major industrial dispute, and keep newspaper and magazine cuttings dealing with it. Once the dispute is over, write its history, showing how it affected the work of other sectors of the economy.

Unit Two

The Distribution of Goods from the Producer to the Consumer

2.1 Introduction

The chief effect of the division of labour is that the people working in an industry produce more goods than they themselves need. For example, in 1983 the number of cars produced per worker in Britain was about 14, far more than any individual employee could have produced or needed. It is the function of commerce to ensure that these vehicles reach the people who want them. (Commerce will have already played an important part in their production by providing transport for raw materials and finance for machinery.) There are a number of different routes from the producer to the consumer, and we summarize them in Fig. 2.1.

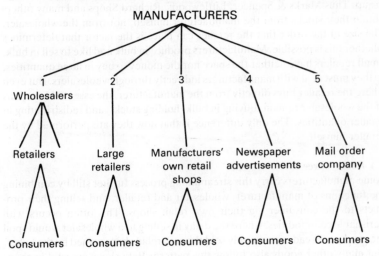

Fig. 2.1 *Routes from producer to consumer*

2.2 The Pattern of Distribution

(a) Route One

This is the traditional and most familiar route. As soon as a manufacturer has produced the goods he sells them in large quantities to the wholesaler, who redistributes them in smaller quantities to a large number of retailers. Small retail grocers obtain the bulk of their supplies in this way. The wholesaler provides a service to the manufacturer by buying in large quantities and relieving him of storage problems, and to the retailer by obtaining goods from a number of different manufacturers and supplying them when required. This method of distribution is important where the demand for the product is seasonal but production takes place throughout the year, as with fireworks or Christmas cards; or where the demand for the product is fairly even throughout the year but, as with many farm crops, output is concentrated into a few weeks. In each case the wholesaler has the important function of balancing supply and demand.

(b) Route Two

Great changes have taken place in the structure of the retail trade, with the rapid development of transport and communications. Retail shops tend to be larger than they were 25 years ago, when the manufacturer-wholesaler-retailer-consumer pattern of trade prevailed. This increase in size has in turn led to changes in the pattern of distribution. It is now quite common for route two to be adopted. Retailers can frequently afford to buy direct from the manufacturer. This is particularly true where the retail shop belongs to a large group. Thus Marks & Spencer, Littlewoods, Richard Shops and many others obtain their stocks from the manufacturer himself, not from the wholesaler. The size of the order that the retailer can place is the factor that determines whether this is possible. Manufacturers produce in bulk and like to sell in bulk. Small retailers have neither the space nor the money to buy in large quantities, so they must deal with manufacturers indirectly through wholesalers. But even where the retailer buys directly from the manufacturer, the essential functions of the wholesaler remain: buying in bulk, holding stocks, and redistributing in smaller quantities. The only difference is that now they are performed by the retailer himself.

(c) Route Three

Some manufacturers carry this streamlining process further still by combining the functions of manufacturer, wholesaler and retailer, and selling their products to the consumer via their own retail shops. This often occurs with perishable commodities, where the delay in selling to a wholesaler would spoil the product. Bread is commonly sold through retail shops owned by the baker. But many other goods also follow this pattern: Bata shoes are sold in shops owned by the company, and most beer produced in Britain is sold in public houses owned by the brewers. In each of these instances the manufacturer acts as the wholesaler, holding stocks until they are required by the retail branches.

(d) Route Four

A further way of eliminating the wholesaler and the retailer from the distributive process is for the manufacturer to sell directly to the consumer via newspaper advertisements. This method gives the producer access to a large number of consumers.

(e) Route Five
Another variation is mail order selling, where goods are ordered from an expensively produced catalogue. Here the catalogue, which is carried by an agent or representative of the mail order company, acts as a permanent advertisement. In this case the company combines the roles of wholesaler and retailer.

A more recent refinement of this kind of selling is the marketing of goods through *agents*, who demonstrate them at parties in the homes of potential customers. Cosmetics and kitchen equipment are notable examples, but some clothes, jewellery and pottery are also sold in this way.

2.3 The Distribution of Primary Products

Most manufactured goods reach the consumer by means of one of the routes we have just outlined. There are often special difficulties with primary products or raw materials, and several variations of the basic pattern have had to be evolved. This is partly because most of these materials are very localized, and often occur far from the factories or consumers who need them. The difficulties of marketing certain industrial raw materials have resulted in the establishment of specialized *commodity markets* where the materials can be obtained, and often ordered in advance of requirements. (They are discussed in Section 4.5.) The disposal of agricultural produce also requires special facilities because of its perishable nature. Most of it is sold in one of the ways shown in Fig. 2.2.

Fig. 2.2 Disposal of agricultural produce

(*a*) A small amount can be sold in the locality where it is produced. You are probably familiar with the stalls and small shops at farm gates, where the farmer disposes of some of his produce.

(*b*) A substantial proportion is taken by road to local or regional markets, where it is sold either to wholesalers or direct to retailers.

(*c*) Some farmers send their produce to national markets, the most important of which is Covent Garden in London, for fruit and vegetables. Goods from all over the United Kingdom and indeed from abroad are sent to Covent Garden for redistribution. Other notable markets in London are Smithfield, for meat, and Billingsgate, for fish.

(*d*) It is now quite common for farm crops to be sold direct to manufacturers for processing, for we buy an increasing amount of our food in a frozen or dehydrated state.

(*e*) Sometimes the farmer may be compelled by law to sell his crop or produce direct to a *marketing board*. These are organizations set up to control the output and sale of a particular product. An important example is the Milk Marketing Board. Such boards are really performing the function of wholesalers.

Having made this preliminary survey of the ways in which finished products reach the consumer, we shall examine the processes involved more closely in the following Units.

2.4 Questions and Exercises

(*a*) Short Answers

1. What are the distributive trades?
2. What is the traditional pattern of distribution of goods from producers to consumers?
3. By what other means may goods reach the consumer?
4. Name four goods where production is seasonal but demand is steady throughout the year.
5. Name four goods where demand is seasonal but production may be steady throughout the year.
6. Which branch of the distributive trades overcomes the problems referred to in Questions 4 and 5?
7. By which distributive route would you expect your daily newspaper to reach you?
8. In what ways may fresh vegetables be distributed to consumers?
9. What is meant by mail order selling?
10. How have supermarkets contributed to the decline of the wholesaler?

(*b*) Essay Answers

1. Explain and comment upon the various ways in which finished goods may reach the consumer.

2. What difficulties arise when manufacturers dispense with the services of wholesalers and sell direct to retailers?
3. In what respects has the growth of large retail firms affected the traditional pattern of distribution?
4. In what ways do (*a*) wholesalers, (*b*) retailers benefit consumers?
5. 'The services offered by the wholesaler are essential to the efficient distribution of manufactured goods.' Discuss, showing what happens if the wholesaler is eliminated.

(*c*) **Projects and Assignments**
1. Examine in detail the facilities that exist for the distribution of milk from farmers to final consumers in the United Kingdom.
2. Select a number of household goods that you buy regularly. Compare the prices over a number of weeks or months in (*a*) two supermarkets, and (*b*) a small retail shop. What differences do you notice? Comment on the reasons for the differences.
3. Choose the main product of a local factory. Discover what you can about the raw materials and components needed to make this product (where they come from and how they arrive). Try to find out where the product is sold and what problems are involved. Show how commercial services provided by outside organizations are essential to its production.
4. Describe the work of *either* Billingsgate Fish Market *or* Smithfield Meat Market, showing how it is important to producers and consumers for the smooth distribution of fish or meat. (You may find it helpful to consider the problems that would arise if the market ceased to operate.)

Unit Three

The Retail Trade

3.1 The Definition of the Retailer

To many of us the most familiar business units are the retail shops from which we normally buy the things we need. The word *retail* originally meant *to cut a piece off*, and a retailer is still a businessman who sells things in small quantities. He may *buy* packets of detergent in their hundreds or thousands, but he will sell them to us one at a time.

3.2 The Functions of the Retailer

The retailer is a *middleman* and he performs functions for two groups of people. The first group are the manufacturers and wholesalers who provide him with goods, the second, the consumers who buy the goods from him. In fact, retailers exist to provide a link between the consumers and the producers of goods. As we shall see in the rest of this Section, in providing services for consumers the retailer necessarily relieves manufacturers and other producers of several burdens.

(a) Providing Local Supplies

Procter and Gamble, the producers of a large proportion of our household soaps and detergents, have factories in Essex, Lancashire and Northumberland. It would be impossible for consumers to go to one of these factories every time they wanted to buy a bar of soap, nor would the firm be pleased to see them. Wholesalers would not welcome them either, for they like to sell in large quantities. Retailers, however, by establishing their shops in towns and villages and on housing estates throughout the country, provide consumers with a local and easily accessible supply of goods. As well as performing this important service for us, they also form an indispensable part of the producers' distribution system.

(b) The Breaking of Bulk

Manufacturers and wholesalers deal in very large quantities. Retailers provide goods in single units.

(c) Providing a Variety of Goods

Each manufacturer of, for example, wrist watches, makes his own particular brand. The retail jeweller obtains supplies of watches from a number of manufacturers, and thus provides a variety of goods for consumers to choose from.

(d) Advice and Information

In many fields of the retail trade this is less important than formerly: most of us don't need advice when buying our weekly groceries and household goods. But if we are decorating the house, the local supplier of paints and other materials may be able to give us some useful tips about new products that are available. Similarly, we may receive helpful advice from the chemist about medicines, while the photographic dealer spends much of his time discussing the suitability of equipment for different purposes. Then, in the other direction, the retailer may well be able to give information to the manufacturers' representatives who call on him, especially with regard to how well certain products are selling. This may affect the future production plans of the manufacturer.

(e) Other Services

Retailers may provide a *pre-delivery service* for some goods: motor cars, bicycles and many kinds of electrical equipment should not be sold without the retailer checking over them to ensure that they are in good condition. Some retailers provide *credit* for their customers. This may be on an informal basis in the case of the daily purchase of groceries (see Section 3.3(b)) or on a formal basis in the case of consumer durables (see Unit 6). Retailers provide a *delivery service* in respect of most *consumer durable goods* (goods intended to last a long time, such as television sets or cars). It would be very inconvenient if furniture stores, for example, did not deliver goods for us.

Many retailers provide an *after sales service* for their customers. This applies particularly to the sale of consumer durables. In the event of the television set breaking down, your retailer should be able to send an engineer to repair it.

Finally, some small shops open very early or close very late as a service to their customers. Not all retailers provide all these services, but they do all try to provide goods at a time and in a form convenient to consumers.

3.3   Types of Retailers

Retailers take a variety of forms in providing the services we have just outlined in Section 3.2. The majority of these forms can be found in any shopping centre.

(a) Street Markets

Many towns have street markets, but very few of them are open every day. There are three kinds of retailers who sell in these markets.

(i) The owners of shops who hope to increase their sales by renting a stall at a market in a neighbouring town.

(ii) The producers of agricultural goods who prefer to market their goods in this way rather than through other channels (see Unit 4). (This practice is much less common than it used to be.)

(iii) Traders who rent stalls at a number of different markets on different days.

The advantage of the market trader is that his *overheads* are low. (Overheads are expenses that have to be met whether goods are being sold or not, such as rent, rates and heating.) In the market heating and lighting are not usually needed. Since overheads are low the market trader often sells goods at cut prices. Frequently he will go out of his way to obtain goods direct from manufacturers, which also helps him to sell at low prices. The disadvantage to the customer is that the stallholders do not normally provide the same kind of after sales service as you would expect from other retailers.

(b) The Independent Retailer

This is the name we normally give to the person who owns and operates his own shop. Independent retailers are not commonly found in the town centre these days, for the expense of maintaining a shop there is considerable. Large profits can be made in high streets, because thousands of consumers do their shopping there, but the owners of shop sites can charge high rents, which only large firms can afford. But as you move out of town towards the suburbs you will normally find a number of independent traders, including newsagents, butchers, tailors and florists. These small retailers, as we may call them, may enjoy any or all of the following advantages.

(i) They have complete control of the business, so any decision regarding development may be made quickly.

(ii) Outside the town centre the proprietor often knows his customers personally, and can retain their custom by going out of his way to accommodate them.

(iii) In some trades independent retailers can also offer convenience to the customer. Small newsagents, confectioners and general stores are frequently found open either early in the morning or late at night, or both. The same shops also tend to open on Sundays, as do independent motor car accessory dealers. Not only is this convenient for the customer, but also it enables the proprietor to compete with larger businesses which have strict opening hours.

It would be a mistake to think that *all* small retailers open at these unusual times, however. Only in important tourist centres are you likely to find clothes shops, for example, open on a Sunday, nor are they likely to open at unusually early hours on shopping days.

(iv) It was once common practice for the proprietor of a small general shop on a housing estate to allow informal credit to his trustworthy customers, which meant that they could pay at the end of the week. While this practice undoubtedly continues here and there, it is not all that widespread nowadays.

It certainly cannot be said to give small retailers, as a group, any real advantage over their competitors.

(v) More significant is the ability of the small retailer to provide particular goods or services for minority groups of customers, especially in the grocery trade. Go into the local supermarket and you will probably find a choice of three or perhaps four different kinds of cheese. But visit the nearby delicatessen, specializing in the provision of exotic foods, and you may be offered a dozen or more different cheeses.

Again women are often upset when they find someone else wearing a dress identical to their own: both dresses are probably bought at a branch of the same large store. If they bought their clothes at smaller shops, the possibility of this coincidence would be reduced. It is true of men's suits: buy them ready-made by a nationwide firm, and you may find many others wearing the same; have one made to measure by an independent tailor, and the problem is overcome.

(vi) Some small retailers give a free delivery service, but we cannot regard this as a special advantage, because it is also available from the larger types of retailer.

(c) Voluntary Chains
In recent years the independent retailers in the grocery trade have lost ground to the very large supermarkets (see Section 3.3(f)). Many have sought survival by joining one of the voluntary groups such as Spar or Wavy Line. These groups are normally organized via wholesalers, and they allow independent retailers to enjoy some of the advantages of the large scale retailers, which we shall discuss later. There are four main advantages to joining a voluntary chain.

(i) Individual retailers place their orders with wholesalers within the group, who can then place very large orders with manufacturers and secure important discounts. (By discount we mean, in this context, a reduction in price.)

(ii) National advertising can be undertaken by the group as a whole. Of course, for this to be effective the shops have to be recognizable as members of the group. This inevitably leads to a loss of individuality, but the group symbol does become a kind of guarantee to the public.

(iii) The group often finances the renovation and decoration of members' premises by means of a loan.

(iv) The groups often lay down minimum standards for members, thereby making them more attractive to consumers. For example the group may insist that members carry a certain level and range of stock.

In return for these advantages the retailer has to sacrifice some of his independence, for many policy decisions are taken by representatives elected to the management committee of the organization. The retailer may have little say in decisions about local advertising, his window display and even what goods he sells.

While voluntary chains are found mainly in the grocery trade, many independent photographic retailers now combine in a similar way to compete with large multiple firms.

(d) Multiple Shops

The tendency today is towards large scale retailing, and there are a number of large scale retailers which are known as multiple shops. Some of them specialize in a narrow range of goods, others sell a large variety of goods under one roof.

Among the specialist multiples are Halfords (motoring, cycling and camping accessories), Richard Shops (women's clothes) and W.H. Smith (magazines, books and stationery). Although each of these shops will have a branch manager responsible for the performance of the individual unit, the general policy of the shop (and that of all others in the group) is laid down by head office. These are centralized organizations: branch managers do not have the power to negotiate with manufacturers or wholesalers, and they are not responsible for the decor of their shops. These matters are all left to head office. (You will notice that multiple shops are recognizable by their uniformity.) In this way the business secures considerable *economies of scale* (by this we mean that the cost per unit of production falls as the size of the business increases). The business can afford to employ specialists whose greater efficiency reduces costs. Individual units within the multiple chain need not advertise either: this is normally done on a national scale by head office.

Other multiples offer a much wider range of goods. In shops like Tesco you can obtain the bulk of your weekly shopping: food, household goods, hardware, clothes, some electrical goods and many other things. Like the specialist multiples they enjoy very large discounts and can frequently sell at lower prices than smaller organizations.

Some shops, for long regarded as specialist multiples, have in recent years begun to diversify by selling a broader range of products, in order to increase their profits. Boots, the chemists, sell far more goods than the traditional chemist. Marks & Spencer have established themselves as food retailers and are now selling soft furnishings as well.

Some retail outlets which look like multiples are, in fact, *franchises*. Franchising is the process whereby the owners of a business allow others to run it for them in return for certain payments. Wimpy and Kentucky Fried Chicken are examples. The people who operate the retail outlets (the franchisees) pay the owners a substantial sum for the privilege of using the name, and have to buy or rent the premises. There is an agreement that the franchisee pays the franchisor either by purchasing all materials from him or by paying a royalty (a fixed percentage of sales). The parent firm has the advantage of attracting capital from enterprising individuals and in effect receives a share of their profits; the franchisee has the advantage of being able to use a well-known and widely advertised name without having to build up his own reputation, and he can receive other assistance from the parent company, for example in the form of cheap supplies.

(e) Department Stores

These are like many shops under one roof (and the same ownership), and they are normally found in town centres. The most famous example is Harrods in London; Selfridges and Debenhams are others. Some stores, such as Boots, which were once specialist multiples, have now taken on many of the characteristics of department stores. Within these stores separate departments cater for consumers' wants: electrical goods, furniture, clothing, glassware, china, books, toys and many other things will be found. Each department is under the control of a buyer or manager responsible for making the department profitable. The department store offers luxury shopping, because many facilities are provided for customers: there is often a car park for customers only and a café or restaurant.

Many department stores are owned by very large firms, even where they retain their original names. This has resulted in the independence of the stores and of individual departmental buyers being reduced, in the interests of centralization.

(f) Supermarkets

A supermarket is generally defined as a self-service shop with over 186 square metres of floor space. Many of them may be regarded as multiples as well, for they operate on a wide scale. They concentrate on food and household goods, and only stock goods which they know they can buy in bulk and sell quickly. Since they rely on rapid sales, they need to be in busy shopping centres. Their goods are normally pre-packed and frequently advertised nationally by manufacturers, but sometimes the supermarket chains buy in such bulk that manufacturers are prepared to produce foods specially for them under their own labels (see Section 3.7). Supermarket prices are usually very competitive, because of their high rate of sales, but this is only one of the factors that has led to their rapid growth, as we shall see in Section 3.8.

(g) Superstores and Hypermarkets

There are two kinds of outlet bigger than supermarkets, operated by companies such as Asda, Tesco and Sainsbury.

(i) **Superstores**. These have at least 2 500 square metres of selling space.

(ii) **Hypermarkets**. These normally have over 5 000 square metres of selling space.

Both tend to be single-storey buildings, rely on self service and sell a wide range of food and non-food merchandise. These shops are mainly near urban areas, relying heavily on car-users for their business and they frequently provide large areas of free car parking space.

Stores of this size did not appear in Britain until the mid 1960s, but by 1983 there were about 190 superstores and 40 hypermarkets. Both types provide competitive and convenient shopping. There is frequently opposition to their introduction because of fears that they may have a harmful effect in the long run on more conventional shops.

(h) Retail Co-operatives

The retail co-operative movement began in Rochdale in 1844 to protect working people from exploitation. The movement developed rapidly; today's Societies still retain many of the original features.

(i) Membership is open to anyone prepared to buy a share in the society. This normally costs £1. A member may subscribe up to £5 000 if he wishes, and he will receive interest on his capital. (It is not, of course, necessary to be a member to buy goods from the co-operative shops.)

(ii) The society exists to serve the members, and each member has one vote in the election of the management committee, however much capital he has contributed and however much he purchases from the society.

(iii) The profits of the societies used to be divided between members half-yearly, in proportion to their purchases from the society. This led to a considerable amount of book-keeping, and in most societies it is now the practice to give dividend stamps with purchases instead. Under this system dividends are no longer restricted to members.

The co-operatives resemble department stores in that they embrace the whole field of retail trade within one organization. Indeed, since they often provide milk, bread and coal as well as a laundry service and frequently a funeral service, they are even more comprehensive than most department stores. (Of course, they do not normally provide the same luxurious facilities.) In other respects they resemble the multiple stores, because they have the benefit of centralized purchasing and other services provided through the Co-operative Wholesale Society, which is owned and controlled by the retail societies.

The co-operative societies have broader objectives than the other retail units we have discussed. While they need to make a surplus to pay out interest to their shareholders and to finance expansion and the building of new shops, they also finance a range of educational, political and social activities.

Originally, the main strength of the co-operatives was that they were local societies serving local communities. Recently a process of amalgamation has reduced the number of societies from 1 015 in 1958 to 160 in 1983, and this has caused them to lose their local identity. As a result, local control has been lost as well. Originally the management committees were known to members, who could make their views known and have a feeling of identity with the society. This is impossible in the very large societies which exist now. In addition, the policy of issuing dividend stamps, in imitation of some super-markets, has caused the co-operatives to be regarded as just another retail outlet.

(i) Discount Stores

A recent development in distribution has been the establishment of a number of discount stores. These are really wholesalers who buy in large quantities from manufacturers and sell direct to the public. They are especially common in the electrical goods industry, selling stereo equipment, deep freezers and televisions. They advertise widely in the national and local press. Discount stores are able to sell at very competitive prices by reducing staff and cutting out some of the retailers' profit, and this is their chief advantage to consumers. While the goods they sell are subject to the same consumer legislation as other goods, you should not expect the same services from the discount stores as you obtain from the independent retailer. One of the ways they cut their prices is by eliminating the services they provide with the goods; for example, less trouble may be taken over the display of goods.

(j) Mail Order Firms

The term *mail order* covers a number of different forms of selling. The best known is that used by the nationwide firms who sell via catalogue and local part-time agents. The attractive catalogues, which are expensive to produce, offer a wide range of consumer goods which a customer may purchase on *credit* over a period of 20 weeks (see Unit 6). This is the principal advantage to the shopper, especially as the credit is automatic and involves no formality. Normally the holder of a catalogue shows it to her friends and neighbours and places orders for goods on their behalf, receiving a commission of (usually) 10 per cent from the mail order firm for her trouble. The customers have the additional advantage of having the goods delivered to their door.

The mail order firm itself enjoys several advantages.

(i) It does not need expensive high street premises. Large buildings tucked away on industrial estates are perfectly adequate.

(ii) The catalogues provide it with a permanent and enticing shop window in many homes, though the quality of the goods may be difficult to assess.

(iii) The availability of instant credit persuades many people to buy goods on impulse which they would ignore in an orthodox shop window, even though prices are normally raised by the credit charge. In addition, once a customer gets used to paying perhaps 80 pence per week, she is often quite happy to buy further goods at the end of 20 weeks.

(iv) The firm enjoys the usual economies associated with bulk buying and the profits of both wholesaler and retailer.

Against these advantages must be set the disadvantage of having to meet heavy packaging and postal charges, as goods are sent off in single units, and frequently having to pay the postage on goods returned as unsatisfactory, especially in the case of clothing.

Another kind of mail order selling is where manufacturers or wholesalers advertise in the national press, inviting orders by post. Most weekend newspapers carry advertisements of this kind. It is ostensibly a very convenient method of shopping, and frequently goods are offered at bargain prices. There is, however, the usual difficulty of not being able to inspect the goods in advance. Also, although you may have the right to return them if they are not suitable, there have been cases where customers have had difficulty in getting their money refunded. Such advertisements are covered by the Fair Trading Act 1975, and the national newspapers operate their own Mail Order Protection Scheme.

3.4 Changing Structure of the Retail Trade

In the last 15 or 20 years there has been a significant trend towards large scale retailing. Thus the multiples and, in food retailing especially, the supermarkets have become increasingly important. Of the large scale retailers the co-operatives have benefited least from this general tendency. Another important change has been the increasing share of trade going to the mail order firms which account for over 6 per cent of non-food retail sales. There have been a number of factors at work which have caused changes in the structure of the retail trade, particularly the ending of Resale Price Maintenance and the trend towards branding and packaging.

Table 3.1   The changing structure of the retail trade, 1971–82

Type of firm	1971			1982		
	No. of businesses	No. of outlets	Turnover (£ million)	No. of businesses	No. of outlets	Turnover (£ million)
Single outlet retailers	338 210	338 210	7 076	189 132	189 132	20 050
Small multiple retailers	28 626	83 966	2 134	27 030	72 350	9 220
Large multiple retailers	1 073	71 162	6 524	997	63 526	35 020
Co-operative societies	313	16 480	1 215	149	6 983	4 024
Total	368 222	509 818	16 949	217 308	331 991	68 314

3.5 The End of Resale Price Maintenance

Resale Price Maintenance (RPM) is the practice whereby the manufacturer of a product stipulates the price at which it may be sold by the retailer. It was introduced in the United Kingdom in the late nineteenth century at the request of retailers who wanted an end to the fierce price competition that had developed. One of the consequences of such competition is frequently a reduction in the quality of goods sold, as sellers try to maintain their profits by devious means.

The practice became more widespread after 1945 and particularly in the 1950s and early 1960s, for the large scale retailers, which were already emerging, were eager to cut prices. In order to keep in business, small retail firms exerted pressure on the manufacturers to insist on fixed retail prices. The practice of RPM came to an end in two stages: as a result of the Restrictive Practices Act 1956 and the Resale Prices Act 1964. Only if the Restrictive Practices Court found Price Maintenance to be in the public interest could it continue. Only in the case of books and medicines has RPM been found to be in the public interest. This was recognized in the Resale Prices Act 1976 which abolished the practice while still allowing manufacturers to publish recommended prices (see Section 7.3).

3.6   Self Service

The ending of RPM facilitated the growth of self-service shops. These can be time-saving to customers and are convenient in that goods are well displayed and individually priced. There is, of course, a loss of personal service. For retailers the self-service system can be labour saving (smaller wage bills) and the use of clever display techniques may increase sales through impulse buying: this occurs when shoppers buy goods in addition to those they originally intended to purchase; for example, sweets are often strategically placed near check outs where customers in the queue may be tempted. A disadvantage to retailers is the increase in shoplifting and pilfering that accompanies the growth of self service.

3.7   Branding and Packaging

The traditional function of the retailer was to buy fairly large quantities of sugar, cheese or vegetables from a wholesaler and weigh them off as consumers demanded them. Today almost anything we buy from the grocer or greengrocer can be pre-packed and pre-weighed. The packaging may be done by the manufacturer, the wholesaler or the retailer himself, but whichever is the case, the retailer can display his goods on fixtures from which the customer can help himself. Even meat and vegetables may be pre-packed in this way, which has encouraged self-service shops and large scale retailing.

The pre-packaging of goods has been accompanied by the *branding* of goods so that they are readily identifiable. There are two kinds of brands.

(a) Manufacturers' brands, where the goods bear the manufacturer's name.
(b) Retailers' brands, where the goods bear a name that is readily associated with a particular retailer. Large scale retailers are able to order in such bulk that manufacturers will produce goods and label them specially for individual firms. In each case national advertising will periodically remind consumers of the brand names.

Branding and packaging have the advantages of making goods readily identifiable and of facilitating self-service retailing. They do not necessarily benefit the large retailer at the expense of the small, for many small retailers are now using the self-service system. There are other factors, however, which have given the large retailer a distinct advantage.

3.8 Advantages of Large Scale Retailing

(a) Economies of Scale

The effect of economies of scale, which we discussed in Section 3.3, is to reduce the cost per unit sold. The most important economies are the discounts obtained by buying in bulk, especially where retailers have their own brands. There are also considerable savings in labour for those large retailers who use self service, though there is still much work to be done behind the scenes.

(b) Specialization

The small retailer is responsible for all the decisions that have to be taken: what to sell, where to sell, whether to advertise, where to obtain goods and so on. The large firm can afford to employ specialists to cover all these functions and many more. Each specialist devotes all his time to his job: efficiency increases, profits rise and expansion continues.

In addition to these economic advantages, there are several other factors which have contributed to the large retailers' success.

(c) Convenience

Perhaps the biggest advantage the large scale retailer has for the customer is the convenience which is offered. Many people do not have time to stand in queues while customers in front of them discuss the weather with the shopkeeper, nor do they want to rush from shop to shop in order to get the week's shopping. Large scale supermarkets overcome both obstacles: people can shop at their own pace, and the bulk of the food and household goods that they need can be bought in one place. The combination of these two factors has been of overwhelming importance to the growth of the supermarket sector.

(d) Growth of Private Transport

The week's groceries for an average family constitute a fairly hefty load. The small grocer may be prepared to deliver such a load for you, but if you have your own transport you no longer need his assistance. You can drive perhaps a few miles to the supermarket, place your purchases in a large box, which is usually available, and transport the goods yourself. The fact that there are 15 million private cars on the road now, compared to 5 million in 1960 indicates that many more families are now able to shop in this way. This is very much to the benefit of the large scale retailer.

(e) Promotions

Retailers today find themselves in a very competitive situation. As a result, they place great emphasis on 'special offers' and price cutting to promote sales. Until the mid 1970s much of this price cutting took the form of the issue of trading stamps which the consumer saved until he was ready to exchange them for goods or cash. They constituted, in effect, a delayed price reduction.

3.9   Disadvantages of Large Scale Retailing

As you would expect from the rapid development of large retailers, their advantages heavily outweigh their disadvantages but it is important not to lose sight of the latter. There are three main disadvantages.

(a) Decline in Personal Service

The nature of large scale retailing means that the customer cannot normally deal directly with the proprietor or indeed the manager. It is unlikely that the supermarket manager will be prepared to accept special orders: he is only interested in buying goods that he can sell very rapidly to a large number of people. Likewise delivery and after sales service are not usually provided by supermarkets. Generally, the customer has to work harder in the supermarket than in other stores.

(b) Staffing Problems

Although the supermarket may require fewer staff in relation to its sales, the jobs that it can offer are generally routine and involve little contact with the general public.

(c) Pilfering

Pilfering is a distinct problem in the supermarkets, and for most of the large retailers. Convictions for shop-lifting are frequent, and the temptation is much greater in large self-service stores than elsewhere. The large retailer has the choice of either accepting heavy losses through shop-lifting or installing cameras and employing extra staff. Both alternatives are very expensive. In 1984 it was estimated that over £1 300 million of goods were stolen by shop-lifters.

There are some trades, such as jewellery and bespoke tailoring, for which the very large outlet is not entirely suitable and in these areas the small retailer still prevails. But elsewhere it is probable that the trend towards the large store will continue. The emergence of hypermarkets covering several acres shows this.

3.10   Questions and Exercises

(a) Short Answers

1.   Make a list of the functions of retailers.

2. Which of these functions are not normally provided by supermarkets?
3. Make a list of the main kinds of retailer.
4. Why are there so many different kinds of retailer?
5. Give three reasons why traditional small retailers are disappearing, especially from the grocery trade.
6. What are voluntary groups of retailers? What advantages do they have for their members?
7. Give five reasons why multiple shops have grown in recent years.
8. What is a department store? What are its advantages?
9. What are branded goods? Give some examples.
10. How has the growth of car ownership affected the retail trade?

(b) Essay Answers

1. Comment upon the statistics given in Table 3.1, giving reasons for the changes shown.
2. Outline the difficulties faced by a small retail grocer in competition with a nearby supermarket. What steps can he take to protect his trade?
3. What are the main advantages and disadvantages of the retail co-operative societies?
4. Distinguish between department stores and multiple shops, showing the advantages of each.
5. Examine the factors which have led to changes in the structure of the retail trade in recent years.

(c) Projects and Assignments

1. Make an analysis of all the retail shops in your local shopping centre, separating them into the categories we have examined.
2. Make a comparison of two or three local supermarkets under the following headings: location; prices of certain essential items; special offers; branded goods; choice of goods (e.g. how many brands of coffee?); advertising in the local or national press, or on television.
3. Select some goods from mail order catalogues and compare their prices with those of similar goods available locally. What explanations are there for the differences?
4. Over a period of, perhaps, six months, compile a collection of news cuttings about the retail trade. Use your collection to write a commentary on the current developments in retailing.
5. If you can, visit a hypermarket or superstore, and (a) give an indication of its scale and the scope of its sales; (b) show what problems and benefits there are for consumers; (c) find out what you can about the problems of organizing such an enterprise.

Unit Four

The Wholesale Trade

4.1 Introduction

Specialization and division of labour are the main characteristics of the industrial and commercial systems of the advanced countries. These two factors
have led to mass production and the standardization of output. Firms and
factories turn out their goods in thousands and hope to sell them rapidly, so
that they do not have too much capital tied up in stocks of finished goods. On
the other hand, final consumers only want to buy small quantities of goods at
any one time. For consumers this problem is overcome by the existence of
retailers. Producers are helped over this problem in many industries by the
existence of wholesalers, who buy in very large quantities from manufacturers
and sell in smaller amounts to retailers. The wholesaler thus acts as a kind of
reservoir, which is kept topped up by large inflows of goods from a limited
number of manufacturers and emptied by smaller outflows of goods to a large
number of retailers.

There are, however, several variations on this pattern of distribution, as we
saw in Unit 2. As retail units get larger they may deal directly with the
manufacturer, buying in large quantities and redistributing the goods to their
branches in smaller amounts. Sometimes the manufacturer may himself sell
direct to the consumer, cutting out both wholesaler and retailer. But whether
there is a separate wholesaler or not, the job of holding stocks and releasing
them in small quantities still has to be done. It is important, therefore, that we
examine the role of the wholesaler in detail – the more so as he is frequently
accused of being unproductive. First let us look at the different kinds of
wholesaler that there are.

4.2 Types of Wholesaler

The channel of distribution for any given commodity depends upon a number
of influences.

(i) The nature of the product: perishable goods have to be treated differently from durable ones; some goods are mass produced, while others are
made to order by craftsmen.

(ii) The conditions of production: manufactured goods are normally produced on a steady, continuous basis with some goods being completed every

day, but agricultural produce may be harvested in only one month of the year. Some goods are home produced, while others are only obtainable from over-seas.

(iii) The demand for the product: demand is continuous for many goods, but for others, such as Christmas cards or swimming costumes, it is seasonal.

You can imagine that a large number of combinations are possible and it would be surprising if all goods could be treated alike on their way from the producer to the retailer or consumer. We can, in fact, identify six types of *middleman* or *wholesaler*.

(a) General Wholesalers
General wholesalers may operate on a national or regional basis; some serve a strictly local market. General wholesalers normally stock a wide range of goods and need a substantial amount of capital to finance their large ware-houses, stock and advertising, and to pay the salaries of the salesmen they send round to obtain orders from retailers.

(b) Specialist Wholesalers
Specialist wholesalers or merchants restrict their activities to a particular trade and to a particular area. There is almost certainly a builders' merchant in your home town who carries a wide range of materials for resale to local builders or 'do it yourself' shops. In large cities there are often wholesale fruit and vegetable markets selling to retailers over a fairly wide area.

(c) Cash and Carry Wholesalers
These wholesalers have developed rapidly in recent years. Their name indi-cates their method of trading: they do not allow credit purchases and they do not usually offer transport facilities. Since the customer has to transport his own goods, cash and carry wholesalers usually have local markets. Sometimes they deal with the general public as well as with retailers. In the electrical goods and household furniture trades this has led to the rise of *discount stores*, which are a mixture of wholesaler and retailer. Like orthodox wholesalers they operate from large, often sparsely decorated premises and they buy in large quantities; like retailers they sell to the public in small quantities.

(d) Brokers
Brokers are also middlemen. They are *agents* who work on behalf of a *princi-pal*: their job is to find buyers for the seller's goods. They are not responsible for the delivery of the goods, for they do not normally have them in their possession; the buyer and seller make their own arrangements over this. Brokers, like all agents, receive a commission for their services.

(e) Factors
These are a special kind of agent in that they do not merely bring buyer and

seller into contact with each other, but they actually have the goods in their possession. They are especially important in the export trade (see Unit 19).

(*f*) Del Credere Agents
These agents guarantee a sale for their principals. They charge a higher commission for their services because they run the risk of being left with goods on their hands. The ordinary broker does not carry this risk.

4.3   The Functions of the Wholesaler
We know that the general purpose of wholesalers is to facilitate the flow of goods from the producer to the consumer. In fulfilling this role they provide a number of services both to producers and retailers.

(*a*) Warehousing
We have seen that manufacturers produce goods in large quantities and need to sell them quickly. The wholesaler enables them to do this, by undertaking to buy their output in bulk and store it in his warehouse until it is required by retailers. If the wholesaler did not exist, either the manufacturer would incur the expense of warehousing goods or retailers would have to buy in much larger quantities. The provision of warehousing by the wholesaler involves many incidental benefits for both producers and retailers and, indeed, for consumers; we shall discuss these in the rest of this Section.

(*b*) Marketing
To some extent the wholesaler relieves the producer of the task of finding a market for his goods. Retailers often visit the wholesaler's warehouse or showrooms, which gives the wholesaler the opportunity of promoting the sale of goods by means of effective displays. He may also undertake other kinds of advertising on behalf of the manufacturer, thereby helping his sales. Nevertheless, most producers do have their own representatives and sales force to visit shops and promote their products. They need to keep an eye on market trends.

(*c*) A Reservoir
Just as he provides a market for the manufacturer, the wholesaler also serves as a source of supply to retailers. By offering them a wide selection of goods from a number of different manufacturers, he saves them a lot of effort: retailers do not have to visit each individual manufacturer to choose their goods. Without wholesalers the distribution of goods from manufacturers to retailers would require a number of separate journeys and transactions, as Fig. 4.1 shows. Wholesalers reduce the number of transactions and journeys, and all the clerical work which goes with them. Some of the benefits of this should accrue to the consumer, in the form of lower prices.

(*d*) Breaking Bulk
One of the essential functions of the wholesaler is that of breaking bulk, that is,

buying large quantities of goods and dividing them into smaller quantities for the retailer. In the past the wholesaler would often have been responsible for the packaging and branding of goods as well, but today this is more commonly undertaken by the manufacturer. In some trades, however, notably the tea trade, wholesalers are still responsible for *blending*: teas are bought in bulk from various sources and mixed by the wholesaler to produce the correct blend. It is at this stage, too, that the grading of goods sometimes takes place. This is especially important in the commodity markets where, as we shall see in Section 4.5, dealers may be buying or selling materials which have not yet been produced.

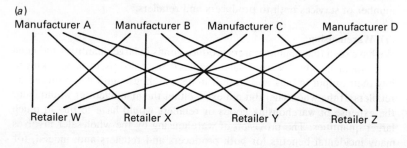

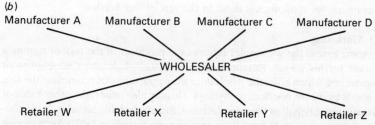

Fig. 4.1   The importance of the wholesaler: (a) wholesaler omitted;
(b) wholesaler included

(e) Price Stability

In Section 4.3(a) we saw that warehousing is important to the smooth marketing of those goods where production or demand is seasonal. An incidental role of the wholesaler in carrying large stocks of such goods is that he may be able to control the price fluctuations that would otherwise occur. If no one were prepared to hold stocks of, say, seasonal agricultural produce, we could expect their price to be very low when they were being harvested and exceptionally high at other times of the year. By buying the produce at harvest time and releasing it gradually over the year, the wholesaler can eliminate the wilder price fluctuations. On the other hand it is still possible for unscrupulous dealers to hold stocks of goods and wait for market prices to rise, so that they can then sell at an unusually high profit.

(f) Risk Bearing

In holding large stocks of goods or materials, the wholesaler also removes a number of risks from the shoulders of producers and retailers. First, he may find that the goods he has bought in bulk fall in price, so that he makes a loss. In these circumstances the manufacturer is glad to have had a ready market for his output. It is also possible that the goods will go out of fashion before the wholesaler can pass them on to the retailer. Heavy losses may be involved. (This is a problem for the retailer too, but a less important one for him, since he carries smaller stocks.) The wholesaler also bears the risk that goods will deteriorate or be damaged while in his care. He must take appropriate steps to prevent this from happening.

Many of the risks that the wholesaler takes are related to the financial arrangements that he makes. The manufacturer spends large sums of money on raw materials, components and wages in order to produce goods. Once he has delivered them to the wholesaler, he likes to be paid fairly promptly or, in commercial terms, he allows the wholesaler a short period of credit. He needs prompt payment so that he can finance the production of the next batch of goods. On the other hand, the small retailer cannot usually afford to pay cash for his supplies from the wholesaler until he has sold the goods to the consumer. He therefore needs a longer period of credit, which is normally allowed by the wholesaler, who thus takes the risk that the retailer will default on his debt. You can see, therefore, that the wholesaler needs a large amount of capital if he is going to make this kind of arrangement with his suppliers and customers.

(g) Delivery

It is normal for wholesalers to deliver goods to retailers, thereby saving them the expense of running their own van or lorry. In addition they often make it their job to collect goods from suppliers.

(h) Information

It is sometimes said that the wholesalers are a useful source of information to producers and retailers, and to some extent this is true. They can, for example, tell retailers about new products that are becoming available. However, this is more likely to be done either through the trade press (see Unit 16), or by representatives making direct contact with the retailers. Wholesalers might also let producers know which of their goods are selling well and which are less acceptable to the public. But the producers can make their own assessment of this from the orders they receive, so the importance of the wholesaler in this respect should not be exaggerated.

We can now see that the wholesaler provides a wide range of services to producers, retailers and, indirectly, to consumers. Without these services the distribution of goods would be far less efficient than it is.

4.4   Elimination of the Wholesaler

There is no doubt that the wholesaler is declining in importance, although the small retailer still needs his services. There are five main reasons for this.

(a) The growth of large retailers who can undertake their own wholesaling, and who buy direct from manufacturers.

(b) The tendency of some manufacturers to establish their own retail outlets and to sell direct to the consumer.

(c) The growth of pre-packed branded goods.

(d) Large retailers do not need a long period of credit.

(e) Manufacturers prefer to sell direct to retailers so that they can push their own product more than the wholesaler would.

However, even if the wholesaler is eliminated, his functions remain and either the producer or the retailer must undertake them, so we cannot expect his decline to result in spectacular price reductions.

4.5   The Commodity Markets

We saw in Section 4.2(b) that some wholesalers specialize in a narrow range of goods. This specialization is absolute for some commodities and raw materials. There are a number of *commodity markets*, based mainly in London, where dealers buy and sell large consignments of certain commodities, using a variety of different systems. Most of these markets originated in the nineteenth century, when Britain dominated world trade. Britain exported manufactured goods and imported large quantities of the raw materials needed to make them. Since these imported raw materials came from many different areas, it was necessary to develop centralized markets for them. London was the most convenient place for this, as most of the goods were brought in through the Port of London.

(a)   The Baltic Exchange

The main business of the Baltic Exchange is the chartering (hiring) of ships and aircraft, or space on them, but there is also a long established trade in grain, seeds and oils. Trade is by description only: there are not even any samples for dealers to inspect. Wheat, for example, can be graded according to its type and quality. All the dealers know what is implied by the various gradings, and business proceeds on this basis. This itself means that only approved persons can deal: the public – in this case the industrialists who need raw materials – always deal through agents or brokers.

(b)   The London Commodity Exchange

Here a vast number of commodites are bought and sold: cocoa, coffee, tea, sugar, sisal, rubber, jute and vegetable oils, to name a few. The method of dealing varies according to the commodity. Some are sold by sample, some by description; some sales are by auction, others by private treaty between brokers and dealers.

Tea is one of the commodities which cannot be sold by sample, because it varies in quality and cannot be graded. Each consignment of tea is sampled individually by potential buyers who wish to determine its value, and is sold by auction. This method of sale is also used for tobacco and wool, and other products which cannot be finely graded.

(c) The London Metal Exchange

A number of metals are bought and sold here, where the method of dealing is known as *ring trading*. The members assemble around a ring painted on the floor. Each metal is traded for five minutes, and dealers call out their bids or the prices they want for the metal in question. Clerks keep a record of the deals made in this rather unusual way. The process is repeated for each metal several times a day. Between these sessions a great deal of private trading occurs between members. Ring trading, which is not confined to the Metal Exchange, ensures that prevailing prices are well known to all interested parties.

(d) The London Corn Exchange

Established in the middle of the eighteenth century, the London Corn Exchange provides a centralized market for all kinds of cereals produced in the United Kingdom.

There are many other markets, but these four are the most important. Before we conclude this Unit, we must examine a technical feature that is often found in the commodity markets – the *futures* market.

4.6 Futures

You may want to buy metal for machinery that you are going to produce in three months' time. You would like to be sure that you can buy that metal at a fixed price, but during the next three months its price may rise, causing you a loss. You could overcome this problem by buying the metal now and storing it until you need it, but this would tie up your capital unnecessarily.

The alternative policy would be to buy *futures*, that is, arrange with a dealer to buy the metal from him at an agreed price in three months' time. If the price rises in the interval you are safeguarded by your future agreement; if the price falls you need not worry, for you will have based the cost of the machine on the agreed future price.

This system also benefits the sellers of metals. By arranging future contracts they can safeguard themselves against a fall in price, for their client will have to buy at the agreed price, even if it is higher than the prevailing market price. Of course, if the price rises after the seller makes his future contract, he will be bound to sell at the lower price. On the other hand, he will certainly have other uncommitted supplies that can be sold at the new market price.

4.7 Questions and Exercises

(a) Short Answers

1. What is meant by a middleman?
2. Why is the wholesaler sometimes referred to as a reservoir?
3. Distinguish between the different kinds of wholesalers.
4. What is the difference between a broker and a factor?
5. What extra service is offered by a *del credere* agent to his principal?
6. List the functions of the wholesaler.
7. What is meant by breaking bulk? Why is it important?
8. What risks are undertaken by the wholesaler?
9. What is a commodity market? Give examples.
10. Is the middleman productive?

(b) Essay Answers

1. Describe the ways in which the wholesaler may be eliminated.
2. 'If it were not for the wholesaler the price of goods would be lower.' Comment on this statement.
3. What are the benefits of the cash and carry type of wholesaling to a small retailer? Explain the disadvantages as well.
4. 'The wholesaler's functions are essential to the distribution of most manufactured goods.' Why, then, is the wholesaler being eliminated?
5. Describe the services of the wholesaler (a) to manufacturers, (b) to retailers.

(c) Project

Discover all you can about the London Metal Exchange and its methods of working.

Unit Five

The Technicalities of Trade: the Documents Involved

5.1 Introduction

Millions of business transactions take place every day. The majority of them probably consist of the straightforward sale of goods by a retailer for cash. In these cases there is no need to keep a specific record of the transaction. But many other transactions are complex, and the completion of a deal may be spread over several months. In such a case it becomes important to keep a clear record of each stage of the transaction. This can be achieved by each party to the transaction keeping a kind of diary in which all deals are recorded. In some markets, such as the Stock Exchange, this is exactly what happens (see Section 13.7). But in most branches of commerce a more formal record is needed, so that reference can easily be made to a particular transaction.

There are two types of record. One is the books of account kept by every firm, showing all its income and expenditure, money owed and money owing. The study of these belongs to book-keeping and accounting and does not concern us here. The other type consists of the documents that pass between buyers and sellers: each side keeps copies of the documents it sends, as well as those it receives, so that it can keep track of the transaction.

The best way to learn about these documents is to examine a hypothetical transaction between two businesses. Let us take as our example the manager of a sports shop, who wants to ensure that he has an adequate supply of cricket equipment for the beginning of the season. This is not an industry in which wholesalers are very active, so the retailer has to contact the suppliers of equipment direct. He will do this as early as November, to ensure delivery of the goods he wants at the right time. (Retailers have to look ahead: it is no good waiting until the end of November to order Christmas cards, or until April to order Easter eggs.) Sections 5.2–5.10 take us through the transaction step by step.

5.2 The Inquiry

The sports outfitter will probably be in contact with a number of suppliers. If he is not, he will be able to get their names from *trade journals* relating to the industry, such as the *Boot and Shoe Journal*, or from *trade directories*, which list businesses according to the goods or services they supply.

Having obtained the name and address of the supplier, the retailer will make an inquiry as to whether the supplier can let him have the goods he needs, and on what terms the goods would be delivered. It is quite likely that the inquiry would take the form of a letter, but some retailers have specially printed forms on which to make their inquiries. The retailer will probably make the same inquiry of two or three suppliers to be sure that he is buying on the most favourable terms.

5.3   The Quotation

The supplier will reply by sending a *quotation*, which is a statement of

(a) The prices at which he can supply the goods.
(b) The terms on which he can supply them, including any discounts available.
(c) The costs of carriage of the goods.
(d) The amount of time needed for delivery.

The retailer will now be able to compare the quotations provided by different suppliers and place his order with the firm that offers the best terms.

In practice, there is often no need for such an inquiry followed by a quotation, because many suppliers circulate *price lists* to their established customers, incorporating the terms on which they do business in the list. Larger firms issue illustrated catalogues, both to their regular customers and to potential customers making inquiries. The catalogue is frequently accompanied by an order form, on which retailers can make their orders. Alternatively, the retailer may have his own order forms printed; this will make his filing tidier, for all his carbon copies will be of the same size.

5.4   The Order

An order should always contain the following items as shown in Fig. 5.1.

(a) The names and addresses of the two parties.
(b) A description of each item as well as its catalogue number (to prevent mistakes).
(c) The delivery date required.
(d) The address to which the consignment is to be sent.

The total cost of the order is not shown, in case the suppliers cannot provide all the items listed. If Cricket Supplies already have the goods in stock, they can begin to process the order; if not they will deal with it as soon as possible. In the meantime they may send Thurays an acknowledgment of the order, so that they know it has arrived. If it is the first time that they have dealt with Thurays Sports, Cricket Supplies will probably require a *banker's reference* (see Section 11.12) before they will supply goods on credit. A favourable reference will reassure the supplier that his customer has the means of payment.

```
                                              Order no. 7631

              THURAYS SPORTS Ltd
              High Street
              Graybury                    Tel.: Graybury 72812

To: CRICKET SUPPLIES Ltd                   29. 12. 19. .
    Willow Road
    Haston

Please supply:
```

Item	Cat. no.	No. of units	Unit price
Size 6 bats	6341	25	15.00
Size 9 boots	0418	8 pairs	12.00
Full size cricket balls	2344	6 dozen	40.00 per dozen

```
Delivery: March 19..
To: Above address          Signed:  T. Smith

                                     T. Smith, Director
```

Fig. 5.1   An order

5.5   The Invoice

Perhaps the single most important document in the transaction is the invoice, which is the bill for the goods sent by the supplier to his customer. A typical invoice is shown in Fig. 5.2.

There are several important points to notice about the invoice.

(*a*) An invoice is prepared for each delivery by the company, and is sent to the customer. It can accompany the goods, but is often sent separately.

(*b*) When the invoice is prepared, several copies are made. One copy, identical with that shown in Fig. 5.2, is retained by the supplier's accounts department, so that it can keep track of money owed. The other copies (which we deal with in subsequent Sections) have the prices and terms of business omitted.

(*c*) The invoice contains:

(i) The appropriate names and addresses.

(ii) A reference to the customer's order number, so that Thurays Sports can check the invoice against the goods ordered. Similarly, Cricket Supplies give a reference number of their own, in case Thurays have a query to raise.

```
                              Invoice                          43011

                              CRICKET SUPPLIES Ltd
                              Willow Road
                              Haston
  VAT Reg. no. 834 7651 23    Tel: Haston 3011

  To: THURAYS SPORTS Ltd     Your order no. 7631
      High Street
      Graybury                Our ref. 43011
  27. 2. 19..
                              Dispatched by: Our vehicle
```

Quantity	Description	Unit price	Total	+VAT (15%)	Total
25	Size 6 bats	15.00	375.00	56.25	431.25
8 pairs	Size 9 boots	12.00	96.00	14.40	110.40
6 dozen	Full size cricket balls	40.00 per dozen	240.00	36.00	276.00
			711.00	106.65	817.65

```
       Terms: 5%  7 days
              2½% 1 month                    E. & O.E.
```

Fig. 5.2   An invoice

(iii) The supplier's VAT registration number. This tax is levied on almost all transactions, but most businesses that pay it are entitled to deduct their payments from the VAT that they themselves have collected from their customers, and which they have to remit to the Government. This VAT invoice enables them to prove that they have paid the tax (see Section 22.4).

(iv) A description of the goods, their unit price, the VAT payable and their total price. The total amount due for the order is given at the bottom.

(v) The terms of business. In this example, if the account is settled within seven days, a 5 per cent discount will be allowed (that is, 5 per cent can be deducted from the bill). Payment after seven days but within one month entitles Thurays Sports to 2½ per cent discount.

(d) For convenience we have assumed that the prices shown on the invoice are the trade prices, that is the prices that the buyer has to pay. In this case, he will subsequently add on a percentage to cover his expenses and profit. Frequently, however, the invoice will show the *retail* price of the goods being supplied. Clearly the retailer would be unable to buy and sell at the same price and still make a profit. There would therefore be another entry on the invoice – *trade discount*: 30 per cent. In other words the retailer, being in the trade and not a final consumer, can buy the goods at a discount of 30 per cent of the price stated.

(*e*) Many firms have the letters E. & O.E. printed on their invoices. This is an abbreviation for *errors and omissions excepted* and safeguards the supplier against any clerical errors that may have occurred in compiling the invoice.

(*f*) The invoice is not necessarily a request for immediate payment. Many shops will receive several deliveries each month from the same suppliers and will probably settle their account on a monthly basis.

Now we must see what happens to the other copies of the invoice.

5.6   Advice Note, Delivery Note, Consignment Note

These terms are often used in different ways by different people (there is no legal definition of them).

(*a*) Advice Note
This contains details of the goods being sent. It is sometimes sent before the goods, to inform the buyer that he may shortly expect delivery of his order. If the goods do not arrive within a few days, he can begin to make inquiries about them. Sometimes, on the other hand, the advice note is enclosed with the goods, enabling the recipient to check that the right goods have been sent.

(*b*) Delivery Note
This accompanies the goods, and once they have been delivered it is signed by the buyer or his representative and handed back to the lorry driver as proof of delivery. Frequently the driver brings both the advice note and the delivery note and asks the buyer to sign one copy.

(*c*) Consignment Note
This note is different from the other two, in that it is used when the supplier uses transport other than his own to deliver the goods. The consignment note is a formal instruction to the transport firm to accept the goods and deliver them to the customer. The driver usually wants the customer to sign a copy of the consignment note as well.

5.7   The Debit Note

We saw that invoices often carry the proviso E. & O.E., which entitles the supplier of the goods to correct any errors that have crept into the invoice. The *debit note* is a document sent to a customer when he has been undercharged on an invoice.

If, for example, the typist preparing the invoice inadvertently types £10 instead of £11 the matter can be corrected, once the mistake has been discovered, by sending the customer a debit note. But many firms do not bother to draw up a separate debit note. They find it more convenient to send another invoice to rectify the mistake.

5.8   The Credit Note

The mistake on the invoice may be in the opposite direction: the customer may have been overcharged. In this case, the supplier issues a *credit note* when the mistake is brought to his notice. The credit note is normally printed in red to distinguish it from other documents (for it represents a flow of money in the opposite direction to the usual one).

There are a number of possible reasons for issuing a credit note.

(*a*) There has been an overcharge, as above.
(*b*) Damaged goods have been returned by the retailer.
(*c*) Packing cases or crates have been returned by the retailer. He would have been charged a deposit on these on the invoice.

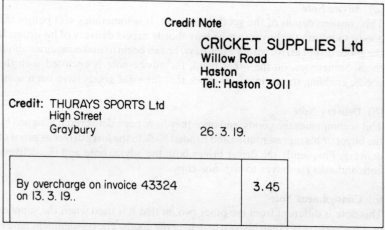

Fig. 5.3   A credit note

(*d*) The retailer has returned gift vouchers or coupons to the supplier. The retailer has allowed his customers a cash discount on these and is entitled to claim payment from the producer. Rather than insist on cash he is normally prepared to accept a credit note, the value of which he deducts from his monthly payment to the supplier.

It is important to understand that the *invoice* must never be altered. This is to avoid giving rise to the suspicion that someone is trying to defraud the company. Errors are always adjusted by the issue of another document –

another invoice or a debit note when the customer has been undercharged, a credit note when he has been overcharged.

5.9   The Statement

At the end of each month Cricket Supplies will send a statement to Thurays Sports, summarizing the transactions that have taken place between them and showing the amount owed by the customer.

Like the other documents, the statement contains the names of the two parties and any relevant reference numbers. The statement (Fig. 5.4) shows that at the beginning of March, Thurays Sports had a debit balance of £121.07. During the month they received two consignments of goods worth £202.62 altogether; they also received a credit note for £2.50 and paid £140 by cheque. The balance at the end of the month was thus £181.19. The manager of Thurays Sports should, of course, check the statement against the invoices and other documents he has received during the month. The statement also contains the terms of payment.

5.10   Payment and Receipt

Normally the customer settles his account through the banking system, paying by cheque or bank giro (see Unit 11). If payment is by cheque, Thurays

---

Monthly Statement: Issued 8. 4. 19..

CRICKET SUPPLIES Ltd
Willow Road
Haston
Tel.: Haston 3011

THURAYS SPORTS Ltd
High Street
Graybury   A/c no. 3435

Terms: 5% 7 days
            $2\frac{1}{2}$% 1 month

Date	Details	Debit	Credit	Balance
1 March	Balance			121.07
8 March	Goods	132.32		253.39
9 March	Cheque		140.00	113.39
14 March	Credit Note		2.50	110.89
23 March	Goods	70.30		181.19

This statement does not include items dispatched or payments received after 31.3.19..

The last amount shown is the amount due

Fig. 5.4   A monthly statement

probably do not want a receipt, as the cleared cheque would be accepted as proof of payment should a dispute arise; if payment is by credit transfer, the bank itself issues a receipt. In the unlikely event of Thurays paying by cash, they would want a *receipt* from Cricket Supplies as proof of payment. Even if they pay by cheque they may insist on a receipt, so as to complete their records.

These, then, are the main documents used in business. Every stage of a transaction between two parties can be traced by these documents and each party to the transaction is careful to keep the documents they receive as well as copies of those they send. They are useful at the end of the trading year when firms make up their books to determine their profits.

5.11   Questions and Exercises

(a) Short Answers

1. Why are business documents necessary?
2. As a retailer, how might you discover the goods and terms offered by a wholesaler or manufacturer?
3. What are the essential features of an invoice?
4. Distinguish between cash discount and trade discount.
5. Distinguish between a credit note and a debit note, showing when each is used.
6. What is the purpose of the statement sent by a supplier to his customer?
7. Why should the customer check the statement carefully?
8. Why do some business documents contain the letters E. & O.E.?
9. 'If you pay by cheque, a receipt is not necessary.' Why?
10. What is a banker's reference? Why is it important to a trader?

(b) Essay Answers

1. Explain the purpose of each of the documents involved when A. Trader buys goods for the first time from A. Wholesaler on credit.
2. Explain the purpose of each of the following, showing the circumstances in which it would be sent: (a) a debit note, (b) a credit note, (c) an invoice.
3. Distinguish between an invoice and a delivery note, showing when each is used.
4. Give examples to show the importance of the proper documentation of business transactions.
5. Describe the various ways in which a manufacturer can inform retailers of his products and their prices.
6. You are holding a village fête. Write a letter of inquiry to a printer regarding the printing of tickets. Give exact details of size, printing, number of tickets, etc.

(c) Assignment

Make a collection of business and commercial documents (invoices, receipts, bank statements, etc.). For each one, write an explanation of its function and importance.

Unit Six

Credit Trading

6.1 Introduction

The purchase of consumer durable goods such as motor cars or televisions usually requires more money than the consumer has available. The goods can, however, be supplied on *credit*. The consumer may borrow the necessary money either from the seller of the goods or from an outside agency, normally a bank. Bank loans and overdrafts, which are usually the best way of borrowing, are dealt with in Unit 11. Here we are concerned with other sources of credit.

6.2 Types of Credit

Credit is available in a number of different forms. The kind of credit you will be able to obtain depends partly upon you and the lender's assessment of your creditworthiness, and partly on your reason for wanting credit.

We must distinguish between short term credit (up to three months), medium term credit (up to five years) and long term credit (up to 25 years). The third type does not concern us here, because it is used mainly for house purchase, but the other two categories are important, medium term (*formal*) credit in particular. But first let us briefly consider the main types of short term (*informal*) credit.

6.3 Short Term (Informal) Credit

(*a*) Trade Credit

If a businessman has the choice between paying as soon as goods are delivered, or in a month's time, and he chooses to pay in arrears he is in effect receiving a loan from his supplier. This kind of credit is mainly available to traders, but some consumers make similar arrangements, when they open an account with a grocer, butcher or garage, for example. They sign for their petrol at the garage as they obtain it and settle the account monthly. They know they can always obtain petrol without cash, and the proprietor is assured of regular custom from his account holders.

As we saw in Section 3.3(*b*) some small retailers offer informal credit of this kind to people they know well.

(b) Credit Cards

Credit cards such as Barclaycard and Access are discussed in Unit 11, but are mentioned here because they are an increasingly important means of obtaining credit. They are not strictly speaking short term, because the holder may elect to repay his debt over a period of years.

A variation of the system has been the issue by large retailers of their own credit cards. Debenhams, Woolworth, and Marks & Spencer are among the many companies which hope to increase sales and win customer loyalty through the use of their cards. These operate in the same way as general credit cards, except for their restriction to branches of the issuing firm.

At present it is estimated that over 40 per cent of adults in Britain have a credit card. In America the proportion is over 80 per cent.

(c) Budget Accounts

This is a somewhat ambiguous term, for some of the clearing banks operate a system of budget accounts, which we explain in Unit 11. In this Unit we are referring to those schemes operated by shops for the benefit of their regular customers. They are frequently found in men's tailoring where, by signing a banker's order for, say, £5 per month, the customer can take delivery of clothes of up to £120 in value (that is, 24 times his monthly payment). He will have to pay either a commission on his purchases or interest on the amount outstanding to his account, depending on the individual scheme. This kind of credit is known as *revolving credit* for once he has paid back some of the £120, the customer can buy more goods up to his personal credit limit. Such schemes also operate in department stores, giving customers access to a wide range of goods.

(d) Check Trading

This is a useful type of informal credit for small purchases. The *checks* are available, in various denominations, from agents who have a regular round and who call to collect repayments. The customer can, for example, buy a check for £20, making an initial payment of 5 pence for each £1 borrowed and 20 subsequent payments of the same amount, making £21 in all. The checks can be used to buy goods at a large number of shops participating in the scheme. The cost to the customer is not exorbitant and he is able to buy the goods he wants at their cash price, without the trouble of filling in documents for more formal credit.

The retailer returns the checks he collects to the issuing company, who redeem him the face value of the checks less a discount of perhaps $2\frac{1}{2}$ per cent. The retailer who joins the scheme must therefore aim to increase his sales sufficiently to offset this fall in his profits.

The biggest of the check-issuing companies is the Provident Clothing & Supply Co Ltd, and so the checks are often known as Provident Checks.

6.4   Hire Purchase

Sometimes the informal types of credit we discussed above are not available to a particular consumer for a particular purchase; he may be unaware of them, or the supplier may not participate in the appropriate schemes. The consumer will then have to arrange more formal credit. The omnibus term *hire purchase* is generally used to describe this more formal credit, and it covers several different kinds of contract.

(a)   Conditional Sale Agreement

Under this type of agreement, the goods remain the property of the seller until the purchase price has been paid by instalments, or until other stated conditions have been fulfilled. It is not normally relevant to consumers, being used mainly for the sale of plant and equipment to industry. As far as consumers are concerned, so long as the amount of credit involved is not more than £5 000, the Consumer Credit Act 1974 has removed any distinction between hire purchase and conditional sales.

(b)   Hire Purchase Agreement

The goods are *hired* to the user, who is given the option to purchase them for a token sum at the end of the hire period; he is not obliged to buy them, but it would be most unusual not to do so. Consumer durable goods such as freezers and stereo equipment are sold in this way, and the finance may be provided either by finance houses (see Section 12.5) or by retailers themselves.

(c)   Credit Sale Agreement

On payment of the deposit or first instalment the goods become the property of the buyer, who undertakes to buy them through five or more instalments. Since the seller has no security for the goods, this kind of agreement is not normally used for expensive items; but it is commonly employed where goods have very little second-hand value and where there would be little point in the seller repossessing the goods in the event of default. This kind of sale is, of course, widely used by the mail order companies.

In the rest of this Unit we shall use the term *hire purchase* to cover all three types of agreement. In all such agreements the consumer undertakes to pay the purchase price plus interest, normally in a number of equal instalments. The seller of the goods may insist on the payment of a deposit of perhaps 25 or 33^1/3 per cent to conform with Government requirements. He may choose to finance the sale himself or, more likely, he will act as the agent of a *finance house*. In this case the retailer actually sells the product to the consumer on behalf of the finance house, which pays him the full value of the goods covered. Thereafter the consumer's weekly payments are passed on by the retailer to the finance house.

6.5   Advantages of Buying on Credit

(a)   Without hire purchase many people would be unable to obtain consumer durable goods. (There is frequently over £8 000 million outstanding on hire purchase agreements.) It is true that they could save up for the goods for a number of years, but the self-discipline needed for this is too great for many people. Hire purchase enables them to do their saving retrospectively: once they are committed to their repayments, most people will honour them.

(b) If hire purchase were unavailable it would be the poor who would suffer. The wealthy would be able to pay cash anyway. There is no reason why some groups should be prevented from enjoying the comforts of modern living, provided they are willing to pay for them. Refrigerators, deep freezers and modern heating equipment are all ways in which the general standard of living can be raised.

(c) We saw in Unit 1 that mass production needs a mass market. If you are mass producing packets of detergent, your customers can afford to pay cash, but if you are mass producing kitchen furniture many of them cannot. For consumer durable industries hire purchase is essential to maintain an adequate turnover. This is true for retailers too: by offering hire purchase facilities, they can attract more customers and increase their profits.

(d) A more obscure advantage is that hire purchase helps to maintain employment. If no one can afford to buy automatic dishwashers, there is no point in employing people to make them. When people buy dishwashers on hire purchase, they are helping to maintain employment in the industry.

(e) Hire purchase is a constructive way of using people's savings. They deposit their savings with a number of financial institutions, which relend the money to other people. The finance houses, incidentally, find hire purchase very profitable. (You, as a consumer, might regard this as a disadvantage!)

6.6   Disadvantages of Buying on Credit

(a) Although hire purchase seems very simple – a deposit plus a fixed number of instalments – it is in fact very complex; the calculation of rates of interest is a jungle in itself. It is common for consumers to pay a higher rate of interest than is necessary because they do not shop around enough. A requirement of the existing legislation is that consumers shall be informed in writing of the true rate of interest they are being charged.

(b) Consumers may be tempted to overburden themselves with hire purchase repayments, especially when they do not have to pay a deposit. Unscrupulous salesmen, perhaps paid by commission, can more easily persuade people to buy goods they don't really want. When this happens the customer, who has signed a contract to make the repayments, may find that he cannot meet them. The supplier or the finance house will then try to repossess the goods, and the customer may finish up in court. But there are safeguards against this, as we shall see in Section 6.7. Many people believe that hire purchase encourages people to be spendthrifts, and is undesirable for this reason alone.

(c) Selling on hire purchase leads to more paper work for the retailer: records have to be kept, and reminders sent to slow payers.

(d) Ultimately there is the risk of the adverse publicity involved in taking a customer to court. (Even though it is the customer who is at fault, the trader may often appear in a bad light.)

(e) Retailers who operate their own hire purchase schemes have more of their capital tied up in debts. They will have paid their supplier for the goods, but will not yet have received full payment from their customer. On the other hand, of course, the retailer will ultimately receive more money for his goods.

(f) Some goods may be returned to dealers by defaulting customers, and they may have trouble finding a market for such second-hand goods.

You can appreciate that if hire purchase contracts were left to the parties immediately involved – the suppliers and the consumers – enormous pitfalls could develop, especially for consumers. For this reason, and also to protect the supplier of goods from unscrupulous or fraudulent consumers, hire purchase and other forms of credit are controlled by Act of Parliament.

6.7 Hire Purchase Legislation

In 1962 the Moloney Report on Consumer Protection made a large number of recommendations to redress what the committee regarded as the unequal balance between consumers and producers. Some of those recommendations were embodied in the Hire Purchase Act of 1964, which was in the main replaced by the Hire Purchase Act of 1965. This in turn has been repealed and largely incorporated into the Consumer Credit Act 1974, which brought the regulation of a whole range of credit transactions into one act.

The Act applies to all hire purchase agreements where the total sum payable, including interest, does not exceed £5 000. (The purchase of large items of industrial equipment by hire purchase is therefore excluded.) For credit sales agreements anything under £30 is exempt from the protection given by the Act. The safeguards to the consumer can be divided into four groups, which were laid down in the 1965 Act and retained in 1974.

(a) Right to Information
The Act laid down that the customer must be given certain information in writing.

(i) The cash price of the goods, so that he is aware of the extra cost of buying by hire purchase.

(ii) The total hire purchase price.

(iii) A description of the goods.

(iv) The amount, number and frequency of the instalments.

(v) A summary of the consumer's rights and obligations under the Act. This information must be presented to the customer in a form laid down by the

Department of Trade, and the agreement must be signed by the hirer. It must contain a clear warning to the hirer that he is signing a legal document and that he will be legally bound by it. The hirer must be given a copy of the agreement within seven days of its being signed. If the agreement is made at any place other than the business premises of the seller of the goods, the customer must receive two copies of the agreement, one upon signature and one by post within seven days.

(b) Right to Withdraw

If you go to the business premises of a firm and sign a hire purchase agreement, you are totally bound by the agreement. But if you sign the agreement anywhere other than at the business premises of the firm, you have the right to withdraw from the agreement within four days of receiving your second copy of the agreement (which comes by post). Any deposit that you have paid becomes repayable and the supplier is under an obligation to collect the goods from you. Your only obligation is to keep the goods safely for three weeks.

The reason for this provision was that unscrupulous door to door salesmen often persuaded people to sign agreements for goods that they didn't really want, by presenting them in a very favourable light in the comfort of the consumer's own home. It has been said that there were many instances of consumers signing agreements while almost mesmerized by salesmen, and finding themselves overcommitted.

(c) Right to Terminate the Agreement

Despite the safeguards we have already discussed, there are still occasions where the hirer finds that he cannot continue the repayments. The Act gives him the right to terminate the agreement at any time, once he has paid half of the total purchase price. If he has not yet paid half he can terminate the agreement by paying the balance up to 50 per cent and returning the goods, paying for any damage done to them.

(d) Right to Retain Possession of Goods

It has happened in the past that impatient finance companies have taken repossession of goods when hirers have fallen slightly in arrears with their payments. Now, once one-third of the price has been paid by the hirer, the owner cannot repossess the goods without a court order. If the owner applies for a court order, the court has certain extra powers.

(i) It may order that the goods be returned to the owner.
(ii) It may vary the terms of the agreement to enable the hirer to fulfil his obligations more easily.

Thus there are a number of ways in which the Act protects hirers, not only from the suppliers of goods but from themselves. The Act also makes quite clear to suppliers their rights and obligations, as we have seen. Suppliers have the further protection that the hirer is not allowed to sell the goods until they become his.

Despite this fairly elaborate framework, consumers remained exposed to many risks when buying on hire purchase or by credit channels. In 1971 the Crowther Committee reported on consumer credit.

6.8   The Consumer Credit Act 1974

The Crowther Report covered the whole field of consumer credit. The main findings of the report may be summarized as follows.

(a) The existing law on credit was deficient in a number of ways but, in particular, different forms of credit were treated in different ways for no apparent reason. It was proposed that all forms of credit should be brought under one comprehensive Act of Parliament.

(b) Consumers should be protected in a number of ways by new legislation:

(i) Advertisements offering consumer credit should not be false or misleading.

(ii) Any interest rate quoted should be the *annual percentage rate*. This is important, for interest rates are often quoted in such a way as to mislead the borrower. Suppose you buy a spin drier on hire purchase, and when you have paid the deposit you borrow £100 from the finance company for one year at a quoted rate of interest of 16 per cent. You agree to repay your total debt of £116 in twelve equal instalments of £9.67. Each month you repay one-twelfth of the interest (£1.33) and one-twelfth of the sum borrowed (£8.34). So at the end of the first month you pay £1.33 interest for borrowing £100 for one-twelfth of a year. At the end of the second month you pay £1.33 interest again, but you have not borrowed £100 for two months. Since you repaid £8.34 at the end of the first month you have borrowed only £91.66 for two months. The interest rate is therefore higher than the quoted rate. In the last month you only owe £8.34 (one-twelfth of £100), and yet you still pay £1.33 interest. If you were to average out the rate of interest paid on each monthly instalment, you would find that the true rate of interest is approximately double the quoted rate. If you bear in mind that on average over the year you are borrowing only £50, you will understand why the quoted (or nominal) rate differs from the true rate.

(iii) The information which now has to be given to consumers under the Hire Purchase Act should be compulsory for all forms of credit transaction.

(iv) Early settlement of a credit transaction should entitle the debtor to a rebate, on a scale laid down by parliament.

(v) The Government should appoint a Credit Commissioner to supervise the whole field of consumer credit. His job would be to control the institutions providing credit and to educate the members of the public who wanted it.

(vi) All those providing credit should be licensed by the Credit Commissioner, who should have power to withdraw the licence for offences such as overcharging.

In 1974 the Crowther Committee's recommendations were embodied in the Consumer Credit Act which is administered by the Director-General of Fair Trading. However, the provisions of the Consumer Credit Act are being introduced in stages, and technically the Hire Purchase Act of 1965 is still in force.

6.9   The Economy and Hire Purchase

As well as trying to protect consumers from a variety of abuses through the Hire Purchase Act, the Government has the broader duty of controlling the level of activity in the economy. We saw in Section 6.5 that one of the benefits of hire purchase is that it increases the demand for consumer durable goods. If the Government feels that the demand for these goods is already too high, it may decide to reduce demand by changing the terms on which goods can be purchased through hire purchase.

If I want to buy some furniture costing £500 and there are no hire purchase restrictions, the retailer may ask for a deposit of 10 per cent of the price and allow me to repay the balance plus interest over a period of four years. But suppose that the Government issues a directive that all hire purchase transactions require a 25 per cent deposit: the necessity of putting down £125 instead of £50 might deter me, and many others, from buying the furniture, or other goods. Furthermore the Government might insist that no hire purchase agreement should run for more than two years. In this case the weekly repayments would have to be larger than if the contract could run for three or four years. This would be another reason to defer the purchase, and the Government would have achieved its objective. Likewise, if it wished to *increase* the sales of consumer durables, the Government could reduce minimum deposits and increase the period of repayment.

While this is a convenient and reasonably successful method of influencing the level of demand, it does have the distinct disadvantage that it is felt more by the poor than by the rich, who normally have alternative ways of financing their purchases.

6.10   Rental Agreements

A rental agreement is an alternative to credit. The object of hire purchase and credit sales is that the goods are finally owned by the customer. In recent years, a large proportion of people have preferred to rent a television set rather than buy it. The ownership of the set never passes to the customer under such agreements. He pays a fixed weekly or monthly sum which may be reduced when he has been renting the set for a year or two. It is the responsibility of the owner of the set to keep it in working order, and since repairs can be expensive one suspects that this is the main reason for the popularity of the system.

Strictly speaking, a rental agreement is not a credit transaction, but it is included here because it is generally regarded as an alternative to hire purchase, not only by many consumers, but also by the Government. Whenever the Government alters the deposit and terms of repayment on hire purchase transactions, it makes similar changes in respect of rentals – requiring, for example, six months' rent to be paid in advance.

6.11 Where Else Can I Borrow?

We outlined the main sources of credit above, but there are a number of other sources of which you should be aware.

(a) *Building societies* lend money for up to 30 years to finance house purchase or improvements to property, such as the installation of central heating.

(b) *Insurance companies* operate similar schemes by advancing money against endowment policies (see Section 18.4).

(c) *Local government authorities* also lend money for house purchases.

(d) *Moneylenders and pawnbrokers* are always available to make loans, the former often without security, but interest rates may be very high and borrowers are better advised to keep to the channels we outlined earlier in this Unit.

6.12 Questions and Exercises

(a) Short Answers

1. Explain the difference between cash sales and credit sales.
2. What sort of goods are sold on credit to final consumers?
3. What is a credit card? Show briefly how it works.
4. What is meant by the term *revolving credit*?
5. Give three differences between a hire purchase agreement and a credit sale agreement.
6. What are the main advantages of hire purchase to the consumer?
7. What is the function of a finance house in hire purchase?
8. What protection does the consumer have if he buys goods under a hire purchase agreement?
9. In what circumstances can a finance house repossess the goods under a hire purchase agreement?
10. What is meant by the *true rate of interest*?

(b) Essay Answers

1. Explain the advantages and disadvantages of hire purchase to (a) a retailer, (b) a consumer.
2. Why do consumers need protection when entering into hire purchase agreements? What protection do they receive under hire purchase legislation?
3. J. Smith wishes to buy a tape recorder. Explain to him the advantages of

buying (a) by paying cash, (b) through hire purchase, (c) by using his credit card.

4. Why was the Consumer Credit Act 1974 necessary? What protection does it give to the consumer?

(c) Projects and Assignments

1. By answering advertisements and making inquiries at local banks and shops, compare the terms on which you can buy an automatic washing machine. (What deposit is required? How high are the repayments? What is the rate of interest? Will the bank lend money? How much do you save by paying cash?)

2. Find out how hire purchase and other forms of credit trading have increased in recent years. (Use the *Annual Abstract of Statistics* or *Financial Statistics* in the reference library.) Plot your information on a graph. Compare your results with figures for the growth of retail trade and incomes. What conclusions can you draw?

3. Write two speeches: (a) advocating the abolition of all kinds of hire purchase and credit sale, (b) demanding easier credit facilities.

Unit Seven

Consumer Protection

7.1 Why Do Consumers Need Protection?

In a free enterprise system firms can only stay in business if they sell their products to the public at a profit. Firms need to keep their costs as low and their revenue as high as possible. There are many ways of doing this, and if firms were left entirely to themselves there are many ways in which consumers could be deceived and exploited. The following come readily to mind.

(a) Prices might be fixed artificially high either by one firm or, worse still, by a group of firms acting together.

(b) Spurious price cutting might occur: recommended prices may be unnecessarily high so the retailers can offer 'attractive' reductions.

(c) Customers might not receive the correct weight or quantity of goods.

(d) Advertisements might make false claims for goods.

(e) Inferior and even dangerous ingredients and components might be used in production to keep costs down.

You can probably think of other ways in which producers could deceive consumers. Gradually legislation has been introduced to control the worst abuses which, in any case, were characteristic of only a minority of firms. In these areas it is clear why the consumer needs protection. But there are other situations in which the consumer may find it difficult to determine whether he is being offered a fair deal, even though the honesty of the producer or supplier is not in question. Many goods are not sold in standard measures: you can buy a pint of milk or a pound of potatoes but it is not so easy to buy a standard amount of some things. It is largely through Government pressure that many commodities are now sold in standard sizes. Until recently you needed a pocket calculator to determine which was the best buy: a bottle of shampoo containing fluid ounces, centilitres or grams.

Do you want to buy a vacuum cleaner? The price of any one model varies from shop to shop, which is one problem. But even if you are trying to choose between two similarly priced machines, how do you go about it? You could take the retailer's advice, but he might be tempted to recommend the model that gives him the best profit, irrespective of the actual merits of the machines. If this is true of a relatively inexpensive item such as a vacuum cleaner, the difficulty of making a rational choice between two or three new motor cars is far greater.

Even if legislation is completely comprehensive in controlling abuses, the consumer is still faced with difficult choices. To help him there are now a number of official and unofficial bodies which examine various goods and assess their merits objectively. We shall be looking at some of these bodies later in this Unit.

We may summarize by saying that there are two broad reasons why consumers need protection. First, some producers are dishonest, and Governments have a responsibility to protect the public against them. Second, it is impossible for the consumer to make an objective assessment of many of the goods he wishes to buy.

7.2   How the Government Helps

We have already seen how the Government helps consumers over hire purchase and credit purchases. Consumers are protected from other abuses, too, by a whole range of legislation, and this is the main way in which the Government helps them. It has also given them further help by establishing official bodies to cater for consumer interests in particular fields. First we deal with the legislation.

7.3   The Government and Prices

One area in which the public is often at the mercy of producers is that of prices. We saw in Section 3.5 how legislation in 1956 and 1964 resulted in the ending of Resale Price Maintenance for most goods. Retailers could no longer be compelled by manufacturers to sell goods at prices higher than they wanted.

In many trades the practice of RPM has been replaced by that of *recommended prices*. The manufacturer supplies goods and recommends the retail prices at which they should be sold. There is nothing to prevent retailers selling at lower prices if they want to, and in fact the existence of recommended prices amounts to an incentive to cut prices. If consumers see that a packet of soap powder has a recommended price of 26 pence but is being sold at '2 pence off' for 24 pence, they are tempted by an apparent bargain. They have no way of knowing if the recommended price has been artificially inflated in the first place, although their suspicions may be aroused when they see that the cartons often have '2 pence off' *printed* on them.

It is easy for consumers to be misled by the price markings on goods which they are thinking of purchasing. Sometimes abuses in pricing become so widespread that the Government is forced to intervene. This intervention can take several forms.

(a) The Government may establish a commission to examine existing prices and proposed increases. A Price Commission was in existence from 1974 to 1980; it had the power to reject price increases, but in practice seemed only to postpone them.

(b) On occasion the Government has forbidden price increases, though this step has usually been taken in an attempt to control inflation rather than as a measure of consumer protection.

(c) In 1979 the Government issued *price marking orders*. The purpose of these orders was to outlaw bogus claims about prices – 'Worth £40, our price £25'; to prevent comparisons with prices charged by 'other traders'; and to ban comparisons with recommended prices in the case of a wide range of consumer durable goods.

There are many areas other than pricing in which it is felt that consumers need protection.

7.4   Legislation to Protect Consumers

(a) The Sale of Goods Act 1893
Under this Act

(i) Goods must suit the purpose for which they are sold.

(ii) Goods sold by description must fit the description.

(iii) Goods sold by sample must correspond with the sample.

In the event of any of these conditions not being fulfilled the buyer normally has the right to claim a refund from the seller.

This Act formed the basis of consumer protection for three-quarters of a century, but it became apparent in the 1950s and 1960s that it was inadequate to deal with the sale and distribution of highly sophisticated products in the modern business environment.

In 1962 the Moloney Report on Consumer Protection was published. It pointed out that the greatest difficulty facing consumers was the fact that they were unorganized, while groups of manufacturers and traders formed tightly knit groups to serve their own interests. The report made many recommendations to help redress the balance, and in the period since then there have been a number of pieces of legislation, many of them directly inspired by the findings of the Moloney Committee.

(b) Weights and Measures Acts 1963 and 1979
The 1963 Act lays down the standard measures by which goods can be sold, and there is a trading standards officer in each area to enforce the regulations. You can imagine the difficulties that might arise if there were no precise definitions of terms like *pint* or *ounce, litre* or *kilogram*.

The main effect of the 1979 Act was to remove the necessity for each packet of goods to be exactly a prescribed weight. So long as the weight of a batch of the packets averages out at the prescribed amount, no offence has been committed by the producer or seller.

An important aspect of the Weights and Measures Acts is the requirement that certain prepacked goods be sold in packets which indicate the weight of the contents.

(c) The Food and Drugs Act 1955

This earlier Act is of the utmost importance to consumers. It controls the contents of food products, their labelling, and the conditions under which they are manufactured and sold. The more obvious requirements are that there should be no smoking where food is handled, and that running hot water and hand basins must be provided for washing, but if you consult the Act itself you will find an enormous range of detailed regulations. The Act is enforced by the local environmental health department, and anyone who thinks he is the victim of breaches of the Act should report the matter to that department.

The Food and Drugs Act is also concerned with the amounts of various ingredients found in food products. In this respect it is reinforced by the *Labelling of Food Regulations*. A few examples will show you the effects.

(i) Jam must contain a minimum proportion of the named fruit: blackcurrant jam, 25 per cent blackcurrant; strawberry jam, 38 per cent strawberry.

(ii) Meat pies must contain at least 25 per cent meat.

(iii) At least 50 per cent by weight of sausages must be meat (65 per cent for pork sausages).

(d) Trading Stamps Act 1964

This Act provided a minor but significant safeguard to consumers. It lays down that where stamps are used every stamp must have its cash value printed on it, and that the holders of stamps can choose to exchange them either for cash or for goods. This ensures that people can easily tell how much of a discount the stamps really offer.

(e) The Trade Descriptions Act 1968

Since 1887 a number of Acts have been passed to control the marking of goods. Their object has been to ensure that labels on packets give a true description of the contents. They were replaced by the Trade Descriptions Act of 1968. This Act lays down heavy penalties for traders who deceive the public by making false claims for their goods or services, or who make inaccurate price comparisons. Before the Act was operative it was quite common for shops to offer large price cuts at sale times, when in fact the reductions were minimal. Now it is an offence to claim, for example, that the price of an article has been cut from £10 to £7 unless the article has actually been offered at £10 for a continuous period of 28 days during the previous six months. This is obviously helpful to consumers, but you will now find shops that publish a disclaimer to the effect that a price reduction does not indicate that the goods have been on offer at the higher price for 28 days in the previous six months!

But the Act, which is enforced by the trading standards officers, is concerned with more than prices. The producer or trader must not describe goods as waterproof or unbreakable unless they really are waterproof or unbreakable. Some dealers in the second-hand car trade used to make a practice of rewinding mileometers to deceive potential customers about the distance covered by a vehicle. This practice is now an offence under the Trade Descriptions Act.

(f) The Fair Trading Act 1973
Consumers were given further protection by this Act, which established the Office of Director-General of Fair Trading. He has wide-ranging powers to control trading practices which are considered unfair to consumers. The Director-General is assisted by the Consumer Protection Advisory Committee. The Office of Fair Trading has investigated and made recommendations on matters such as:

(i) Comparative pricing, which is the practice of advertising goods at '2 pence off' the recommended price, when it is virtually impossible for the consumer to discover the recommended price. Retailers of consumer durable goods are no longer allowed to quote manufacturers' recommended prices.

(ii) The denial by shopkeepers of the right of consumers to obtain their money back if they have been supplied with unsatisfactory goods. Notices such as 'No cash refunded' mislead consumers as to their rights. This practice is now forbidden under the Unfair Contract Terms Act 1977.

(iii) Traders who are selling goods must not pretend to sell them as private citizens, since consumers might then believe that their legal rights are less than they are.

(g) The Supply of Goods (Implied Terms) Act 1973
Some producers and suppliers of goods used to try to avoid their obligations to customers by getting them to sign guarantees that effectively took away their rights under the Sale of Goods Act 1893. Now this cannot be done: any guarantee or warranty offered by producers can only be additional to their obligation to supply goods which are of *merchantable quality* and fit for their purpose.

(h) The Sale of Goods Act 1979
Many of the recommendations of the Moloney Committee found expression in this Act which also incorporated most of the 1893 Act, the 1973 Supply of Goods Act and parts of the Consumer Credit Act and the Unfair Contract Terms Act.

(i) The Consumer Safety Act 1978
Apart from the possibility of being misled or even defrauded, consumers also face the risk of being endangered by goods they buy. This 1978 Act gives the Government power to make regulations governing goods which may injure or kill the public.

(i) Household fires (gas, electric or oil) must be fitted with a guard which prevents clothing touching the flame or element.

(ii) The wiring on electrical goods must be in accordance with the regulations laid down and they must be sold with a label explaining the code.

(iii) There are other regulations which deal with the safety of children's nightwear, cosmetics, toys, pencils, electric blankets and so on.

(*j*) **The Supply of Goods and Services Act 1982**
Most of the legislation discussed above dealt with goods but not with services. This was remedied by the 1982 Act which extended the provisions of the 1979 Supply of Goods Act to contracts for the supply of services and to hire purchase and rental agreements.

7.5 Government-sponsored Bodies

In addition to this legislation introduced to protect consumers, there are various bodies sponsored by the Government which assist consumers in general or the customers of particular industries.

(*a*) **National Consumer Council**
One of the immediate effects of the Moloney Report was the establishment of the Consumer Council in 1963. It promoted consumer rights by a number of methods, but, in 1970, it was wound up for reasons of economy. The Office of Fair Trading took over many of the Council's areas of interest after 1973, but did not exist to put the case of consumers.

Consequently, in 1975, the National Consumer Council was established with a Government grant to make representations to the Government and other public bodies on behalf of consumers. Members are drawn from trade unions, parliament, industry, commerce and independent consumer organizations. The Council has involved itself in a number of activities: for example, the Government's campaign to encourage and subsidize loft insulation followed pressure from the NCC. The NCC has a special role to play in speaking up on behalf of poorer consumers. Its main purpose is to draw attention to injustices.

(*b*) **Nationalized Industries**
The public corporations or nationalized industries are among the largest suppliers of goods and services in the United Kingdom. We examine them in detail in Unit 9, but it is appropriate to examine one feature of them here. Since they are so large and remote from individual customers, the Government has insisted on the establishment of a *Consumers' Consultative Council* for each one of them, to enable the voice of consumers to be heard.

The Councils consist of representatives of local government, local industry and other interested bodies. They certainly provide a mouthpiece for consumers and sometimes make important representations to their industries, but they lack real power and need to be strengthened if the consumers' interests are to be fully safeguarded.

The address of each Council can be obtained from the local office of the nationalized industry concerned, and customers in dispute with the industry can obtain assistance from the Council.

7.6 Independent Assistance to Consumers

The Government clearly makes an enormous contribution to the protection of consumers, but there are many other ways in which they are helped. These methods of assistance fall into two broad categories.

(*a*) Services undertaken on a national scale and covering a wide range of trades and industries.

(*b*) Services concentrating on one trade or industry, and often established by the members of that industry to lay down and maintain minimum standards of production or behaviour.

(*c*) Services run by local authorities, such as consumer advice centres.

We shall now examine some of these independent bodies.

7.7 The Consumers' Association

This entirely independent and non-profit-making organization is probably the best known consumer information institution, with a membership of over 600 000. It operates mainly by conducting comparative tests on goods and publishing the results of them in its monthly magazine *Which?* When a particular product is going to be tested it is bought from an ordinary retailer, who is not told about the purpose of the purchase. A number of different brands of the product are bought, and all are subjected to the same detailed and controlled tests.

In its report, *Which?* lists the good points and the bad, and often suggests which products offer good value for money. The Consumers' Association goes a long way towards redressing the imbalance between producers and consumers, for it provides consumers with an objective assessment of a range of goods. It is not unusual for producers to modify their products after adverse criticisms from *Which?* Where a particular injustice to consumers becomes apparent, the Consumers' Association may adopt a campaigning attitude, exerting pressure on the Government to put things right. The Association also provides a personal service for its members, enabling them to obtain advice on consumer problems.

While *Which?* deals with almost any product, the Consumers' Association also publishes four other more specialized magazines: *Money Which?* where complicated financial, banking, insurance and tax matters are examined; *Motoring Which?*, where the Association's tests on motor cars and related products are reported; *Handyman Which?*, dealing with a whole range of tools and equipment; and *Holiday Which?*, investigating all kinds of holidays at home and abroad.

7.8 The British Standards Institution

This institution is another non-profit-making body. It lays down minimum standards in the manufacture of consumer goods. But while it can specify the desirable quality, performance and dimensions of certain goods it has no authority to enforce its recommendations, as it is independent of the Government.

The influence of the BSI is often demonstrated, however, when the Government compels manufacturers to produce goods to the institution's standards. Electrical goods and motor-cycle crash helmets are notable examples.

The kite-mark of the BSI is now well known, and rightly regarded as a sign of quality. Consumers know that any product bearing the kite-mark has been the subject of extensive tests by BSI inspectors.

7.9   Newspapers and Television

Some newspapers have been running their own consumer protection service for many years. It is not easy for an individual consumer to make a complaint to the head office of a national company; it is even more difficult for him to get satisfaction. But a telephone call from the consumer adviser on a national newspaper or a television programme, and the threat of adverse publicity that it carries, will very often produce results.

The press and television are not only important in dealing with individual complaints. They also play a vital *educational* role, making consumers aware of their rights and of the sharp practices to which they might be subjected. One television programme performed a valuable service in drawing attention to the practice of repricing existing stock when a new consignment came in at a higher price. The practice has more or less disappeared as a result.

7.10   The Citizens' Advice Bureaux

The role of the Citizens' Advice Bureaux is much wider than that of consumer protection, but in areas where there is no local consumer protection organization, the CAB often acts as a mediator between consumers and traders, with considerable success. In this respect the CAB has the advantage of an up-to-date knowledge of the law and is also probably in regular contact with retail trade organizations in its area.

7.11   Protection by the Industries

Many industries establish codes of practice of their own, for the guidance of their members and the protection of consumers.

The *Advertising Standards Authority* is an example. Although the consumer is already protected by the Trade Descriptions Act, the ASA tries to maintain high standards in advertising. Its Code of Advertising Practice is examined in Section 16.8. The *Retail Trading Standards Association*, and the *British Electrotechnical Approvals Board for Household Equipment* are other examples, and there are many others associated with different industries.

7.12   Self-protection

You will frequently find that the best kind of consumer protection is self-protection. If you have cause for complaint about goods or services supplied to you (or which should have been supplied to you) you should raise the matter with the supplier. Since he will normally realize the legal position, you will probably be able to come to an amicable agreement if your complaint is not a spurious one, and provided you adopt a reasonable approach.

The majority of retailers are prepared to correct genuine mistakes, even if the consumer is partly to blame, for two reasons. First, they are jealous of their reputation and it is good for them to be known as fair traders. Second, it is a cheaper way of dealing with the problem than becoming involved in a lengthy dispute which could finish up in court. Further, where faulty goods are involved the retailer himself will probably be able to return them to the manufacturer.

It is also possible for individuals to conduct a campaign against producers on behalf of consumers. The most notable example is an American, Ralph Nader, who campaigned vigorously against the dangerous features of certain American cars. Although almost all his arguments were denied by the powerful American car manufacturers, he eventually had the satisfaction of seeing the United States Government take his side by laying down stringent safety requirements for motor vehicles sold in America.

7.13 Questions and Exercises

(a) Short Answers
1. Name three ways in which consumers may be exploited.
2. What is Resale Price Maintenance?
3. How does the Fair Trading Act help consumers?
4. Give an example to show the usefulness of the Trade Descriptions Act 1968.
5. Why was it necessary to pass the Supply of Goods (Implied Terms) Act in 1973?
6. What is the principal way in which the Consumers' Association helps consumers?
7. In what ways may the process of metrication be to the disadvantage of consumers?
8. What are price marking orders? Why are they necessary?
9. How are consumers protected within the nationalized industries?
10. What is the purpose of the British Standards Institution?

(b) Essay Answers
1. Outline the main forms of consumer protection available in the United Kingdom today.
2. Why is it necessary to protect consumers? Show how they are assisted by (a) the Consumers' Association, (b) the Fair Trading Act.
3. 'Successive Governments have had to take measures to protect consumers.' What measures have been taken since 1968?
4. What protection exists for consumers against abuses in connection with the following: trading stamps; high prices; dangerous electrical goods; second-hand cars whose mileage is falsely stated?
5. Distinguish between the following, showing the purpose of each piece of

legislation: (a) the Sale of Goods Act 1893 and the Sale of Goods (Implied Terms) Act 1973; (b) the Trade Descriptions Act 1968 and the Fair Trading Act 1973; (c) the Consumer Credit Act 1974 and the Consumer Safety Act 1978.

(c) Projects and Assignments

1. Examine several back numbers of *Which?* Show how the Consumers' Association sets about testing products and making its recommendations.

2. Read some *Which?* reports and (a) explain how consumers who intend to buy durable goods can benefit from these reports; (b) choose any piece of equipment and devise your own *Which?* report on it, showing the kind of examination and tests that might be necessary.

3. Visit your nearest consumer advice centre. Examine the leaflets and show why consumers need to be protected, and what facilities are available to them.

4. Construct your own primitive price index by selecting half a dozen everyday items and noting their prices for three or four months. Calculate the average price change. Show why your index is inadequate as a measure of changes in the cost of living.

Unit Eight

Business Units: the Private Sector

8.1 Introduction

Production and distribution are in the hands of a very large number of business enterprises which vary immensely in their scale and organization. The reason for this variety of business organizations is that some activities can only be carried out by large firms, while others are best conducted by small ones. There are two main problems facing any firm.

(a) Capital

First the owner must obtain the capital necessary to run his business. The *initial capital* is the money that he sets aside for the use of the business, and the amount needed varies enormously. On the one hand the business could be a very small enterprise, with the owner buying shirts at a wholesale market and selling them on a casual basis to his friends and workmates: the capital needed for this is very small and easily accumulated. If, on the other hand, the object of the business is to generate and distribute electricity to a community of 800 000 people, far more capital is needed, probably more than one man can raise. Between these two extremes lies a whole range of possibilities, explaining to some extent why so many different business forms exist.

(b) Control

The second problem is the control of the business. The man dealing in shirts has few problems of control: he knows his source of supply, he probably has a very limited stock and he knows his customers. The same is true of many small retailers. But consider the manufacture of steel. The manufacturing plant probably occupies a site of several square miles. Raw materials have to be gathered from all over the world and arrangements made for them to arrive at the site at the correct time and in the right condition. Several thousand men are employed in the process of turning the raw materials into finished steel sheets or tubes. Finally arrangements have to be made for storing the finished products and distributing them to purchasers. An operation of this sort is highly complex and much more difficult to control.

It is not surprising, then, that many different types of business unit have evolved. Since 1945 this diversity has been increased by the division of the British economy into two sectors – the public and the private. The main differences between the two sectors concern ownership and motive.

Business enterprises in the private sector have a clearly identifiable owner or group of owners, whose principal objective is to make a profit. Businesses in the public sector have no owners, but belong to the community as a whole; and the pursuit of profit, or *surplus* (as it is called in this context), has to be reconciled with consideration for the public interest. In the United Kingdom economic activity is divided fairly evenly between the two sectors, but elsewhere things are different. In the United States, the majority of enterprises are privately owned, and decisions are taken by the owners of capital or their elected representatives within the firm. At the other extreme, in Russia, there is hardly any private enterprise, most enterprises being controlled by the state. In this case the decision-making procedure is highly centralized and ultimately in the hands of the people's political representatives.

There are five forms of ownership to be found in the private sector.

(i) Sole traders: 1 owner.
(ii) Partnerships: 2 to 20 owners.
(iii) Private limited companies: at least 2 owners.
(iv) Public limited companies: at least 2 owners.
(v) Co-operative societies: any number of members.

(It is important to remember that *public* limited companies are found in the *private* sector. It is surprising how many people fail to appreciate this; see Section 8.7.)

In the public sector we can identify two groups of enterprises.

(i) Public corporations.
(ii) Municipal undertakings.

We examine these in detail in Unit 9. In this Unit we shall examine the different types of business in the private sector in detail.

8.2   The Sole Trader

The simplest and most common form of business organization is that of the sole trader. He starts business with his own capital and labour, assisted perhaps by one or two employees, and takes the profits as his reward. Such enterprise is not confined to the retail trade, although it is very widespread there. In any local newspaper you will see advertisements from builders, plumbers, hairdressers, printers and others in business on their own account, while in the public announcements column of the same paper you will probably read notices of the bankruptcy hearings of other similar sole traders.

It is easy to establish such a business, for there are no formal procedures, and it has two great advantages: the owner makes independent decisions, and he has personal contact with employees and customers. There are, however, many difficulties associated with this form of business.

(a) The owner does not have the advantage of *limited liability*: he is liable for the debts of the business to the full extent of his private assets. Thus insolvency could even force him to sell his own home to pay creditors. (In other forms of business, except partnership trading, the owners are only liable to the extent of the capital they have committed to the business.)

(b) Legally no distinction is made between the owner and the business, so not only does he face unlimited liability, but also there is often a lack of continuity in the event of the owner's death. Many businesses have to be sold to meet death duties.

(c) The sole trader usually has difficulty in raising capital. Initially he will probably use his own savings, and later he can expand by ploughing back profits. He may also be able to borrow from a bank, but in times of economic restraint small businessmen often find overdraft facilities withdrawn. In addition the sole proprietor may have to pay a higher rate of interest than larger firms. Private loans are possible, but the sole trader is not allowed to appeal to the public for capital.

(d) Business is very competitive nowadays, and success demands hard work, long hours and not inconsiderable worry. In most forms of business these burdens can be shared, but the sole trader must bear them alone.

(e) Technological progress is often out of the question for the sole trader because he can seldom afford the heavy capital outlay. But it is often this progress that increases efficiency, so the gap between small and large firms widens, and the markets of the small firms shrink as customers patronize the more efficient larger firms.

If the sole trader can overcome these difficulties he may wish to expand. In this case he will need

(a) More capital, which he obtains by setting aside the profits of the business for reinvestment.

(b) More employees, which are not usually difficult to find.

(c) More expertise in various aspects of the work.

(d) Assistance with the management of the business.

A convenient way of overcoming these problems is to form a *partnership* with another interested party.

8.3   Partnerships

Partnerships do not necessarily grow out of sole proprietorships. Sometimes a business begins life as a partnership, when two or three employees of one firm decide that they would rather work for themselves than for their employer. Many partnerships in accountancy and the building trade begin in this way.

The main features of a partnership are as follows.

(a) There may be between 2 and 20 partners, except in a professional partnership (e.g. solicitors) where there is no upper limit.

(b) Profits or losses are shared between the partners by agreement (either written or oral). If there is no agreement the Partnership Act of 1890 states that:

(i) Profits and losses must be divided equally.

(ii) No interest is payable on capital contributed to the firm.

(iii) Partners cannot claim a salary for work they do.

(iv) Any loans that a partner makes to the partnership carry interest of 5 per cent per year.

(c) Any agreement made by one partner on behalf of the partnership is binding on all the partners.

(d) All partners are entitled to be involved in the management of the firm.

(e) The partners, like a sole trader, have unlimited liability: if the firm goes bankrupt they are all liable for its debts to the extent of their personal wealth.

The risk of unlimited liability used to deter many people from entrusting their capital to a partnership. But in 1907 Parliament passed the Limited Partnership Act, which allows partners to assume limited liability on the following conditions.

(a) They take no part in the running of the business (though they do share in the profits, of course).

(b) There must be at least one general partner who has unlimited liability for the debts of the business.

(c) The partnership must be registered with the Registrar of Companies.

Clearly there are more formalities involved in establishing a partnership than a sole proprietorship. Why do people go to this bother? There are three main advantages to be gained.

(a) More capital is available.

(b) The introduction of new partners allows specialization, and can add a new dimension to a business. A general builder, himself a trained bricklayer, may improve his business and offer a better service if he takes a plumber and a carpenter as partners. Of course he can simply employ them, but if they become partners their interest is identified with that of the firm. Besides, if he just employs them they make no contribution to capital.

(c) Unlike alternative forms of expansion, the partnership can keep its affairs to itself. Its annual accounts do not have to be submitted to anyone other than the Inland Revenue.

Despite these benefits that accompany the formation of a partnership, there are several drawbacks that need to be considered.

(a) As with the sole proprietor there is no distinction between the owners and the business. They too face unlimited liability. (There are very few limited partnerships, for it is usually better to form a private limited company.)

(*b*) Because the business is identified with its owners, a partnership also suffers from a lack of continuity. If one of the owners dies or leaves the partnership for some reason, the partnership is at an end, and a new one has to be formed. This is not an especially difficult operation, but it is an irritating necessity.

(*c*) Since any undertaking of one partner binds the others, it is important not to enter a partnership with someone whose business judgment is suspect.

(*d*) Since each partner is entitled to a say in the management of the firm, there may well be disagreements. This may cause delays damaging to the business.

(*e*) As the business grows the partnership may well face the same problem over capital as the sole proprietor. There is a limit to the amount of capital that can be obtained from 20 partners or by ploughing back profits. Further expansion may require the establishment of a limited company.

8.4 Limited Companies

It is not inevitable for businesses to begin life as partnerships or sole proprietorships. Where large scale operations are involved the limited company is the normal business unit. Its principal attraction is that the shareholder's liability is limited to the nominal value of the shares held. This facility was conferred by Act of Parliament in 1856. In this way, by buying shares, a large number of people can contribute funds to an enterprise without risking all their personal possessions. Furthermore, as the company has its own legal existence quite separate from that of the shareholders, its continuity is not threatened by the death of one of them. There are many formalities involved in forming a company and we can only look at them in outline.

Limited companies must be registered with the Registrar of Companies. To comply with his requirements, which are laid down by the Companies Acts of 1948 to 1981, the promoters of the company must present the following.

(*a*) Memorandum of Association
This governs the company's relationship with the outside world. Its main contents are

(i) The company's name, which must contain the word *limited*. This is a warning to anyone dealing with the company that they cannot look beyond the company and its resources for the redress of any grievance.

(ii) The address of the company's registered office.

(iii) The objects of the company. Prospective shareholders then know what they are committing their funds to, and they have a legitimate claim against the company if their money is used for anything else.

(iv) A statement of the limited liability of members (for the benefit of potential creditors as well as shareholders).

(v) The amount of capital to be raised by issuing shares, and the types of shares to be issued (see Sections 8.5 and 13.4).

(vi) The agreement of the founder members that they wish to form a limited company, and that they will purchase the stated number of shares.

(b) Articles of Association

These control the internal running of the company. They will usually follow the model articles set out in the Companies Act 1948 instead of formulating a tailor-made set of articles. These articles cover such things as

(i) The procedure for calling a general meeting.
(ii) The rights and obligations of directors.
(iii) The election of directors.
(iv) The borrowing powers of the company.

When these documents are complete they may be sent to the *Registrar of Companies*, together with a *statutory declaration*.

(c) Statutory Declaration

This states that the promoters of the company have complied with the requirements of the Companies Acts. If all is in order the Registrar will then issue a *Certificate of Incorporation*, which establishes the firm as a separate legal entity (incorporation means *making into a body*). The firm can now do anything that the sole proprietor can do. The important thing from a legal point of view is that the firm can now sue and be sued in the courts.

In the case of a *public* limited company, a *certificate of trading* is needed before the company can begin its operations. This is issued by the Registrar when he is satisfied that the company has raised the minimum amount of capital required to fulfil its plans. If the company finds that it cannot raise this minimum amount the certificate is not issued. It is also necessary to convince the Stock Exchange Council of the wisdom of the project and the integrity of the promoters, before shares can be sold in the Stock Exchange.

8.5   The Capital of Limited Companies

The promoters of a limited company can raise capital in a number of different forms. They try to attract contributions from all kinds of people and insti-tutions, by offering them *shares* in the business. Some shares carry a fixed rate of interest and a guarantee of repayment, while others have no fixed return and no offer of repayment. Every person who buys a share becomes a part owner of the company, and is entitled to a share of the company's profits.

The term capital is a confusing one, and we shall return to it in Unit 13. For the time being you should note the following three meanings of the word.

(i) *The nominal or authorized capital* of a Company is the maximum amount of money the company is allowed to raise by issuing shares to the public.

(ii) The company may not wish to issue the maximum amount of shares at the outset. The amount that they do issue is referred to as the *issued capital* of the company.

(iii) When the shares are issued, the company does not always need the full amount to be paid immediately. The proportion of issued capital that is actually paid for is the *paid up capital* of the firm. If the company fails, the holders of shares which are not paid up are required to pay the difference between the nominal value and the paid up value of their shares. For example, if a company has an authorized capital of £800 000 in £1 shares, it may decide to issue them all. If it does not need all the money immediately, it may call for payment of 75 pence on each share, giving it a paid up capital of £600 000. The shareholders would then have to pay a further 25 pence for each share held.

(a) Ordinary Shares
These represent the risk capital of the business. The holders of such shares are not guaranteed a dividend at the end of a trading year because this depends on whether or not the company makes a profit. However, they do have voting rights, and elect the board of directors, who are responsible for the general policy of the company.

(b) Preference Shares
While ordinary shares provide an attractive investment for those who do not mind the risk of getting no reward in some years, others find that preference shares offer a safer investment. Preference shares fall into several groups. There are *basic preference shares*, which receive a fixed dividend out of profits before anything is paid to ordinary shareholders. With *cumulative preference shares* a dividend missed in one year is carried forward to the next. Most preference shareholders have no say in the control of the company as they have a privileged position with respect to dividends. *Participating preference shares* not only carry a fixed rate of dividend, but also entitle their holders to a further share of the profits once they reach a certain level.

A company can also issue *debentures*. These are not shares. Debenture holders do not share in the ownership of the company. Debentures are simply loans to the company, on which a fixed rate of interest is paid before preference or ordinary shareholders receive anything. They are normally secured against property owned by the firm, so that in the event of the company's bankruptcy debenture holders are assured of getting their money. If debenture holders do not receive their annual interest, they can force the company into liquidation.

8.6   The Private Limited Company

As we have seen, when a small business expands there is a need for extra capital. The partners or sole proprietor may decide to turn the business into a limited company to raise this capital. Until the Companies Act 1980, the normal procedure was to establish a private company with a maximum of 50 shareholders. The 1980 Act effectively reversed the standing of companies.

Prior to this Act, all companies were public companies unless they met the special requirements for private companies. Now all companies are private unless they meet the requirements laid down for public companies.

The main points to note about private companies now are: (*a*) their name must end with the words Company Limited; (*b*) they are not allowed to issue shares or debentures to the general public; (*c*) there is no longer any limit to the number of shareholders. Let us look at the advantages of forming a private company.

(*a*) The main advantage of a limited company is its independent legal status, and hence the limited liability enjoyed by its shareholders.

(*b*) With limited liability the company is able to attract capital from people who would not otherwise be prepared to invest.

(*c*) In a private company the founders of the business can usually keep control of it, by holding a majority of the shares.

These advantages have led to the creation of many private companies, the majority of them operating on a purely local basis, but many of them nationally known. Indeed the publishers of this book are formed into a private limited company.

Like all business units, however, the private company also has its disadvantages. There are three main drawbacks.

(*a*) The shareholder in a private limited company can only transfer his shares to someone else with the consent of the company.

(*b*) The company is not allowed to appeal to the public for extra capital.

(*c*) The accounts of the company must be filed annually with the Registrar of Companies. They are then available to anyone on payment of a nominal fee.

8.7   The Public Limited Company

The largest and most important units in the private sector are the public limited companies. Some of them are enormous. In 1979 Imperial Chemical Industries employed 151 000 people, had machinery and buildings worth more than £4 000 million and sold goods to the value of £4 500 million.

Until the 1980 Companies Act, only the largest businesses became public companies (about $2\frac{1}{2}$ per cent of all companies were public in 1979). As we have seen, the situation now is that companies have to meet certain conditions in order to be regarded as public limited companies.

(*a*) It must be stated in the memorandum of association that the company is public.

(*b*) The name of the company must end with the words 'public limited company'.

(*c*) The issued capital of the company must be at least £50 000.

(d) The company must have at least two owners (seven before the 1980 Act).

Like the private company, the public limited company has the advantage of independent legal existence, limited liability for shareholders and continuity of the business. It also enjoys the extra benefit that it is allowed to appeal to the public for funds, whereas the promoters of a private company have to rely on friends and relations for capital. There is no restriction on the transfer of shares.

The other benefits that used to be associated with public companies were those of large scale production. While it is still true that the largest firms will benefit from economies of scale and that the largest firms will be public limited companies, it is not true that all public companies will be large and therefore not necessarily true that they will benefit from economies of scale.

There are disadvantages associated with public limited companies.

(a) The formalities of forming a public limited company are quite involved, and raising capital can be very expensive.

(b) Sometimes a public limited company grows so big that it becomes difficult to manage, though this problem can also occur in other forms of business organization.

(c) Even established public companies have to comply with many regulations. Extra requirements are frequently put upon them by the Government, to protect either shareholders or the general public.

(d) The accounts of the company must be published, so there can be no secrecy or privacy about its affairs.

(e) Perhaps the most important disadvantage of this kind of business is that the owners can normally exercise little control over it. This is so important that it deserves a Section to itself.

8.8   The Control of Companies

If a business is run by a sole proprietor, it is quite clear that he contributes the capital, takes the decisions and enjoys the profits. But these functions are divided between different groups of people in a limited company, and especially a public limited company.

(a) Ownership

A public limited company is owned by its shareholders, and there may be several thousand of them in a large company. Their rights vary according to the kind of shares they own, but it is quite clear that they cannot all be consulted about every decision that needs to be made in the running of the business. If they were, nothing would ever get done. Therefore arrangements are made to delegate the control of the company to a small group of shareholders.

(b) Control

Each year the company holds an annual general meeting, one of the purposes of which is to elect a *board of directors* responsible for running the business. Each ordinary shareholder will have one vote for each share he owns, so it follows that if someone owns 51 per cent of the ordinary shares he can control the business. This does not occur very often and, in fact, most shareholders' meetings are sparsely attended, which to some extent reflects their lack of real power. (In many companies the lack of shareholder participation means that the holder of 25–30 per cent of the shares has control.)

The directors elect a managing director from their number, and together they are responsible for the general policy of the company. Of course they must always act within the terms of the memorandum of association.

(c) Management

When a company employs tens of thousands of people it is of course impossible for a board of directors of perhaps two dozen people to take all the necessary decisions. The directors therefore lay down the general policy of the firm, and each of them assumes a particular area of responsibility. One may be responsible for marketing the product, another for safety and so on. The firm also employs full-time managers to make the day-to-day decisions in running the firm. Each of these managers has a team under him to run his department, and many decisions are taken by quite junior people, who have no financial interest in the company.

You can see, therefore, that there may be a great split between the owners of the business and those who control it: while it may be necessary for the directors to have shares in the company, there is nothing to say that the managers must. Some people argue that the aims of the managers do not always coincide with those of the owners, and that this is a serious weakness of the public limited company.

8.9   Other Kinds of Companies

There are two other kinds of company, but there are very few of them left nowadays.

(a) Companies created by Royal Charter, such as the Hudson's Bay Company.

(b) Companies Limited by Guarantee, in which members guarantee to provide a fixed sum of money in the event of the company going into liquidation.

8.10   The Growth of Companies

All the enormous public companies that are familiar household names today began as very small undertakings. There are three main ways in which companies can expand and most of our large firms have expanded in all three ways.

(a) An Expanding Market
If the economy is expanding, many firms grow simply because their market is growing. A company producing motor vehicles or television sets in 1950 can hardly have failed to increase its turnover since then. A firm may also actively seek new markets for its product, perhaps overseas, and so increase in size. In either case we should expect the turnover and capital employed to increase.

(b) New Products
A further possibility is that the firm will grow by producing new goods. Thus firms in the electrical goods industry have diversified into electronics and a whole range of new products has not only been developed but has come into widespread use. The popularity of pocket calculators and video recorders suggests that firms producing those goods will have expanded in size.

(c) Mergers
The most rapid expansion is achieved by taking over, or merging with, other companies. Mergers fall into four main groups, though few of them fit these categories precisely.

(i) **Horizontal mergers** occur where the two companies are engaged in the same stage of production: a merger between two retailers would be in this category. The creation of the British Leyland Motor Corporation (now known as BL) was achieved through a horizontal merger.

(ii) **Vertical mergers** occur when one company merges with another which is engaged in a prior or subsequent stage of production. Thus the takeover by a retail grocery chain of a firm of food processors would be a vertical merger. Similarly Cadbury Schweppes safeguard their supply of raw materials by owning their own cocoa plantations.

(iii) **Lateral mergers** involve two companies producing goods which are related to each other but not in direct competition. The creation of Cadbury Schweppes was in many ways a lateral merger, taking advantage of raw materials and marketing outlets common to both parent companies. The common link may be at only one end of the process: distilling and brewing, for example, are two quite separate processes, but the lateral merger of a brewer with a distiller should lead to important marketing economies.

(iv) **Diversifying mergers** are probably the most widespread these days. They occur where the products of the companies are unrelated. The acquisition of a cosmetics or potato crisp manufacturer by a tobacco company constitutes a diversifying merger. Such mergers are frequently defensive, by which we mean that the acquiring company is anticipating a decline in its principal market.

A more aggressive kind of diversifying merger is that which makes the acquiring business a *holding company*. This is a company which controls a number of other companies by holding at least 51 per cent of their shares, but not necessarily taking an active part in their management. In this way companies in a variety of industries may benefit from the financial skill and prestige of the holding company, without losing their separate identities. By careful selection a holding company can establish a closely integrated group, with each section complementary to the others. On the other hand, there is more than a suspicion that many of today's diversifying mergers are inspired by speculative rather than economic motives, and that loss-making activities in one part of the group are subsidized by profitable activities in the others.

One result of expansion by all these methods has been the development of *multinational companies*. The multinational company is one with productive facilities in more than one country, but under ownership based in one country only. Many of the largest firms in the British economy come into this category, for example, Shell, Unilever and Ford. A deeper study of such companies belongs to the field of economics, but we may note here one important reason for their development: when domestic markets become saturated, firms have to look elsewhere for outlets for their capital and their products. Unfortunately, the multinational company sometimes arouses suspicion in its host country because its loyalties and interests do not necessarily coincide with those of the host country.

8.11 The Survival of Small Firms

From what we have said so far, it would seem that limited companies, especially large ones, enjoy most of the advantages. The fact remains that the majority of firms are small, and they do manage to survive despite their problems. A Government inquiry into small firms (the Bolton Committee) found many reasons for their survival.

(a) The entrepreneurial spirit of people who value independence and who probably make a greater contribution to the economy by running their own businesses than they would if submerged in a larger organization. There are many firms which could expand but do not, either because the owner wishes to retain control or because he does not want the greater pressure of a larger organization.

(b) Small and geographically dispersed markets are best served by small firms. Moreover, large firms are often not interested in the production of custom-made goods.

(c) Small firms frequently provide an important service to large firms. By providing them with components, and thus relieving them of the task of organizing the production of those components, they enable them to concentrate on their main tasks.

(d) Small firms are often responsible for important innovations. The managers of small firms, being in many ways closer to the market than top managers in large firms, are sometimes quicker to spot and appreciate the significance of new developments. Small firms are more flexible, and often more amenable to the wishes of their clients.

(e) The Government often gives special assistance to small firms especially those just establishing themselves. For example, there are many tax concessions available to them which are not given to large firms.

8.12 Co-operative Societies

In Section 3.3 we examined the retail co-operative societies in some detail. *Producers'* co-operatives are not very common in the United Kingdom, but they are very popular in many parts of Africa and Asia, and indeed in some parts of Europe. They are useful because they enable farmers, for example, to join together to buy and share large items of capital equipment that they could not afford individually. Moreover they can achieve further economies by linking together for the marketing of their products.

What agricultural co-operation there is in Britain is fostered by the *Central Council for Agricultural and Horticultural Co-operation*. This runs a scheme which provides grants for co-operative production and marketing.

8.13 Questions and Exercises

(a) **Short Answers**
1. Explain the difference between the public sector and the private sector.
2. Explain the difference between the public company and the private company.
3. Name the business forms in the private sector.
4. Explain the importance of limited liability to shareholders.
5. What advantage does the private limited company have over the partnership?
6. Who owns a limited company?
7. 'A limited company is a *corporate body*.' What does this mean?
8. Distinguish between the articles of association and the memorandum of association of a limited company.
9. Why is it necessary for some companies to have ordinary shares, preference shares and debentures?
10. Distinguish between nominal, issued and paid up capital.

(b) **Essay Answers**
1. Compare public limited companies and co-operative societies as business units.
2. Show how the functions of the sole proprietor are divided between different groups in the public limited company.
3. Explain the importance of the following in the formation of a limited company: the memorandum of association; the articles of association; the certificate of incorporation; the certificate of trading.

4. Explain the stages by which a sole proprietor's business may expand until it becomes a public limited company.

5. Distinguish between partnerships and private limited companies under the following headings: ownership; formation; distribution of profits; liability.

(c) **Projects**

1. Gather as much information as you can about the formation of companies. (Much can be obtained from the business pages of the newspapers.)

2. Write to or visit your local co-operative society, and write a report on the origins, growth, and recent developments of the co-operative movement.

Unit Nine

Business Units: the Public Sector

9.1 Introduction

While most of the economic and commercial activity in Britain is conducted by the types of firm we examined in Unit 8, some goods and services are provided by central or local government authorities, either directly or through specially appointed agencies. We discuss the reasons for this in Section 9.5, but first we shall simply consider the various types of public enterprise.

(a) The Government as Trader

Sometimes the Government's trading activities are under the direct control of a Government department. Her Majesty's Stationery Office, for example, is under the control of the Treasury, and the Post Office was until 1969 directly controlled by the Postmaster-General, who was a Member of Parliament. Local authorities often provide local transport services and are involved in catering on a commercial basis.

(b) The Government as Shareholder

The Government may hold a large number of the shares of a public limited company and it does, in fact, hold 39 per cent of the shares in British Petroleum. But this does not happen very often. When the Government provides finance to a firm in difficulty, it may take a shareholding on either a temporary or a permanent basis, as in the case of Rolls-Royce. Occasionally the Government sets up a limited company under its sole ownership, where there is an important service to be performed but not much profit to be made: Remploy, the agency which finds employment for handicapped people, is such an example.

The British Technology Group is a public sector organization which acts as a holding company for the Government, and supervises the Government's investments in companies in general. (In 1981 the Group took over the National Enterprise Board which was set up in 1975 to promote and finance improvements in efficiency.)

(c) The Public Corporations (Nationalized Industries)

Public corporations are the most prominent form of public enterprise in the United Kingdom. Their development has been gradual, though none of them is more than 80 years old. The establishment of the Port of London Authority in 1908 was an early example, but the peak of the movement came in the period 1945–51, with the nationalization of the transport, energy and iron and steel industries. We may divide the public corporations into two groups.

(i) Those which sell a product or service directly to the public, charging each customer for what he uses. This group consists of the basic nationalized industries, which supply coal, steel, electricity, gas, transport and all the services of the Post Office.

(ii) Those which provide a service, but do not charge for it directly. Into this category we may put the British Broadcasting Corporation, the Independent Broadcasting Authority (which has the task of supervising the private sector firms who actually provide the broadcasting services), the United Kingdom Atomic Energy Authority, the Arts Council, the Forestry Commission and a number of others.

We shall be primarily concerned with the first group in this Unit, since they form by far the largest part of the public sector. Many people seem to have a rather hazy idea of what goes on in the public sector, and it might be useful to raise and answer the questions they most commonly ask about the nationalized industries.

9.2 What Are Public Corporations?

First let us clear up one ambiguity. In the United States the term *public corporation* refers to what we in the United Kingdom call a public limited company, and it is therefore part of the *private* sector. In the United Kingdom however, a public corporation is a separate legal form found only in the *public* sector. Each one is set up by an Act of Parliament to run the whole of, or at least most of, an industry. Each corporation has a legal identity separate from the Government, and has its own management board selected by the Government. Like the limited company it may sue and be sued in its own name.

The *general policy* of a public corporation is laid down by the Government, in consultation with the board of the corporation. For example, the decision to switch from town gas, manufactured from coal, to North Sea gas was not made by British Gas; it was a matter for the Government.

The day-to-day management of a corporation is theoretically free from Government interference. Matters such as the negotiation of wages with trade unions, and the determination of prices were intended to be left to the corporation. In practice there are many occasions when the Government decides that it must intervene in these matters.

9.3 Who Does the Shareholders' Job?

In a public limited company individual members of the public are the shareholders and hence the owners of the business. The public corporation has no such group of owners. The best description of its ownership is that it is owned by the Government in trust for the community as a whole. This can lead to difficulties with regard to *control* and the subscribing of *capital*.

The shareholders in a limited company have these two important functions. They exercise control over the board of directors: if the company is not running effectively, the shareholders have the power to get rid of the directors and elect replacements; and it is to the shareholders, as owners, that the annual accounts and report of the company are presented. The shareholders also subscribe capital.

(a) Control

Since the public corporations have no shareholders in the ordinary sense, alternative arrangements have had to be made. Over the years successive Governments have built up a system through which the public corporations are accountable to parliament, which thus fulfils part of the role of the shareholders. Control is exercised in several ways.

(i) Each corporation must publish its accounts annually. These are the subject of close examination by the *Public Accounts Committee* of the House of Commons, a group of specialists who may well be more demanding than the shareholders of a limited company.

(ii) Other parliamentary committees, known as *Select Committees*, have the power to make more general investigations into the affairs of the corporations. Members of their boards are sometimes called before the Select Committee to report on procedure and policy. This again may provide a more formidable control than the shareholders of a company do. But criticism is not the sole object of these committees: they come up with many constructive suggestions as well.

(iii) There is supposed to be an annual debate in parliament on the affairs of each corporation. In practice, the pressure of parliamentary business means that these are often cancelled in favour of other debates, but if a corporation is experiencing difficulties the debate is held. This is a useful way of examining problems, and provides another example of the way in which parliament takes over the role of shareholders.

(iv) A more continuous control is exercised by the appointment of a Government minister to have political responsibility for each industry.

(v) Since 1980 the corporations have also been subject to investigation by the *Monopolies and Mergers Commission*, a Government-appointed body which looks into the activities of business organizations which may be behaving in ways that are against the public interest.

(b) Capital

The other important function of the shareholders in a limited company is to subscribe capital. In the case of the public corporation the capital has come or may come from a variety of sources.

(i) The corporations used to issue their own securities to the public. For example, the Gas Council once issued British Gas Stock, on which it paid a fixed rate of interest. All the proceeds from issuing the securities went to the gas industry. The holders of these securities were in no sense the owners of the industry, nor were they taking any risks. They received their interest whether the industry made a profit or not, because it was guaranteed by the Government.

(ii) In 1956 the practice of each of the corporations issuing its own securities was ended, and now they borrow direct from the Treasury to finance capital projects that cannot be met out of current income. If necessary the Treasury issues *gilt-edged securities* (see Section 13.4) to raise the money required. (Sometimes, however, the Treasury may be unwilling or unable to lend them the amounts they want at the time they want it. This is another way in which the activities of the nationalized industries are controlled.)

(iii) More recently some of the corporations have been allowed to raise considerable sums of money from EEC countries, mainly Germany. One of the important side effects of this is to bring a temporary improvement to the Balance of Payments (see Unit 21). These loans are guaranteed by the British Government.

(iv) If the corporation makes a profit, the money can be reinvested.

9.4 What Happens to Their Profits?

As we shall see in Section 9.6, the public corporations are not profit-making bodies in the normal sense. Any profit made is called a *surplus*, and is disposed of in the following ways.

(*a*) It may be used to make interest payments on capital. All the nationalized industries began with enormous capital debts, because compensation had to be paid to the previous shareholders. Interest on all that capital has to be paid at a fixed rate. (This situation is quite different from that of the limited company, which may have some fixed interest capital, but does not have to pay a dividend on the ordinary shares if it has a bad year.)

Recently a new kind of security has been issued by British Airways, on which interest is payable only if profits are above a certain level. At the moment these securities are held only by the Government, but they could well become available to the public at a later date.

(*b*) It may be set aside for the future repayment of loans.

(*c*) It may be reinvested, to finance expansion in the industry.

Should the industry fail to make a surplus, so that it is unable to meet its interest payments, the stockholders do not suffer, for the Treasury will pay. In effect this means that the taxpayers will pay the interest, since it is from them that the Treasury obtains most of its revenue. These interest payments are added to the accumulated debt of the industry. If this debt itself goes on increasing, because the industry is unable to make a profit, it will eventually be *written off* (cancelled), to allow the corporation to make a fresh start.

9.5 Why Are Industries Nationalized?

There is no single answer to the question of why industries have been taken into public ownership. Many influences have been at work, and we shall look at some of the more prominent reasons for nationalization.

(a) Financial Necessity

Sometimes an industry may be so run down that only vast sums of money from the Government can save it. This was an important factor in the nationalization of both the coal industry and the railways after the Second World War. More recently Rolls-Royce came into this category.

(b) Strategic Necessity

Some industries are essential for national well-being and security. Again the coal industry and Rolls-Royce are good examples. In 1947 coal was the United Kingdom's only indigenous source of power, so it was essential for the industry to be placed on a sound footing. Rolls-Royce makes an important contribution to the defence programme of the United Kingdom and other western countries, and likewise could not be allowed to go out of business.

(c) Safety

Nuclear energy is too dangerous to be left in the hands of private developers. Nationalization was seen as a public safeguard.

(d) Basic Industries

There are some industries on which the whole economy depends: the fuel, power, transport and steel industries are examples. If these are not working efficiently, all the other industries suffer. Some Governments have felt that the importance of these industries is so great that the decisions about their investment programmes and their rates of expansion should not be left to boards of directors who only represent the interests of a relatively small number of shareholders. Nationalization was seen as the best way of protecting the interests of the community as a whole.

(e) Natural Monopolies

Although competition is appropriate to most industries, there are certain circumstances in which a *monopolist* may be more efficient. (A monopolist is someone who has exclusive control of a commodity or service.) At one period in the nineteenth century there were three different railway companies, with separate lines running trains between London and Brighton. Not one of them was profitable, for their trains were never full. In this situation it makes better economic sense to have just one operator. The same applies to many public services: for example, we do not want two or three firms competing to sell us gas, each with its own elaborate system of pipelines. Industries like this *need* to be monopolized. It is generally thought that if there is to be a monopoly at all, a publicly owned monopoly is preferable to a privately owned one.

(f) Economies of Scale

Some industries need to be very large to take full advantage of economies of scale (see Section 8.7). The generation of electricity is an example. Once again, if very large units of production are going to be established, many people feel that they should be publicly owned.

(g) Political Belief
Some people believe that the private ownership of the means of production is wrong in itself, and that nationalization is the only way of returning industry to its rightful owners, the community as a whole.

9.6   What Are the Aims of Public Corporations?

The main aim of a limited company is to make a profit for the satisfaction of its shareholders, but the public corporation finds itself in a more ambiguous position. In the early post-war years, when most nationalization occurred, the public corporations were required to cover their costs, taking one year with another. Thus they could make a loss one year as long as there was a profit to offset it later. Since 1961 it has been the Government's general objective that the nationalized industries should be self-financing and should, as far as possible, avoid drawing subsidies from the taxpayer. In consultation with the corporations, the Government hopes to set specific financial targets for each industry. Since the corporations are not straightforward profit-seeking firms, it is often difficult to set appropriate targets for all of them.

In an effort to keep industrial costs down, successive Governments forbade the corporations to increase their prices by large enough amounts to meet their targets. However, in November 1974 the Chancellor of the Exchequer gave a specific instruction that they were to raise prices so that eventually they would no longer be subsidized by the taxpayer. This instruction was reinforced from 1979 when the Government insisted on a policy to make the industries self-supporting.

However, these financial requirements have to be balanced against the corporations' responsibility for performing public services. There is often, for example, a statutory obligation to provide a *comprehensive* service. A private sector firm supplying electricity might refuse to supply the service to outlying areas, on the grounds of economy, but the nationalized industry cannot be so selective.

While it is not laid down in law, it has turned out that a further aim of the corporations is co-operation in the implementation of certain Government policies. For example, if the Government is trying to keep prices down, it will insist that the corporations keep their prices steady, and thus set an example to other firms.

9.7   How Are Public Corporations Organized?

The public corporations are among the largest business units that we have. The five biggest employers in the United Kingdom are all public corporations. Table 9.1 gives an indication of the size of the main corporations. Organizing such enormous units to ensure that goods and services are available to the public at the right time and in the right place is a very difficult task. The approach has been different in each of the industries, because each has different problems to solve: the steel industry has other industrial concerns as its main customers, while British Gas not only has to deliver gas to industrial consumers but to millions of private homes as well.

It is not therefore surprising that the two corporations are organized differently. The Steel Corporation is organized according to the various products that are made, and the gas industry is organized on a regional basis.

9.8   How Does the Public Benefit from Public Corporations?

(*a*) Industries that are essential to our economic well-being can be kept going even if they are not profitable in a narrow economic sense. The railway system is an example. Though hardly comprehensive as it is, the railway network might be smaller still by now if it had been left to private enterprise. The railways provide many benefits, such as speedy travel between the major centres and less crowded roads, and most people think it is worth paying extra taxes for things like this.

Table 9.1   The size of public corporations, 1982/83

	Sales (£ million)	Capital employed (£ million)	Profits (£ million)	Employees (thousands)
Electricity	8 417	32 605	639	147
British Telecom	5 708	8 437	1 010	246
British Steel	3 443	2 635	−207 (loss)	112
National Coal Board	4 727	3 960	−82 (loss)	210
British Gas	5 199	10 996	394	105
British Rail	2 816	1 348	−87 (loss)	220
British Airways	2 241	758	10	49
National Bus Company	665	256	35	52

(*b*) Factors other than profits are taken into account when planning these industries. For example, for many years uneconomic coal mines were kept open to avoid massive regional unemployment.

(*c*) A more comprehensive service can be provided.

(*d*) Often enormous economies of scale are available, which should result in lower prices for consumers.

(*e*) The public corporations are under ultimate, if very remote, democratic control.

9.9 Why Are the Corporations so Heavily Criticized?

(*a*) Many of the corporations have little competition, so there is a danger of complacency, which leads to inefficiency.

(*b*) It is sometimes said that some public corporations are treated more favourably than their private competitors. It has been suggested, for example, that British Airways has undue influence with the Government over the allocation of routes.

(*c*) The very size of the corporations inevitably leads to faults in the services they provide. While these faults must be admitted, the corporations suffer from several handicaps which are sometimes overlooked.

(*d*) When the corporations fail to make a profit, the press and the public often draw unfair comparisons with the large limited companies. They forget the obligations that the Government places upon them. (Frequently the Government has refused to allow a public corporation to increase its prices.)

(*e*) One important difficulty is that of salaries. The corporations are unable to pay salaries which are as high as the large limited companies, so it is possible that they do not attract the most dynamic managers and thus fail to achieve their optimum efficiency.

(*f*) Some of the industries, as we have seen, were in a very poor way when they were taken over. They have still not fully recovered.

9.10 Privatization

The Government elected in 1979 began to reverse the process of nationalization. This policy is known as *privatization* and it stemmed from the Government's belief that private sector industries are more efficient than those in the public sector. The Government was also anxious to raise revenue from selling the businesses and to avoid using taxpayers' money to subsidize them in future. This explains why an organization such as British Aerospace, once wholly owned by the Government, is now partly owned by private investors.

9.11 Municipal Enterprise

Most local government authorities undertake some trading activities. Some of their services, for example, education and street lighting, are provided free of direct charge to the actual user, but are paid for indirectly by the whole community in the form of *rates*, or local taxation. For many other services the local authority makes a charge in order to cover costs: swimming pools, sauna baths, golf courses, football and cricket pitches, theatres, dance halls and bus services are just a few of them. However, the income from these services is frequently insufficient to cover costs, and so they too have to be subsidized out of the rates. It is felt that the users of these services should make some direct contribution to the costs.

9.12   Questions and Exercises

(a) Short Answers

1. What is the difference between a public corporation and a public company?
2. What is the difference between a public corporation and a municipal corporation?
3. Give four reasons why an industry may be nationalized.
4. Who owns a nationalized industry?
5. Who controls a public corporation?
6. How do nationalized industries raise additional capital?
7. What is a natural monopoly?
8. Make a list of the nationalized industries.
9. What trading activities are undertaken by your local government authority?
10. How does the Government influence nationalized industries?

(b) Essay Answers

1. Compare a public corporation with a public limited company from the point of view of (a) ownership, (b) control, (c) aims, (d) capital.
2. Why are some industries nationalized? What problems do they face that do not exist for private sector firms?
3. Select any public corporation with which you are familiar. Describe its organization and aims.
4. Examine the ways in which the functions of the shareholders in a public company are performed in a public corporation.
5. Why is it that the supply of gas and electricity is nationalized, but your local hairdresser's is privately owned? How do the problems of each type of organization differ?

(c) Projects

1. Make a collection of news cuttings relating to the nationalized industries.
2. By studying the reports of the public corporations (available in most reference libraries), make a list of those that make a profit and those that do not. Why do some of them make a loss? Who makes good the loss?

Unit Ten

The Monetary System

10.1 What Is Money?

Most of us feel happier if we have some money in our pocket or in the bank or the Post Office. We go to work to earn money. We may spend it on goods and services or we may save it. We value goods in terms of money and we may measure a man's wealth in monetary terms. Few of us, however, pause to ask the question, what is money?

The answer is that money is a claim to goods and services. Another way of putting it is to say that money can be exchanged for the goods and services we need. In itself, contemporary money is practically worthless: the starving man cannot eat it, nor the thirsty man drink it, but each may use it to buy food or drink.

Another answer to the question, 'what is money?' is contained in the saying 'money is as money does'. Let us consider more closely what it is that money does.

10.2 The Functions of Money

If our money ceased to exist tomorrow we should soon discover the importance of the jobs it performs. It has four separate functions.

(a) Money as a Means of Exchange

Without money a normal shopping expedition would become impossible. Consider what happens now: we decide what goods we wish to buy, take the money from our wage packets or bank account, go to the appropriate shops and exchange our money for the goods we want. This is money as a means of exchange, and we probably obtained the money in the first place by exchanging our services for it in the form of labour. Without money our employers would have to pay us in some other way for our services, perhaps by allowing us to take some of the goods we helped produce. While this might solve his problems it would be only the beginning of ours, for we should now have to exchange our 'wages' – wheat or clothes or typewriters – for the goods we require. If we have been paid in typewriters we must find someone who not only wants a typewriter but who is anxious to get rid of food and books in the quantities we wish to buy. Such a coincidence is unlikely to occur frequently. In fact under a system of *barter* a modern industrial society such as ours could not exist.

The great advantage of money is that it does away with the need for this coincidence of wants.

(b) Money as a Measure of Value
Even if the owner of the typewriter were successful in finding someone prepared to accept it in exchange for books, there would be the further problem of deciding how many books should be surrendered for one typewriter. And it would be the same with any other goods: the exchange rate between the two would be the subject of delicate negotiation between the parties. Traders would need to bear in mind exchange rates between all kinds of commodities. In our present society the value of all goods is measured in terms of money so they can easily be compared. It thus becomes much easier to recognize a bargain and to avoid paying excessive prices.

(c) Money as a Store of Value
We do not always wish to spend all of our income as we receive it. If we are paid in money we may keep it to spend in perhaps three or four years' time. If we are paid in the form of, say, fruit, it will quickly deteriorate and become worthless. Money is thus a convenient way of storing wealth. It is quite true that money kept in a tin for a number of years may fall in value because the prices of everything else rise, but this is not the same as fruit quickly going bad.

(d) Money as a Standard for Deferred Payments
All kinds of contracts and agreements are drawn up in monetary terms. Thus when a trader obtains a bank loan, his future repayments are fixed in terms of money. This is money being used as a standard for deferred payments, though once again the falling value of money may cause complications.

We can therefore say that the role of money is to facilitate trade, and that money is at the heart of our economic and commercial system. It is impossible to imagine modern society without it. We must now consider the characteristics of money and the way in which it has developed into its present forms.

10.3   The Nature and Characteristics of Money

(a) Acceptability
It was once the case that money had *intrinsic value*, that is, it was wanted in its own right irrespective of its value as money. Today's money has no intrinsic value; it is valuable because we know that shopkeepers and others will accept it in exchange for goods. Thus the most important characteristic of money is that it should be generally *acceptable*. As long as the public have *confidence* in the money in circulation, it will be generally acceptable, but if that confidence does not exist then it will not. It was some time before the one pound coins were generally acceptable to the public after their introduction in 1983. There have been isolated occasions, fortunately not in our own country, when the public have lost all confidence in money because its value was falling daily – so the price of a loaf of bread might double between breakfast and tea-time. This brings us to its second essential characteristic.

(*b*) **Stability of Value**

Money should have stability of value if it is to facilitate the production and distribution of goods. The present tendency for prices to rise means that our money is correspondingly falling in value and cannot properly fulfil its role as a measure of value. However, since the changes in prices are usually gradual we need not let this worry us too much at this stage, although it is worth looking at Table 10.1 to see how the value of money has changed since 1970. If we assume that a given parcel of goods could be bought in 1970 for £1 we can read from the table what the same parcel of goods would have cost in subsequent years. Thus in 1974 we could have bought the same parcel of goods for 139 pence, and in 1984 for 524 pence. This tendency for prices to rise, which is known as *inflation*, is one respect in which our money does not have all the traditional characteristics that money should have.

(*c*) **Other Characteristics**

There are several other characteristics that money should have, none of them perhaps as fundamental as the two we have already outlined.

(i) **Portability**. It is obviously desirable that money should be portable, so that shopping can be done conveniently. In some societies huge boulders have been used as money. Imagine the difficulty of doing the weekly shopping in such circumstances.

(ii) **Divisibility**. It is also important that money should be divisible, so that small payments can be made. One of the reasons for the use of copper and other base metals in monetary systems was the impossibility of making small payments in gold or silver. Again, we should be faced with great difficulties if the smallest monetary unit in circulation was the £10 note.

Table 10.1 The falling value of money

Year	Amount needed to buy a given amount of goods (pence)
1970	100
1971	108
1972	115
1973	124
1974	139
1975	168
1976	233
1977	273
1978	300
1979	327
1980	386
1981	431
1982	468
1983	488
1984	524

(iii) **Durability**. If money is to act as a store of value it is necessary that it should not deteriorate. In those communities where livestock was used as money, a man would find his wealth depreciating as it aged.

(iv) **Uniformity**. It is generally agreed that money should be uniform in quality, otherwise there would be a tendency for people to hoard those coins with the highest metal content. At one time our coins contained precious metals in varying proportions.

10.4   Types of Money

We have already mentioned some of the commodities that have been used as money in the past. Although a wide variety of commodities have been used as money, most societies have now settled on metallic coins. We conclude this Unit by looking at the kinds of money that have been used in this country.

(a) Gold and Silver
For a long period gold and silver coins with a guaranteed metal content were in circulation. They thus had intrinsic value, and the public were eager to accept them.

(b) Base Metals
The relative shortage of gold and silver, and the difficulty of making small payments, led to the introduction of other metal coins, such as copper and nickel ones. Eventually the use of gold and silver was abandoned altogether. Now our coins are merely tokens which we accept, not because of their intrinsic value, but because we know other people will accept them from us.

(c) Paper Money
It was once the practice of wealthy merchants and traders to leave their gold and silver with a goldsmith for safekeeping. In exchange they received a note from the goldsmith, on which he promised to pay a fixed amount of gold or silver on demand. Such notes were often used to buy goods from local dealers, the dealer then claiming the gold from the goldsmith. These, in effect, were the first banknotes. Most of the holders of such notes never bothered to cash them for gold, and the gold consequently lay idle in the goldsmith's vaults. Before long the goldsmith realized that he could issue notes in excess of the amount of gold in his vault: no difficulty would arise, provided that not everyone wanted to withdraw gold at the same time. These banknotes which were not fully covered by gold were known as *fractionally backed* notes.

The proportion of gold to notes issued fell over the years, and we are now in a position where the entire note issue is unbacked by gold. We accept the notes only because we are confident that other people will accept them from us.

(d) Bank Money
Table 10.2 shows the total amount of money available in September 1984.

You will notice that, while the volume of notes and coins is considerable, it is dwarfed by the second item, bank deposits. Nowadays, most money changes hands through the use of these bank deposits.

Table 10.2   The supply of money, 1984

	£m
Bank notes and coin	12 102
Bank deposits	93 366
Total	105 468

10.5   Questions and Exercises

(a) Short Answers

1. What is meant by *barter*?
2. What are its disadvantages?
3. What are the functions of money?
4. What are the main characteristics of money?
5. Why does money need stability of value?
6. Why has gold often been the basis of a monetary system?
7. What is fractionally backed money?
8. Why does the Bank of England issue £50 notes?
9. Look at a copy of *Financial Statistics* and find out what the size of the money stock is today.
10. What would be the disadvantages of using the following as the only money in Britain: (a) chalk, (b) eggs, (c) cattle, (d) mercury, (e) pound notes?

(b) Essay Answers

1. Give examples to show why money makes trade work more smoothly.
2. What are the main characteristics of money? Consider whether British money today has these characteristics.
3. Write a paragraph explaining to your employer why he should increase your wages to combat the fall in the value of money.
4. Describe the ways in which we might receive and make payments in the absence of money.

(c) Project

See what you can learn about the Retail Price Index. Keep a record of the changes in the Index to show how the value of money changes.

Unit Eleven

The Banking System:
the Clearing Banks

11.1   Introduction

No institution is more important to a businessman than his bank. He may want to borrow money to help him start his business or to finance the purchase of stocks once the business is under way, or he may simply need to settle his debts with his suppliers or collect money from his customers. The bank will help him in each situation. In this Unit we shall examine briefly the early development of the banks and the functions they perform nowadays for traders and the community in general.

First we must distinguish between the different kinds of bank.

(a)   The Central Bank

The Central Bank of the United Kingdom is the Bank of England. It is the Government's Bank and its functions are explained in Section 12.6.

(b)   The Clearing Banks

The Clearing Banks are the subject of this Unit. They are probably the banks with which you are most familiar, because they provide a wide range of services to businessmen and the general public. The best known of them are Barclays, Lloyds, Midland and National Westminster. They are also known as joint stock banks or deposit banks.

(c)   Merchant Banks

As their name suggests, these banks were originally merchants or traders. They became involved in the finance of trade in the nineteenth century, and their interests have spread from there. Now they offer a number of services to commerce and industry, as we shall see in Section 12.3.

11.2   The Development of the Clearing Banks

As we saw in Section 10.4(c), the original bankers in the United Kingdom were goldsmiths and jewellers, whose vaults provided a place of safekeeping for the valuables of local people. Rather than carry large amounts of gold around with them or leave it at home, people would deposit it with the goldsmith, who would make a small charge for the service and issue a receipt to the depositor. The receipt could be exchanged for gold at any time if the depositor wanted to make purchases. Once the newly withdrawn money had been spent, the recipient would almost certainly redeposit it with the goldsmith. It eventually became the practice not to withdraw gold for every purchase but to pass on the receipt to traders from whom you bought goods. As long as the trader recognized the receipt and trusted the goldsmith who had issued it, this was a much more convenient way of making payments, since the receipt represented a claim on an amount of deposited gold.

This benefited the goldsmith too, in that only a small proportion of the gold deposited with him was ever withdrawn. The goldsmiths soon realized that they could turn this situation to their own advantage. Suppose they had £10 000 deposited and knew from experience that a maximum of £2 000 was withdrawn on any one day, and that this would be redeposited within a day or so. They deduced that if the ratio of gold in their vaults to the value of the receipts they had issued was greater than 20 per cent, they need never run out of gold. So they began tentatively to issue *receipts* or *promises to pay* to people who had not deposited any gold but who wanted to borrow instead. Naturally they made a charge for this service. Since these receipts were identical to those issued to the original depositors, they could be used for purchases in exactly the same way. The danger lay in the temptation to issue too many receipts unbacked by gold. When this happened and the ratio of gold to promises to pay fell to, say, 5 per cent, rumours would sometimes grow of the goldsmith's inability to meet his liabilities. The holders of his paper promises would then clamour for repayment, bringing about the collapse – bankruptcy – of the goldsmith.

The next development was the growth of what we now know as cheques. If you had a sum of money deposited with a goldsmith, or a bank as we may now call them, you might instruct your bank to transfer money to someone else. Such orders would be individually written – there was no such thing as the printed cheque that we know today – but the role of these early banks was essentially the same as that of today's banks. We can now examine that role in detail.

11.3 The Functions of the Banks

(a) The Safeguarding of Customers' Money

As we have seen, this was the original function of the banks, and it remains important today. Broadly speaking, you may keep your money in two types of account at the bank.

(i) **A current account**, which is essential to all businessmen. Money or cheques can be deposited into such an account at any time and, more important, withdrawals can be made at any time without giving notice to the bank. Payments can also be made to creditors by writing a cheque in their favour (see Section 11.3(c)). The banks do not normally pay interest on such an account, but if the balance on the account falls below a stipulated level, the bank will make charges for running the account.

(ii) **A deposit account**, on which interest is payable, is usually subject to seven days' notice of withdrawal. In practice you may normally withdraw money on demand, but you lose the seven days' interest on the amount withdrawn. The amount of interest payable on such an account varies from time to time and according to the notice required for withdrawal.

Opening a bank account is not difficult. The current account is the most useful type for general purposes. At the bank you will be asked to provide a specimen signature, so that the bank can see that your cheques are properly signed and to fill in a form, giving the names and addresses of referees (probably two) who are able to vouch for your honesty. Provided that the references are favourable, the bank will accept an initial deposit to open your account. You will then be issued with a cheque book and a paying-in book, and will be able to use the services outlined in this Unit.

An important aspect of the safekeeping of deposits is that the banks must always make sure that they have enough money to meet likely withdrawals by customers, or, in technical terms, that they retain sufficient *liquid assets* to meet anticipated withdrawals. Liquidity in this context means *nearness to cash*, so liquid assets are those that can be turned into cash quickly. In Section 11.11 we shall see how the banks arrange their assets in order to meet this requirement.

(b) Supplying Cash to Customers

If we are going to entrust our money to the bank, we need to be sure that we can withdraw it when we want it. Thus the banks must always have money available for their customers. Since all branches of the banks receive deposits of cash from their customers, you might imagine that they will normally be able to meet their customers' requirements when they want to withdraw. In fact, it is unlikely that the deposits and withdrawals at any one bank branch will exactly balance. For example, in those branches located near industrial estates withdrawals are likely to exceed deposits, as firms draw money to pay wages. High street branches, on the other hand, are likely to experience a net inflow of cash, as shops pay in their takings. There has to be a transfer of cash from the high street branches to the industrial estate branches. Similar transfers may need to be made between urban and rural branches. Other branches may experience seasonal fluctuations in their requirements, seaside branches for example. The banks therefore have to organize the physical transfer of money from place to place.

The banks are also the means of getting new notes and coins into circulation, although these originate at the Bank of England and the Royal Mint respectively. It is also the function of the banks to withdraw badly soiled or mutilated notes from circulation when they are deposited. These are returned to the Bank of England, where they are destroyed.

(c) Operating the Cheque System

A cheque is an order to your bank to pay a stated sum to the bearer of the cheque or a named person. We saw earlier that the original cheques were letters from customers to their banker or goldsmith, telling him to transfer money. Today it is usual to write your cheques on printed forms issued by the banks, though there is nothing to stop you writing a cheque on blank paper. Indeed there are many examples of cheques being written on unusual materials: the friends of A. P. Herbert are said to have written a cheque on a cow as a means of demonstrating that there is no legal obligation to use printed cheques.

Fig. 11.1 shows specimen cheques blank and completed.

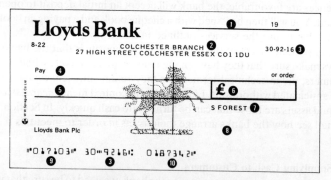

Fig. 11.1 Specimen cheques: (above) blank and (below) completed

(1) **Date.** All cheques should carry the date on which they are drawn (or written out). When you receive a cheque, you should pay it into your bank immediately. The drawee bank will refuse to honour a cheque after six months have elapsed from the date of issue. (An exception is made at the beginning of each year when many cheques appear to have been drawn the previous January or February, having been absent-mindedly dated with the wrong year.) Sometimes cheques are *post-dated*, a practice which is frowned upon by the banks.

Suppose you receive a bill on 15th March and know that you have insufficient funds in your bank account to cover the bill, but that your salary will be paid in on 28th March. You may be able to keep your creditor quiet by sending him a cheque dated 28th March, in which case you will have gained two weeks' delay. This is a post-dated cheque. The bank will not process the cheque until 28th March.

(2) **The drawee.** The cheque is said to be *drawn* on the bank. All cheques carry the name of the bank and the address of the branch on which it is drawn. This is the branch at which the account is held. The bank is known as the drawee. If there is a query about the cheque, reference can easily be made to the drawee bank.

(3) **Branch code number.** This appears in the top right hand corner of the cheque and again at the bottom, where it is printed in magnetic characters to facilitate the automatic handling of the cheque.

(4) **Payee's name.** This must be written on the top line of the cheque. United Stores can then pay it into their account. If the cheque is an open cheque, as it is in Fig. 11.1, United Stores can cash the cheque over the counter at a bank (see Section 11.4).

(5) and (6) **The amount** that is to be paid must appear both in words (5) and in figures (6). It is important that these figures agree. If there is a discrepancy between the sum in words and the sum in figures the cheque will not be honoured by the bank.

(7) **The drawer's name** is often printed beneath the box in which the figures are written.

(8) **The drawer's signature.** The drawer must also *sign* the cheque, to authorize the bank to pay the money out. Again, if the cheque is not signed, or if the signature does not correspond with the specimen signature provided by the client when he opened his account, the bank will not honour the cheque.

(9) **The cheque number** appears in the bottom left hand corner of the cheque, and again it helps the sorting of cheques within the branch. The bank keeps a record of the cheque book numbers issued to each customer, and can therefore debit the appropriate account. The cheque number also appears on the customer's bank statement, to help him check the details of his statement.

A further figure will appear at the bottom of the cheque once it has been paid into the bank. This will be the amount of the cheque, printed by the bank on the basis of the figures written in by the drawer.

(10) **The account number** appears at the bottom of the cheque, again in magnetic characters, to facilitate the automatic handling of the cheque. Each

customer has his own account number which appears on all his cheques and on his paying-in slips (see Section 11.5).

11.4 Types of Cheques

(a) Open Cheques

The cheque shown in Fig. 11.2 is an open cheque. Anyone who finds an open cheque can take it to the bank on which it is drawn, pretend to be the payee and obtain cash by endorsing the cheque on the back with the payee's name. Obviously it is not normally safe to write such cheques, but it may be necessary if you wish to pay someone who does not have a bank account.

(b) Bearer Cheques

These are very rarely used today. They are made out 'Pay Bearer', as in Fig. 11.2, and anyone in possession of such a cheque can demand cash from the bank without even identifying himself, since the name of the payee is immaterial.

Fig. 11.2 A bearer cheque

(c) Crossed Cheques

If two parallel lines are drawn across the face of a cheque it becomes a crossed cheque. (Figs. 11.3–11.6 are all crossed cheques.) The bank will not pay cash over the counter on a crossed cheque, because the crossing indicates that the cheque must be paid into a bank account. Should a thief pay a crossed cheque into the wrong account, it will be possible to trace the account to which it has been credited. The fact that a crossed cheque is made payable to J. Smith does not mean, however, that it has to be credited to J. Smith's account. He may want it paid to his *order*. Thus if he owes money to B. Jones he can endorse the back of it *in favour of B. Jones*, and Jones can then pay it into his own account.

The cheque in Fig. 11.3 carries a *general crossing*. Other general crossings appear on the cheques in Figs. 11.4 and 11.5. Some people maintain the old practice of writing '& Co.' between the parallel lines. This dates from the days when, if the drawer of the cheque was uncertain of the name of the payee's bank, he would write in the words '& Co.' leaving it to the payee to complete the banker's name.

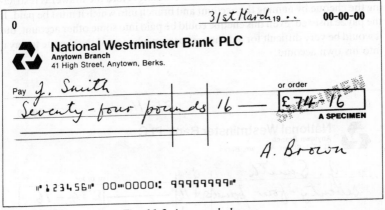

Fig. 11.3 A crossed cheque

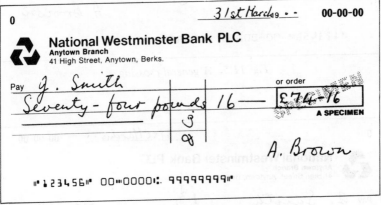

Fig. 11.4 A general crossing

Sometimes a cheque is crossed *A/C Payee Only*, as in Fig. 11.5. This is an instruction to the bank that the cheque should be paid only into the account of the named payee. In fact, if the payee desires, he *can* endorse the cheque in favour of someone else, but the bank will always take care that the authorization is genuine, for the bank will be liable if it credits the wrong account.

Not negotiable crossings are also quite popular. The effect of such a crossing is that the payee cannot negotiate the cheque to someone else (i.e. he cannot make the cheque payable to someone else by endorsing it). In fact this is *not* the case: the payee can still transfer the cheque if he wishes. But the crossing is a warning to the recipient to ensure that the transferer is the real owner of the cheque. If he is not, and has stolen the cheque, the recipient has no more right to claim the money than the thief.

The cheque in Fig. 11.6 bears a *special crossing*. Here the drawer is restricting the cheque by naming the account and branch into which it must be paid. If the payee insisted, even this cheque could be paid into some other account, but it would be very difficult for a dishonest person who found the cheque to pay it into his own account.

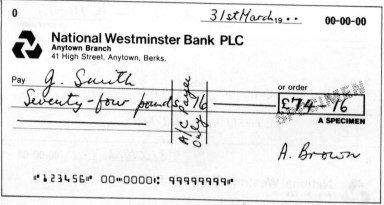

Fig. 11.5   *A general crossing*

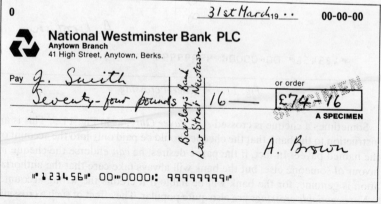

Fig. 11.6   *A special crossing*

11.5 Clearing a Cheque

When you write a cheque in favour of your creditor, you are instructing your bank to transfer money from your account to his. The process of dealing with the cheque once it has been paid in to your creditor's bank is called *clearing* the cheque. The actual process will vary according to whether the drawer and payee share the same bank or live in the same town. Three examples will show you what happens.

(*a*) H. Brown, who banks at National Westminster, Ipswich, pays £20 by cheque to R. Smith, who banks at National Westminster, Reading. Smith pays the cheque into his account, using a paying-in slip like that shown in Fig. 11.7.

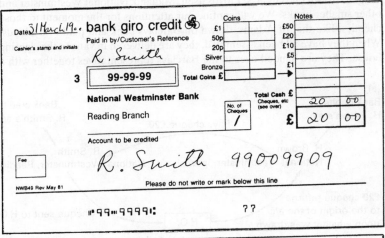

Fig. 11.7 A paying-in slip (front and back)

The counterfoil of the paying-in slip is stamped by the bank and kept as a receipt by Smith, who thus has a permanent record of his in payments. Smith's bank sends Brown's cheque to its head office (together with all the other cheques that have been paid into the branch that day). At the head office Brown's cheque is bundled together with all the other cheques drawn on the Ipswich branch and is then sent there. There Brown's account is debited with £20 and the cheque filed for future return to Brown.

(b) L. Adams, who banks at Barclays, Brighton, sends a cheque for £25 to B. Jones, who banks at Lloyds, Margate. The cheque is paid into Jones's account in the same way as before, the account is credited with £25 and the cheque sent off to Lloyds head office. Lloyds divide all the cheques they receive according to their bank of origin. Thus there will be great racks of cheques drawn on Barclays, Lloyds itself, Midland, National Westminster and other smaller banks. We will confine our attentions for the moment to those cheques, like that of Adams, drawn on Barclays bank and paid into Lloyds. When they have all been assembled, they are delivered in vans to the clearing house. They are handed over to the Barclays representatives together with a

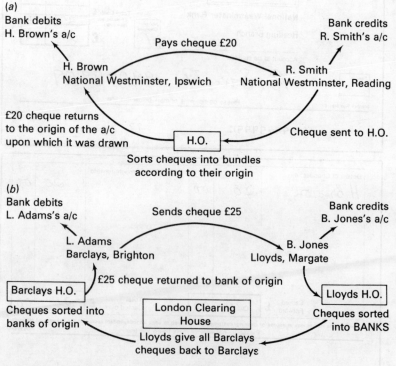

Fig. 11.8 Cheque clearing: (a) between branches of the same bank;
(b) between different banks

note of their total value, for this is the sum that Barclays owe to Lloyds. At the same time the Barclays representatives present Lloyds with cheques received by Barclays, drawn on Lloyds. (The question of the settlement of the debt between the banks is dealt with in Section 12.7.)

Adams's cheque is now taken back to Barclays head office with all the others they have received, and from there it is returned to Barclays Brighton branch, where Adams's account is debited £25.

(c) L. Adams, who banks at Barclays, Brighton, pays £15 by cheque to A. Green, who uses the same bank. This is the simplest case, for the bank merely reduces Adams's balance by £15 and increases Green's by the same amount.

11.6 Dishonoured Cheques

It sometimes happens that when the cheque arrives back at the drawer's branch via the clearing system there is insufficient money in his account to cover the payment. In this case it may be sent back to the payee marked 'RD', which means that the payee should 'Refer to Drawer' for an explanation. In fact the bank will normally honour the cheque, provided the amount involved is not large and provided the customer is expected to pay money into his account fairly shortly.

Lack of funds is not the only reason for cheques being dishonoured by the banks, and we mention three other possibilities.

(a) The amount written in words and the amount written in figures may be different. In this case the drawer will be asked to remove the discrepancy.

(b) The signature may not correspond with the specimen given to the bank when the account was opened (see Section 11.3). This will arouse the bank's suspicions, and they will ask the account holder to verify that he did sign the cheque. Some accounts need the signatures of two people before money can be transferred, and cheques will be dishonoured if there is only one signature on them.

(c) If more than six months have elapsed between the date of the cheque and the day it is presented to the bank, the cheque is stale. It is possible that the cheque has passed through many hands in this time, and the bank will want to make sure that the drawer knows what is happening to his cheque.

11.7 Bank Giro Credit System

Cheques are the most important method of payment provided by the banks but there are others, and the bank giro credit system is one of them. Figs. 11.9 and 11.10 show the main documents involved. This system allows payment to be made at any branch of any bank to any other branch in the country, and it is available to those who do not have a bank account as well as to those who do. The system is also known as the *credit transfer system*.

In the case of Bloggs & Co shown in Fig. 11.9, they are paying £228.24 to the account of A.J. Smith, who has presumably supplied them with goods to this

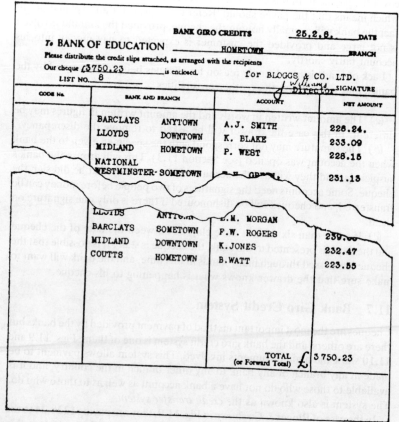

Fig. 11.9 A bank giro credit slip

Fig. 11.10 A multiple bank giro credit slip

value. The cheque will be cleared in the ordinary way outlined in Section 11.5, and Smith's account will be credited with the amount in a few days. The bank giro system offers several advantages.

(a) You do not need a bank account to pay by this method, although your creditor must have one.

(b) Since you pay your cheque (or money) directly into the bank, you do not have to worry about it going astray in the post.

(c) The bank will make a charge to people not holding an account at the bank, but this is considerably cheaper than the fee on a postal order and the postage necessary to send it to your creditor.

(d) If you are an account holder you can pay money into your account from any part of the country.

For businessmen there may be considerable economy in using the bank giro credit system to pay wages and salaries. Fig. 11.10 shows what happens. Bloggs & Co Ltd want to pay the monthly salaries of their eight branch managers. The firm *could* instruct the wages department to send eight separate cheques to these employees. Instead, the bank giro credit form is completed as shown, with the code number, bank branch and name of each payee as well as the amounts with which they are to be credited. At the same time an individual slip is prepared for each payee, but this does not need signatures. The main form is totalled and signed, probably by a director of the firm, and a single cheque drawn to cover the total salary bill. Thus by using a multiple bank giro credit slip, the director has to sign one cheque instead of eight. Imagine the saving of time if there are 5 000 employees to be paid.

11.8   Standing or Bankers' Orders

If you have to make regular payments of a fixed amount, you can instruct your bank to pay the money out of your current account on a given day each month or year. You might have standing orders covering the payment of your house mortgage, life insurance and cricket club subscription. The advantage to you is that once the form has been completed you can forget about these annual or monthly payments. A slight disadvantage is that the bank will not inform you each time they make the payment, so if you keep only a small balance in your account you may inadvertently overdraw the account and not realize this until the bank sends you a statement.

The advantage to the payee of a standing order is that he does not have to send a reminder to the payer, and this saves him much paperwork. The only disadvantage is that if the payments have to be increased, a new form has to be completed by the account holder, and many people are notoriously slow at completing the forms. This problem has been overcome by the introduction of the direct debit system.

11.9 Direct Debit

This system is a cross between the credit transfer and the standing order systems, but here the initiative lies with the creditor. It is up to him to inform the debtor's bank of the amount owed, which is then transferred to the creditor's account. Of course he must obtain the debtor's prior authority for this system to be used. Its main advantage over the standing order system is that it can be used when the size of the payments is likely to vary from month to month. Also, if the payment is an annual subscription which has to be increased, it can be done without the necessity of a new form being filled in. To the payee there is the further advantage over the credit transfer system that he does not have to rely on the debtor's punctuality to secure payment. When this system is used, the payer should of course safeguard himself by instructing his bank not to accept a direct debit above a stipulated level without specific authority from himself.

11.10 Bank Draft

This method of payment is used where large sums are involved and where the payee is not happy to accept his creditor's cheque because he does not know him. If Retailer Co. Ltd owes Wholesaler Co. Ltd £500 he can obtain a bank draft like that in Fig. 11.11 by paying £500 to the bank. The draft is sent to the wholesaler, who now has a cheque drawn on the bank itself. This is clearly much safer than a cheque from a little known retailer. Once regular transactions are taking place between the two, it is likely that payments will be made by cheque.

The *traveller's cheque* is a more familiar kind of bank draft. If you are travelling abroad you may not want to carry large amounts of foreign currency with you. Instead, you can buy traveller's cheques, like the one shown in Fig. 11.12, from a bank. As a safeguard you should sign the cheque immediately. When you want to exchange it for foreign currency, you countersign the cheque at the top, and it will only be cashed if the two signatures are identical. (The fact that the second signature has to be at the top of the cheque makes the forger's task more difficult, because the lower signature is covered by his hand.) The recipient now has a cheque drawn on the bank itself: this is much more acceptable than a cheque drawn on the account of an unknown recipient.

Although traveller's cheques are normally used abroad, there is no reason why you cannot use them in your own country. In Britain, however, there is generally no need to carry large amounts of money on your person because you can nearly always find a branch of your bank which will provide you with cash, even if they have to telephone your branch to get authority first.

11.11 Loans and Overdrafts

An important role of the banks is to lend money to persons and businesses temporarily short of funds. The early bankers soon found that they had surplus

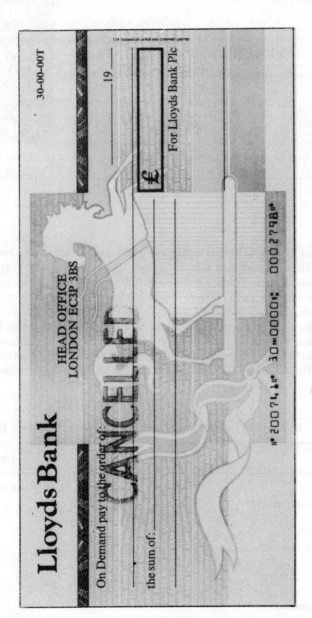

Fig. 11.11 A bank draft

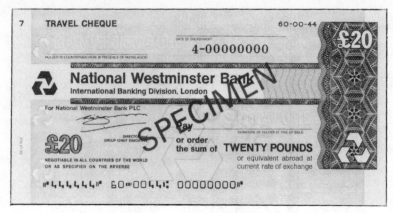

Fig. 11.12 A traveller's cheque

funds on their hands which could be lent at a profit, and this activity has been the basis of their business ever since. You must remember that most people, once they have deposited money in the bank, will not want to withdraw cash. They are normally happy to make payments by cheque or credit transfer. As long as the bank retains sufficient money in its tills to meet its day-to-day requirements, it will be able to use the balance to its advantage. Experience has taught modern bankers that they need to keep between 2 and 5 per cent of their assets in the form of cash. As you can see from Table 11.1, the position of the main British banks in December 1983 was that cash accounted for about 2 per cent of their assets.

Table 11.1   Abbreviated Balance Sheet: main British banks, December 1983

Assets	£m	Liabilities	£m
Cash	2 000	Total deposits	88 000
Money at call and short notice	4 000		
Treasury bills	300		
Commercial bills of exchange	2 500		
British Government stocks	5 200		
Other investments	3 000		
Loans	76 000		

The banks have to be careful not to tie up too much of their remaining money in long term loans, otherwise a sudden demand for large sums of cash might leave them with dangerously low cash reserves. To maintain a sufficient level of *liquidity* (see Section 11.3(*a*)) they make a number of *short term loans*, which take various forms.

(i) *Money at call and short notice* is lent mainly to highly specialized financial institutions called *Discount Houses*. The loans may be made for only 24 hours and are frequently repayable on demand (*at call*). The banks earn only a low rate of interest on these loans because of this, but it is preferable to keeping cash reserves idle in their tills and vaults.

(ii) *Treasury bills* are paper securities issued by the Government for three months. They are extremely useful to the banks in that, having Government backing, they are absolutely safe. The banker knows that he will get his money back (with interest) in three months at the most.

(iii) *Commercial bills of exchange* are also issued for three months. They are a means of financing trade and industry, and as they carry a slightly greater risk than Treasury bills they earn the banks a higher rate of interest.

These short term loans provide the banks with a second line of defence in case there should be heavy and unexpected cash withdrawals. While liquidity is essential, the banks' main objective must be *profitability*. This is provided by the next two items on the list of assets in Table 11.1. *British Government stocks* are longer term securities issued by the Government to raise money, and are very profitable to the banks, although the price obtained for them may vary from time to time. However, the banks obtain most of their revenue from *advances* made to customers in the form of loans and overdrafts. Since these account for over two-thirds of the banks' assets, we must look at them in detail.

(*a*) **Forms of Advances**
The bank may allow you to borrow by means of an overdraft or by a loan.

(i) **An overdraft** is an informal way of borrowing from the bank for a short period. Thus, if a trader's bills are greater than his cash and bank balance at a given moment, he may ask the bank manager to allow him to *overdraw* his account for a few weeks to cover the difference. If the bank manager agrees to an overdraft of £100, the trader is entitled to draw cheques totalling up to £100 more than he has in his account. He will have to pay interest, but only on the exact amount by which he overdraws his account. If the rate of interest goes up during the period of the overdraft, the trader will have to pay at the higher rate. When money is paid into the account the overdraft is reduced, and the bank manager will expect it to be paid off entirely by the stipulated date.

(ii) **A bank loan** is a more formal means of borrowing. If a trader wants to spend £750 on a van, but has only £250 available, he may apply to his bank manager for a loan to cover the difference. He will have to fill in an application form stating the amount he needs, the purpose of the loan, and the length of time for which it is required. Whether or not the loan is granted depends on the factors discussed in Section 11.11(*b*). Assuming that the bank agrees to the loan, the trader's current account is credited with £500, and the rate of interest is fixed for the duration of the loan. He is normally expected to pay it off in equal monthly instalments. When the money is credited to the trader's account, the bank also opens a *loan account* in his name, and this is debited with £500 plus the interest. The monthly payments are then credited to the loan account until the total has been repaid.

(*b*) Who Receives Advances?

Banks cannot lend to everyone who approaches them. Before granting a loan or overdraft they must take two sets of considerations into account.

(i) **Government requirements and bank policy.** In the past the Government has issued directives to the banks on their lending policy. The Government could say that bank lending may increase by only 5 per cent in the next 12 months, or indeed that it must be reduced. Alternatively, they may insist that the banks deposit money with the Bank of England in the form of *special deposits*, so that it cannot be lent to businessmen or individuals.

These special deposits have not been required by the Bank of England for some years now, but the Bank retains the right to call for them if the need arises. If it holds such deposits and wishes to expand economic activity, the Bank releases the deposits.

(ii) **The suitability of the applicant.** There are a number of factors to be taken into account with every applicant for a loan. First the manager will need to be assured of the applicant's honesty and general creditworthiness. Since he must hold an account with the bank, the manager will have some idea of this already. The amount of the loan and the likelihood of the customer being able to meet the repayment will also be considered. The manager will not be keen to lend either to individuals or businesses if the repayment of the loan is likely to place too great a burden on them. Where the loan is to a business, the most important factors are its past record and the likelihood of its continuing profitably. It is the manager's job to assess the risk involved.

The banker will often want some kind of *security* for the loan. This means something that is left in his possession until the loan is repaid, and which he may easily sell if the borrower defaults on the repayment of the loan. Stocks and shares quoted on the Stock Exchange are usually acceptable because they are easy both to value and to sell; life assurance policies or property deeds are equally acceptable. If none of these is available, the borrower may have to find a personal guarantor for the loan, that is, someone who will undertake to repay the loan himself in the event of default by the borrower.

However, not all loans are secured in this way. Many businesses in their early days possess no acceptable securities, and the bank manager may take a calculated risk in lending to them. Furthermore, most of the banks run a personal loan scheme under which they lend to private individuals for a variety of reasons without security. Fig. 11.13 shows the pattern of bank lending in the United Kingdom. You can see that the manufacturing sector is the main recipient of bank loans, but that personal borrowing also accounts for a large slice.

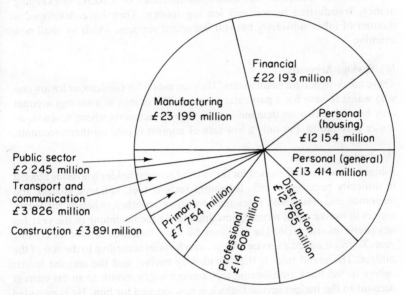

Fig. 11.13   Bank lending in the United Kingdom by sector, August 1983
(£116 050 million)

(c) How Do the Banks Make a Profit on Loans?

Like all financial institutions, the banks aim to make a profit by charging a higher rate on the money they lend than they pay on the money they borrow. Approximately half of their deposits are held on current account, on which they have no interest to pay. If they relend this money it is not difficult for them to make a profit. However, when money is left in deposit or savings accounts, the bank must pay interest on it. Whenever they make loans, however short term they are, they will want to receive a higher rate than they pay out on these deposits. In general they follow this principle: the greater the risk, the higher the rate of interest; also long term borrowers can expect to pay a higher rate than short term. All the banks work from their own *base rate*, which they establish in the light of prevailing economic conditions. The rates they offer on deposits, or charge for loans, are then related to this base rate. As a matter of interest, in those years when rates of interest are high (perhaps because the Government wants them to be) the bank will make good profits because of the big gap between the zero interest paid on current accounts and the rates charged on loans and overdrafts to borrowers.

11.12   Other Functions of the Bank

We have now looked at the traditional functions of a bank: safekeeping money, transferring money and lending money. They have developed a number of other subsidiary but still important services, which we shall now examine.

(a) Savings Accounts

These are designed for small savers. They are useful for children, or for anyone who wants to save for a particular purpose. The money in a savings account may be withdrawn on demand, unlike deposit accounts where seven days' notice is required, but only a low rate of interest is paid on these accounts.

(b) Budget Accounts

Budget accounts are designed for the current account holder who finds himself in difficulty because his bills for things such as fuel, holidays, car tax and insurance and household rates tend to arrive together, whereas his salary arrives in twelve equal monthly instalments. At the beginning of the year (or any twelve-month period) he works out his likely commitments for the coming year. To this is added a service charge, which varies according to the size of the budget. The grand total is then divided by twelve, and the account holder agrees to the bank transferring this amount every month from his current account to the budget account which is now opened for him. He is provided with a separate cheque book with which to pay the bills included in the budget. In this way the burden of bill paying is spread conveniently over the year. The bank has the advantage of extra business and the use of the customer's money when the budget account is in credit. The customer has the advantage of being able to overdraw the account for at least part of the year without the bank manager complaining.

(c) Safeguarding Valuables

As well as looking after cash for its customers, a bank provides facilities for the storing of valuable documents such as property deeds, wills, and items of jewellery. It is sometimes possible to rent special safe deposit compartments from the bank for storage purposes.

(d) Night Safe Facility

The clearing banks are normally closed to the public after 3.30 p.m., and are not usually open on Saturdays or Sundays. Many businesses collect money from their customers after the banks have closed and do not have the facilities to keep it safe until the banks re-open. The night safe facility overcomes this: the trader is provided with a wallet, into which he locks the cash he wishes to deposit in the bank. This is taken to the bank, where the customer unlocks a small trapdoor in the outside wall. The wallet is 'posted' inside, and slides down a chute to the strong room. When the bank staff arrive, the wallets are unlocked and the money credited to the appropriate accounts.

(e) Bank Statements
Statements are provided at regular intervals, to help customers keep a check on their finances. Of course, they should do this anyway but the bank statement provides a double check. It is particularly useful where standing orders or direct debits are regularly drawn on the account, or where credit transfers are paid in.

(f) Credit Cards
A credit card enables the holder to obtain instant credit. They are very widespread in the United States but not yet as popular in the United Kingdom. The two best known here are Barclaycard, which is run by Barclays Bank but is available to people holding accounts at other banks as well, and Access, run jointly by Lloyds, Midland and National Westminster. Other cards are available but they all operate in basically the same way. Let us consider what happens with Access.

The Access Company enrols a large number of suppliers of goods and services, who agree to supply goods and services to cardholders without receiving immediate cash payment. Each cardholder has a credit limit, which is the maximum amount he can have outstanding on his account. He signs for any goods supplied to him and is given a copy of his bill. Another copy, bearing his signature and card number is kept by the shop and later sent off to Access. Access deduct a small percentage commission from the total they owe the shop, and then remit a cheque for the balance. Each month the cardholder receives a statement from Access, telling him how much he owes. He may pay either the whole amount or, if he prefers, only part of it. The minimum payment is fixed by the Government, and changes from time to time. They might, for example, insist that cardholders repay £5 per month or 5 per cent of the total owing, whichever is greater.

The card may also be used to obtain a cash advance from any of the banks operating the scheme, up to the cardholder's credit limit, and there is a small percentage service charge payable. Such advances are subject to the same rules of repayment as ordinary purchases, and in both cases interest is charged on a monthly basis on any outstanding balance on the account.

The advantage of credit cards to the holder is the availability of instant credit. Not for him the formalities involved in buying goods on hire purchase. The disadvantage is the temptation to buy too much and then spend many months in making repayments. Also retailers may increase their prices to cover the commission which they pay to the credit card company.

The advantage to the trader is the increase in his turnover that results from his participation in the credit card system. The disadvantage is the proportion of turnover that has to be paid to the card company and, to a lesser extent, the extra clerical work involved.

To the banks who operate the schemes they provide a profitable outlet for funds which are temporarily surplus to requirements, but the fraudulent use of cards has sometimes caused them problems.

(g) Cheque Cards

Cheque cards should not be confused with credit cards (although Barclaycard now acts as a cheque card for Barclays Bank). Many shoppers prefer using cheques rather than cash when buying expensive items. But retailers are sometimes reluctant to accept cheques, in case they are dishonoured, which could involve the retailer in considerable work to secure payment. The banks issue cheque cards to their creditworthy customers, guaranteeing to the payee that a cheque drawn by a cardholder will be honoured by the bank even if there are insufficient funds in his account. There are certain conditions which have to be fulfilled.

Fig. 11.14 A cheque card

(i) The cheque must not be made out for more than the limit printed on the card, usually £50.

(ii) The cheque must be signed in the presence of the payee, and the signature must correspond with that on the card.

(iii) The cheque must be drawn on a bank cheque form bearing the code number shown on the card (the cardholder's branch code).

(iv) The card number must be written on the back of the cheque by the payee.

The advantages of the cheque card lie in the guarantee it affords to retailers and the assistance it gives to the banks' customers in getting cheques accepted. This is an example of a service provided by the banks for the benefit of their customers, which really carries no advantages for the banks themselves. A further advantage to customers is that they can with the support of a cheque card withdraw cash from any branch of any of the four clearing banks, and often from banks overseas as well, though there may be a charge if they use a branch of a bank other than their own.

(h) Cash Dispensers

These are a recent innovation. They enable bank customers to obtain some cash quickly, when the bank is crowded, or at any time, even when the bank is shut. Cash dispensers are machines built into the outside wall of the bank. The customer is provided with a coded card and a secret number. The card is inserted into the dispenser and the customer then taps out the number to complete the code. He then receives the cash. There is very little fraudulent use of the card, since the number does not appear on the card in writing.

Newer and more sophisticated are the cash points located *inside* the bank and linked to a computer. They provide quick service to the customer who simply wants to cash a cheque. Again a card is inserted, but this time varying amounts can be selected, and the money is forthcoming only if the account is not overdrawn.

(i) Bankers' References

These are especially important to businessmen. If you are about to sign a large business contract with someone with whom you have not dealt before, you can ask your bank to find out about his financial standing. This they will do either by consulting their own records, if he uses the same bank, or by approaching his bank. They will then be able to give you an assessment of his creditworthiness. Similarly your bank may be willing to issue a reference on your behalf, as testimony of your own financial stability.

(j) Income Tax, Insurance, Executorship

The banks provide services in each of these fields. They employ specialists to help individuals and businesses with advice on taxation. They have contacts with leading insurance brokers and can usually quote you competitive rates for all kinds of insurance. They are also able to help you to draw up your will and, more important, see that the provisions of the will are carried out. The person who sees that this happens is called the executor, and the more experienced he is the better. Many people appoint their bank as executor, because they know that the bank's employees are experts who will do the job properly, and that the bank is always there.

(k) Advice and Information

The banks have built up a wide range of intelligence services.

(i) **Advice on borrowing.** A bank manager cannot always lend to a client himself, but he will probably be able to give expert advice about alternative sources of finance.

(ii) **Advice on investment**. The person who has only a small amount of savings is unlikely to have his own stockbroker (see Unit 13). If he wants advice on how to invest his savings he can consult his bank manager, who is sure to have some useful ideas. Furthermore, if the sum involved is too small to interest an individual stockbroker, the customer can use the bank's stockbroker to obtain his shares.

(iii) **Economic advice** of all kinds is provided to trade and industry. Market advice on individual overseas countries and their economic conditions is one example. Banks will also draw up reports on particular industries in overseas countries on the request of a client.

When customers seek advice from their bank manager on matters such as these, there is sometimes no charge for the service provided. Even on occasions when a great deal of work is involved for the bank, the fees charged are very low when compared with those demanded by other professional people.

(l) Foreign Exchange

This is provided by the banks to account holders and others, within the foreign exchange regulations currently in operation.

As you can see, the banks are heavily involved in the economic and commercial life of the country. Far from being concerned only with the safekeeping and transferring of funds, they have developed a very wide range of financial and economic activities, and are constantly on the look-out for new avenues to explore. We shall find yet another direction in which they have developed when we examine the capital market in Unit 13.

11.13 Questions and Exercises

(a) Short Answers

1. Who were the original bankers in the United Kingdom?
2. What was the original function of the banks?
3. Distinguish between current accounts and deposit accounts.
4. Distinguish between loans and overdrafts.
5. Distinguish between the following in connexion with a cheque: payee, drawee, drawer.
6. Explain the difference between open cheques, cheques with a general crossing, cheques with a special crossing.
7. Why are cheques sometimes dishonoured?
8. Explain the differences between a standing order and direct debit.
9. What is collateral security?
10. Distinguish between a credit card, a cheque card and a cash card.

(b) Essay Answers

1. In what ways can you borrow from a bank? What factors must the bank manager take into account before making a loan?

2. What services does the Clearing Bank offer to the small trader?
3. Explain the importance of cheques as a means of payment. What steps can be taken to ensure that a cheque reaches the correct account?
4. What means of payment are provided by the Clearing Banks? Show the advantages of each method.
5. Examine the functions of the Clearing Banks, showing how they make a profit.

(c) **Projects and Assignments**
1. Make a collection of the advertising material issued by the banks, so that you can study their functions. (You can obtain much of this material by visiting local branches of the banks and by reading the press.)
2. Write to the main banks for a copy of their annual reports, so that you can make a comparison of the size of their deposits, the amount of their loans, and the level of their profits.
3. Banks were originally organizations for safeguarding depositors' money. Using any material you can find, give examples of other services provided by the banks in the United Kingdom.

Unit Twelve

The Banking System: Other Financial Institutions

12.1 Introduction

The Clearing Banks, which we examined in Unit 11, are probably the most important financial institutions to the trader. But there are also many other institutions offering a wide range of services to commerce and industry. Some of them are mainly concerned with long-term lending and borrowing, and these will be dealt with in Unit 13. In this Unit we shall look at those which deal in short-term lending and borrowing, and at the Bank of England, which supervises our whole monetary system.

12.2 Discount Houses

Discount Houses specialize in raising money over short periods for the Government, as well as for trade and commerce. There are 11 members of the London Discount Market Association and they are responsible for most of the business conducted. By examining their collective balance sheet in Table 12.1 we can learn something of their activities.

Table 12.1   The Abbreviated Balance Sheet of the London Discount Houses, September 1983

Main assets	£m	Main liabilities	£m
Treasury bills	20	Loans from banks	4 600
Commercial bills of exchange	2 200	Loans from other sources	620
British Government stocks	500		
Local authority securities	400		
Certificates of deposit	1 500		
Other assets	600		

The *liabilities* of the Discount House (or any other institution for that matter) consist of the amounts that the firm is holding which belong to other firms or people. The Discount Houses accept money on deposit from individuals or firms, but the main sources of their funds are the banks. The Discount Houses normally borrow on a very short-term basis, often promising to repay on demand if necessary. This is the *money at call* we saw in Section 11.11. Any firm or bank with large sums of money to spare for short periods might consider leaving it with a Discount House, especially at times when interest rates are high. For example, £500 000 left with a Discount House for one week at 13 per cent per annum interest would earn approximately £1 250 for its owner.

Having obtained money on deposit from various sources, the Discount House must put it to work to earn a profit. The list of *assets* on the balance sheet in Table 12.1 shows how this is done.

(a) Treasury Bills

The Government issues Treasury bills to raise money on a short-term basis. Each week the Treasury calculates how much it will need to borrow in two weeks' time to meet any excess of expenditure over income. The amount is raised by issuing Treasury bills to interested parties with the money to spare. The bills have nominal values of up to £100 000, and the buyers must be prepared to accept at least £50 000 worth. They are always sold below their nominal value (at a discount), and to the highest bidder. Most of the bills go to the Discount Houses, who sometimes keep them until they mature, but more often sell them to the Clearing Banks after a few days or weeks. Whoever holds the bills makes a profit, because of the difference between the amount for which they were bought and the nominal value at which they are redeemed. Another advantage which is very important to the Discount Houses is that Treasury bills are absolutely safe: they are issued by the Government, and any holder knows that he will receive full payment on the specified day.

(b) Other Bills of Exchange

The traditional outlet for the funds of the Discount Houses was in the discounting of commercial bills of exchange. These are examined in detail in Section 19.4, but certain points must be noted here.

Where the purchaser of goods requires temporary credit which the seller cannot afford, the latter may draw a bill of exchange, setting out the debt and demanding payment, normally in three months' time. By signing the bill the purchaser acknowledges the debt and at the same time promises payment in three months. If the purchaser has a good name in the business world, the bill may be accepted by an Accepting House for a small charge (see Section 12.3). The effect of this is to guarantee that in the event of default by the debtor, the Accepting House will settle the account. The supplier of the goods who drew the bill of exchange now has a document which he can pass on to anyone else in exchange for cash.

Suppose the bill of exchange is for £10 000, payable in three months' time and that it has been 'accepted': the drawer of the bill takes it to a Discount House and sells it to them at a discount, the amount of which depends upon the current rate of interest. Perhaps the Discount House offers £9 750 for the bill. The drawer has the advantage of immediate cash (for which he pays £250), and the Discount House can make a profit of £250 by holding the bill for three months and then presenting it to the drawee for payment. In the unlikely event of his being unable to pay, the Accepting House can then be called upon.

In the nineteenth century this was a highly important function, for the sources of finance and credit for industry were much more limited than they are now. In recent years the volume of business in bills of exchange has declined, and the Discount Houses have found other areas for the profitable use of their funds.

(c) British Government Stocks

These represent long term borrowing by the Government, and a small proportion of the Discount Houses' funds is invested in them. Although they are not as liquid as Treasury bills and bills of exchange, Government securities can always be sold on the Stock Exchange, though the prices they fetch tend to vary.

(d) Local Authority Securities

Local government organizations often need to borrow money, and there is now a firmly established market in the securities they issue. As part of their programme of diversification the Discount Houses now deal quite heavily in these securities, specializing in those issued for up to one year.

(e) Certificates of Deposit

These are issued by banks to customers making large deposits (for example, £50 000) for a fixed period. Such a certificate is a promise from the bank to repay the deposit on a specified day. Should the holder of the certificate require cash before the certificate matures, the Discount Houses will normally buy them at a discount and make their profit in the same way as with bills of exchange.

The Discount Houses have a long tradition of integrity in the handling of other people's money. You can see now that they continue to play an important role in the economy by enabling money temporarily surplus to requirements in one part of the economy to be put usefully to work in another.

12.3   The Merchant Banks

The term *merchant bank* is applied to many institutions nowadays, but refers specifically to the 16 members of the *Accepting Houses Committee*, which include such famous financial names as Morgan Grenfell, Rothschild, Hambros and Baring. Such banks grew to prominence through their skill in accepting the bills of exchange used in the finance of international trade. As we have already seen, the Discount Houses advance money against bills of exchange, but are more willing to do so if the bill has been accepted by one of the major Accepting Houses, and thus rendered a *fine bill*. (As the acceptance of a bill is a guarantee that the acceptor will meet the debt in case of default, the Accepting House clearly needs a detailed knowledge of the traders involved.) This is still their most important function: by guaranteeing the value of paper securities, they contribute to the smooth running of the money market.

Nowadays, however, merchant banks have many other activities as well. In addition to their original trading or merchanting functions from which they got their name, and which many maintain today, they provide important financial services for industrial concerns. When a company wants to raise new long term capital, it will normally ask a merchant bank to arrange the issue of the shares. They usually act as general financial advisers to their industrial clients, guiding them not only in connexion with new issues, but also on the timing and scale of investment, and on the merits and demerits of takeover bids and mergers. They also make fixed interest, medium term loans to their clients, for example to finance the installation of new machinery which does not require the raising of extra long term capital. Moreover recent expansion by the merchant banks in the long term markets has included involvement in the *unit trust* and *investment trust* movements (which we discuss in Section 13.3), and in the management of investment portfolios belonging to pension and superannuation funds.

Although they do not hold the same central position in the market as the Discount Houses, the merchant banks nevertheless have close connexions with the public sector. They hold modest amounts of Treasury bills and other Government securities, and also make substantial advances to local authorities. The close relationships which we noticed earlier between the various financial institutions are further underlined by the fact that the merchant banks frequently advance money at call to the Discount Market, and keep substantial balances with other British banks.

To finance this wide range of activities the merchant banks accept deposits both on a current account basis and for a fixed period, from clients at home and overseas. It is in respect of the more important fixed term deposits that the sterling certificates of deposit we mentioned in Section 12.2 are issued. Approximately one-third of merchant bank deposits are from overseas clients. This stems from their traditional involvement with overseas trade, and their former business of issuing bonds on the London Market for overseas Governments and institutions.

12.4 Secondary Banks

Many financial institutions undertake some of the roles of the merchant banks, and are often referred to as merchant banks. They are also called secondary banks. These tend to be relatively new firms, without the size or standing of the Clearing Banks or the Accepting Houses.

These banks normally offer depositors a higher rate of interest than the Clearing Banks, and of course they lend to their customers at a higher rate also. They follow broadly the same trading principles as the Clearing Banks, and at normal times face no special difficulties. At times of economic crisis, however, they are frequently the first to suffer: depositors rush to withdraw funds which have either been lent to borrowers, or invested in shares which have fallen in value and now have to be sold at a loss.

12.5   Finance Houses

We have already examined the role of finance houses in the section on hire purchase (Section 6.4). They obtain their funds from the general public and a variety of financial institutions by offering very attractive rates of interest. The high rates are a form of compensation, because depositors take a greater risk in leaving their money with finance houses than if they leave it with the Clearing Banks, mainly because the finance houses are not so large, do not have the same reserves and do not instill the same confidence. They make their profits by advancing funds to people wishing to buy consumer durable goods. Naturally they have to charge even higher rates than they pay, which is why hire purchase is often one of the most expensive ways of borrowing.

12.6   The Bank of England

The Bank of England is the most important of our financial institutions, exercising a general control of the monetary and banking system on behalf of the Government. It was founded in 1694 as a private institution, but even then it had close links with the Government. These links gradually strengthened until the Bank was nationalized in 1946. Nationalization formally recognized what had long been the case, that the Bank of England was the Government's Bank. But as long as it was a private sector institution there was the possibility of conflict between the Government and the Bank. This did not often occur, but the situation could arise if, for example, the Government wanted interest rates to increase, while the Bank wanted them to fall or remain stable. Now, although there may be differences of opinion between the Bank and the Government about the kind of policies appropriate at a particular time, it is the Government that has the final word: the Chancellor of the Exchequer, advised by the Treasury, can dictate policy to the Governor of the Bank of England.

In most countries the Government's Bank is referred to as the *central bank*, and indeed the functions of the Bank of England are equivalent to those of many central banks. Its most important functions are discussed in this Section.

You will probably find it helpful to refer to Table 12.2, which is a typical weekly return for the Bank of England.

The weekly return summarizes the Bank's position on the stated day. Its division into two parts, the Issue Department and the Banking Department, reflects the traditional organization of the Bank as laid down by the Bank Charter Act 1844. Today the organization is much more complex, but the weekly return retains this form. Let us examine some of the Bank's functions, beginning with those jobs performed for the Government.

(a) **The Government's Accounts**

One of the most important aspects of the work of a central bank is the administration of the Government's bank accounts, which appear under the heading *public deposits* in Table 12.2. There are two principal accounts here: the *Exchequer Account*, into which all taxation receipts are paid and from which all current expenditure is met, and the *National Loans Fund*, the Government's capital account for borrowing and lending. Although there are subsidiary accounts run by individual Government departments, these two accounts between them are responsible for the majority of Government transactions. Since Government expenditure runs at about £100 000 million per annum it is perhaps a little surprising that the public deposits are so small. This is a matter of deliberate policy on the part of the authorities (by which we mean in this instance the Treasury and the Bank): rather than allow a great balance to accumulate in the form of public deposits, they prefer to pay off part of the National Debt (see Section 12.6(c)). On the other hand the Bank takes steps to ensure that there is always enough in the accounts to meet the requirements of the Government, and on rare occasions the Bank itself lends to the Government (overnight) in the form of *ways and means advances*.

Table 12.2   The Bank of England's weekly return, 21 September 1983 (£m)

Issue Department			
Assets		Liabilities	
Government securities	4 062	Notes in circulation	11 388
Other securities	7 338	Notes in banking department	12
	11 400		11 400

Banking Department			
Government securities	388	Capital	14
Advances and other accounts	998	Public deposits	36
Premises, equipment and other securities	861	Bankers' deposits	616
Notes and coin	12	Special deposits	0
		Reserve	1 593
	2 259		2 259

(b) The Note Issue

The Government reserves the right to issue notes and coins, and these reach the public via the Bank of England. The size of the note issue is governed by the Currency and Bank Notes Act 1954, which set a limit of £1 500 million, but this can be increased to meet public demand, subject to Treasury approval. Requirements vary seasonally (demand for notes reaches a peak at Christmas and during the summer holiday periods), and according to the general level of prices and economic activity. There has been a great increase in the issue since 1954, mainly because of rising prices.

At the Bank of England the notes are transferred from the Issue Department to the Banking Department. From there, they are passed on to the Clearing Banks (these are the *bankers' deposits* in Table 12.2) and it is from the Clearing Banks that the notes actually reach the general public. Coins reach the public by a similar route, but they originate at the Royal Mint rather than the Bank of England printing works.

(c) The National Debt

Sometimes, for example during wartime, the Government needs to spend more money than it can raise through taxation. It resorts to borrowing to do this, and the total borrowing is known as the National Debt. In March 1983 the Debt amounted to £125 000 million.

The Bank's responsibilities in relation to the Debt are:

(i) **To issue new securities** when the Government wants to borrow. These may be very short term Treasury bills (see Section 12.2), or longer term *gilt-edged stocks*. The stocks are issued in £100 blocks and the interest on them may be regarded as absolutely secure. The holders of these stocks are guaranteed repayment of their £100 investment on the day stated on the stock. As we shall see in Unit 13, it may in fact be many years before repayment is due.

(ii) **To keep a register of stockholders**, so that the interest can be paid.

(iii) **To pay interest** on the securities every half-year. The rate of interest is fixed for each security and does not vary during its life.

(iv) **To redeem securities** as they mature.

(d) Lender of Last Resort

We saw in Section 12.2 that the Discount Houses often borrow money at call and relend it for longer periods. It sometimes happens that those who have deposited money with the Discount Houses demand immediate repayment, which they are entitled to do. In these circumstances the Discount Houses are in difficulty, for they have committed their borrowed funds for three months or sometimes longer. They try to obtain the money they need from any likely source but in *the last resort*, if all else fails, they turn to the Bank of England, which will always lend them the money they require. When this happens they will have to borrow from the Bank at a rate set by the Bank itself which will almost certainly involve them in some loss, as we shall see in Section 12.6(*f*).

(*e*) External Functions
The Bank also discharges a number of other functions on behalf of the Government which really belong to the international rather than the domestic economy.

(i) **Exchange Equalization Account**. The nation's gold and foreign exchange reserves are held at the Bank in the Exchange Equalization Account. It is from this account that the foreign currency ultimately comes, when it is needed by an importer to buy goods or by a traveller to spend abroad.

(ii) **Exchange control regulations** are operated by the Bank. The Government sometimes wishes to limit the amount of foreign currency spent by residents, and it is the Bank that supervises the arrangements. In 1979 the British Government removed all exchange controls, and residents can now spend or invest their money where they wish.

(iii) **International Monetary Fund**. The Bank's expertise is often called for in complex international monetary negotiations, particularly in connexion with the International Monetary Fund.

(*f*) Monetary Policy
The Government has certain broad economic objectives: it aims to create full employment, to avoid undue inflation, and to achieve a Balance of Payments surplus (see Unit 21). The steps taken to create the economic atmosphere in which these can be pursued are known as monetary policy. This is really a group of policies designed to affect the overall level of demand in the economy, and there are three main controls which the Government can operate.

(i) **Interest rates**. Until August 1981 the Bank of England published the rate of interest at which it would lend to the Discount Houses when acting as the lender of last resort. This rate was known as *minimum lending rate*. Although no longer published, the rate is still in the background when rates are fixed.

The rate at which the Bank lends to the Discount Houses is intended to be a penal rate: if the Discount Houses are forced to borrow from the Bank, they normally lose money, because they are earning perhaps 10 per cent on Treasury bills, but they have to borrow at 10.5 per cent from the Bank. Also the Bank itself has means of influencing the rates of interest on Treasury bills, and when these increase or decrease many other rates move in the same direction. The effect of a rise in interest rates is to discourage people and firms from borrowing, and therefore to reduce the demand for goods and services. In this way the Bank can indirectly influence the level of demand.

(ii) **Special deposits** are designed to influence the amount that the Clearing Banks can lend. If the level of demand for goods and services is too high, the Bank may call for special deposits from the Clearing Banks. They will be told to deposit cash at the Bank of England equal to perhaps 1 per cent of their total deposits. This prevents them lending the money to anyone else, and represents another way in which the Bank of England can try to reduce the overall level of demand. However, if the Government wishes to *increase* the level of demand, the Bank of England can release some of the special and supplementary deposits.

(iii) **Open market operations** are central to monetary policy. As we saw in Section 11.2, our banking system is a fractional reserve system, in which the banks can create deposits much in excess of their holdings of cash. If the Bank of England wants to increase the amount of cash held by the banks, so that they can increase their lending, it undertakes open market operations by buying gilt-edged securities in the Stock Exchange (Unit 13). The sellers of the securities receive cheques from the Bank of England which they pay into their bank accounts, thus increasing the Clearing Banks' holding of cash and enabling those banks to increase their lending. Alternatively, selling gilt-edged rather than buying, the Bank can *reduce* the power of the Clearing Banks to create credit.

By using these policies either individually or collectively, the Bank of England helps to influence the economy. A more detailed examination of the Bank's policies will be found in *Success in Economics*.

(g) The Bankers' Bank

The Bank of England provides an essential link between the Government and the Clearing Banks. Policy initiatives of all kinds reach the banks via the Bank of England. In addition all the banks also run accounts there, which they treat in the same way as private individuals treat their bank accounts, except that the Bank of England does not allow overdrafts. The accounts are used to replenish the banks' stocks of cash if their own holdings – in their tills – are running low. They are also used to settle debts which emerge between the banks themselves as a result of the daily clearing of cheques (see Section 12.7).

(h) Private Customers

These are mainly a legacy from the past, when the Bank of England carried on an orthodox banking business as well as its special responsibilities to the Government. Today the Bank runs accounts for its employees, as well as for some families who have held accounts there for generations.

12.7 The Bankers' Clearing House

In Section 11.5 we looked at the route taken by an individual cheque, which allows the payee's account to be credited and the drawer's to be debited. We saw that the cheque passes through the Bankers' Clearing House, but we did not examine the Clearing House in detail.

Every working day millions of cheques are drawn and paid into bank accounts. It would be impossible for each of those cheques to be cleared individually: the job of the Clearing House is mass clearing. There are two clearings each day, the *town clearing* and the *general clearing*.

(*a*) Town Clearing

This is purely for the benefit of the big financial institutions of the City of London. Large amounts of money are involved and it is important that the cheques are cleared quickly. Only cheques for more than £5 000 can be dealt with at this clearing, and only those drawn on and payable into branches within the City of London are eligible. The total value of cheques dealt with at this daily clearing may be as high as £2 000 million, but the number of cheques is much smaller than at the general clearing. Since the procedure at both clearings is similar, we shall just look at the general clearing.

(*b*) General Clearing

All those cheques which do not qualify for the town clearing are dealt with at the general clearing. A typical day might see around 4 million cheques processed, involving a sum of perhaps £12 000 million.

Each branch of a bank sends the cheques it receives to the clearing department at its head office. There the cheques are sorted and their value added up. If there are four banks in the system, each bank will have three groups of cheques drawn on the other three banks. In order to credit their customers' accounts with the amounts shown on individual cheques, they must obtain the money from the banks on which the cheques have been drawn.

Thus if Barclays customers have paid in cheques worth £10 million drawn on Midland Bank, Barclays must obtain the £10 million from Midland. Meanwhile, Midland customers have paid in £7 million of cheques drawn on Barclays. If Midland pay £3 million to Barclays the books will be balanced. Each bank could deal individually with each of the others on this basis, but the Clearing House eliminates the need for this. Table 12.3 summarizes the position at the end of a hypothetical clearing.

Table 12.3   A hypothetical clearing

Paying Bank	Barclays	Lloyds	Midland	National Westminster
Receiving Bank				
Barclays	—	8	10	3
Lloyds	6	—	4	6
Midland	7	2	—	8
National Westminster	4	1	9	—

We can see the position of each bank in relation to each of the others from this table. Barclays is owed £8 million by Lloyds but owes £6 million to Lloyds, and an adjustment of £2 million is required. But we can also see the net position of each bank: Barclays is owed a total of £21 million (8 + 10 + 3) and owes a total of £17 million (6 + 7 + 4). We may summarize the net position of each bank as follows:

Barclays	is owed £4 million
Lloyds	is owed £5 million
Midland	owes £6 million
National Westminster	owes £3 million

Each of the banks runs an account at the Bank of England through which these debts can be settled. In this example Midland pays £5 million to Lloyds and £1 million to Barclays, while National Westminster pays £3 million to Barclays.

It is not only cheques that are dealt with in this way: credit transfers and other means of payment via the banks also go through the Clearing House. Each day the debts arising from that day's town clearing and the previous day's general clearing are settled. In this way millions of payments are made by a minimum of transactions.

A recent development has been the establishment by the banks of the Bankers' Automated Clearing Services Ltd (BACS), a branch of the Clearing House, which permits large customers of the bank to put their instructions for the transfer of money on to magnetic tape which can be processed by computers without the normal documents being involved.

The organizations that we have been looking at in this Unit are all part of the *money market*, dealing essentially with the short term movement of funds. In Unit 13 we shall examine the bodies which deal with the long term movement of funds and which together form the *capital market*.

12.8   Questions and Exercises

(a) Short Answers

1. What is the central bank of the United Kingdom?
2. What is the purpose of Treasury bills?
3. Why are bills of exchange important in trade?
4. What are the functions of the merchant banks?
5. What is the National Debt?
6. What are the functions of the Bank of England?
7. What is the purpose of the Bankers' Clearing House?
8. What is the purpose of the Discount Houses?
9. What is meant by 'accepting the bill of exchange'?
10. What is meant by 'discounting the bill of exchange'?

(b) **Essay Answers**

1. Explain the ways in which the Bank of England assists *(a)* the Government, *(b)* the Clearing Banks.
2. Describe the operation of the Bankers' Clearing House.
3. What are merchant banks? What services do they provide?
4. Examine the means by which a cheque drawn by A. Smith who banks with Barclays, Cardiff, will be cleared in favour of J. Brown who banks with Midland, Dover.
5. Show why the financial institutions are of vital importance to industry.

Unit Thirteen

The Capital Market

13.1 What Is Capital?

Capital can be defined as goods, physical assets or equipment created in the past but not consumed, and therefore still available for use. As individuals we have a choice between spending all our income on goods and services for immediate use and reserving some of it for future use (savings). The portion saved for future use can be called *capital*, and it may be kept in a number of different forms. It may be kept at home, or, more likely, in one of a number of financial institutions. Capital has two different meanings to a producer.

(a) It may refer to his fixed assets, i.e. the buildings and machinery he uses to produce goods.

(b) It may refer to the money that has been accumulated to buy these fixed assets.

In this Unit we are mainly concerned with (b), and in particular with the *sources* of the funds that producers use for investment in plant and machinery. It is here that we find an important link between the savings of individuals and the capital of firms. When an individual saves some of his income and places it for safekeeping with, for example, a bank or insurance company, that bank or insurance company is free to lend the money to industrial concerns who want to invest it in capital equipment. Thus on one side we have savers, whose income exceeds their current requirements; on the other side we have borrowers, whose income is inadequate to meet their current requirements. The *capital market* exists to bring them together.

13.2 Savers and Borrowers

The capital market consists of a large number of organizations, many of which collect the savings of thousands of individuals and channel them towards business enterprises and other organizations needing to borrow money. In general, however, there is an important difference in attitude between savers and borrowers. Once they have borrowed money, the industrial firms will use it to finance the purchase of machinery, and they normally expect to have permanent use of the money involved. On the other hand, the savers may well want their money back at some time in the future. This clash of interests between savers and borrowers is overcome by the existence of the Stock Exchange, where the owners of shares (i.e. savers) can exchange their shares for money (see Section 13.5).

There are three groups of borrowers in the capital market.

(a) Private Individuals

These are the least important group. They usually borrow to finance house purchase, and there are specialized building societies to help them. They do not really enter the main capital market as borrowers.

(b) The Government

The Government is an important borrower. It is not always possible for the Government to raise all the money it needs through taxation, so it goes along to the capital market to borrow by issuing gilt-edged securities (see Section 13.4). It also needs to borrow periodically to provide funds for the public corporations to finance their investment programmes.

(c) Limited Companies

These are the main borrowers. Remember, however, that it is only the public limited companies that are allowed to appeal to the public for funds. (Private limited companies only really affect the market in the sense that they siphon off some people's savings before they reach the market.) The public limited companies borrow in the capital market by issuing paper securities of various kinds, and we examine these in Section 13.4.

Since savings are unspent income, any of the three groups of borrowers may also be savers. Private individuals deposit their savings with a large number of financial intermediaries, and every year they save more than they borrow. Industrial and commercial organizations may also save by putting aside some of their profits for future use; normally, however, their savings are not as large as the sums they want to invest, so they are net borrowers. The Government and various bodies in the public sector may also save, but they too are usually net borrowers.

The savings of most private individuals are likely to be too small to invest directly in shares. But, as we saw above, the banks and other institutions that collect individuals' savings accumulate large sums, and these can be invested in shares. We examine some of these institutions in the next Section, before looking at the various types of securities and the Stock Exchange itself in Section 13.4.

13.3 Savings Institutions

The capital market depends on a steady flow of funds from savers. A number of organizations exist to provide that steady flow of funds by encouraging personal saving.

(a) Insurance Companies

We discuss these more fully in Unit 18, but they are important to the capital market. Most people have a life insurance policy, whereby the insurance company collects weekly, monthly or annual premiums and undertakes to pay a lump sum, either on a specific date or on the death of the insured person. The company is able to repay more than it collects in premiums because it invests the bulk of the premiums in securities which yield interest or dividends (profits). At the end of 1982, British insurance companies held investments in respect of their life insurance business of almost £80 000 million, distributed as shown in Fig. 13.1.

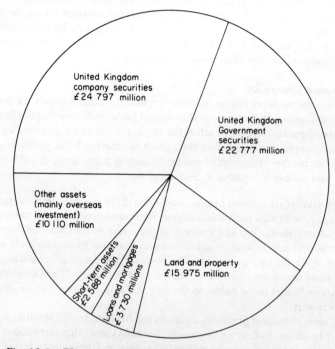

Fig. 13.1 The investments of British insurance companies, 1982 (£79 977 million)

The majority of funds that reach industry and commerce via the insurance companies would not be available to them without the existence of the companies, since individually the contributions would be too small to be worth investing. In any case, the person paying his insurance premium is probably only concerned about the financial security of his family, and not so much about how the money is invested. But there are other organizations where investment is the client's main purpose.

(b) Unit Trusts

While part of most people's savings reach the Stock Exchange via the insurance companies, the number who invest via a unit trust is much smaller. Small savers are able to buy units in the fund, sometimes simply by answering newspaper advertisements. The managers of the trust then use the money raised to buy securities in the particular sectors of industry to which the trust is committed. (The deeds of unit trusts indicate the areas to which funds will be applied.) All earnings on the shares are payable to the trust managers, who then redistribute them to unit holders who may, however, elect to convert them into further units. The chief outlet for unit trust funds are ordinary shares, and at the end of 1983, 90 per cent of unit trust assets were held in this form. The main advantage of a trust is its security, for it is able to spread its investment across a large number of companies and industries, thereby eliminating the danger of complete loss if one company collapses. But for precisely this reason the unit holder cannot expect spectacular returns on his investment, even though he has the advantage of expert professional advice in the handling of his money.

(c) Investment Trusts

These are really *ordinary limited companies* that use their capital to buy shares in other businesses, in order to make a profit for their shareholders. Shares in investment trusts are bought in the same way as shares in other businesses, and are therefore not as easy to obtain as units in a unit trust.

Like the unit trusts they apply the funds mainly to industrial investments, and approximately 90 per cent of their capital is invested in company shares. The main advantage of the investment trust over the unit trust is that it is not restricted in its activities by a trust deed, and thus retains greater flexibility for switching funds from relatively unprofitable to more profitable uses.

(d) Building Societies

These are rather different from the other forms of financial intermediary. People save with them for two reasons: they offer a very safe form of holding as well as a competitive rate of interest; and many depositors hope to be able to borrow money from the society later in order to buy a house. For this reason the societies do not channel much of their funds towards industrial securities. The majority of the money is devoted to house purchase by way of mortgages.

(e) Public Sector Organizations

The National Savings Bank and National Girobank behave in a similar way to organizations in the private sector, investing a proportion of the deposits they receive. As you might expect, they normally direct their funds towards Government securities rather than commercial ones.

(f) Trustee Savings Banks

Since 1976 the Trustee Savings Banks have offered a full range of banking services. They are subject to the supervision of the Registrar of Friendly Societies and the Trustee Saving Banks Central Board. Until 1979 the 19 Banks had to invest their deposits with the National Debt Commissioners; they now have more freedom over the disposition of their funds.

(g) Direct Investors

There are about 2 500 000 people who regularly buy shares directly, without going through any of the intermediaries above. This is a sensible course for people with some detailed financial knowledge who can afford to make a loss on their shares from time to time. For the inexperienced investor it is much safer to invest through one of the institutions. Institutions can afford to invest in many different kinds of share, so that a loss on one can be offset by a profit on another. However, the Government's programme of privatization (see page 84) has significantly increased the number of individual shareholders.

13.4 Types of Securities

When we were considering how private companies raise capital, in Section 8.5, we looked briefly at the types of share that can be issued. It is now time to examine them more closely.

(a) Debentures

These are not really shares, because they do not give their holders any part of the ownership of the firm. They are known as stock, and are in effect long term loans to the company, which normally undertakes to repay the holder on a specific date. Each year debenture holders receive a fixed rate of interest, to which they are entitled whether or not the company is making a profit. If the company goes bankrupt the debenture holders must be paid before any of the shareholders. It is clear, then, that debentures involve very little risk for the holders, but to make them even safer for investors, the debentures are often issued as *mortgage debentures*. This means that a particular part of the firm's property is earmarked for sale in order to repay the debenture holders in the event of difficulty.

One respect in which debentures differ from other loans to a company is in the fact that the lender (the holder of the debenture) can sell his claim against the company to someone else. So if he holds debentures worth £1 000 in a quoted company he can in effect take them along to the Stock Exchange and sell them for the highest price he can get. The company is then in debt to the new holder and will pay the annual interest to him.

(b) Ordinary Shares

These are the most important shares and are issued by all limited companies. They are sometimes known as *equities* because each share entitles its owner to an equal share of the profits of the company. They have several important features:

(i) The money that is handed over to the company in exchange for ordinary shares is never returned to the shareholders for, as we have seen, the companies use the money to invest in plant and machinery.

(ii) The holders of ordinary shares are normally the last to be paid. The return they get on their shares is called a *dividend*. In profitable years the dividend may be very high, while in other years the ordinary shareholders may get no dividend at all.

(iii) The ordinary shareholders thus run the risk that their money will not earn them anything. To compensate for this risk they are entitled to vote at the firm's annual general meeting, where general policy is discussed and the board of directors is elected. It would be an exaggeration, however, to say that the ordinary shareholders controlled the company, for as we saw in Unit 8, this control really rests with the board of directors.

(iv) Some companies issue two or three categories of ordinary shares, one category being entitled to receive a dividend before the rest. A special category is known as *deferred ordinary shares* or *founders' shares*. As their names imply, these shares are issued to the founders of a business, often when it becomes a public company, and they are the last to receive a dividend. But founders' shares often carry disproportionate voting rights, to enable the founders of the business to retain control over it.

(c) Preference Shares

These are designed to attract funds from investors who do not want to take the risks associated with ordinary shares, and who want to be certain of an annual income from their investment.

(i) They carry a fixed rate of dividend per year, payable before ordinary shareholders receive any payment, but after interest has been paid to debenture holders.

(ii) Similarly, if the company is wound up, the preference shareholders will receive their share of the proceeds before the ordinary shareholders.

(iii) *Cumulative preference shares* differ in that if the company cannot afford to pay a dividend one year, it must be carried forward to the next year and be paid before the ordinary shareholders are paid.

(iv) *Participating preference shares* carry a fixed rate of dividend, but they entitle their holders to a further share of the profits once they reach a certain level.

(v) *Redeemable preference shares* can be bought back by the firm in a few years' time. They are issued when the company wants money only temporarily, and this is an inexpensive way of doing it.

(vi) The voting rights of preference shareholders vary according to the articles of the company, but generally where the shareholder has a fixed return to his investment he does not have a voting right. If preference share dividends are in arrears, however, the shareholders normally can vote. In some companies preference shareholders have limited voting rights – perhaps one vote for every five shares, as against the ordinary shareholders' one vote for every share.

(d) Gilt-edged Securities

As we have seen, when the Government or the public corporations need to borrow, the Treasury issues gilt-edged securities. These, like debentures, are generally known as stock rather than shares. Stock is traded in £100 lots, while shares are traded by number. Thus if you buy stock you might buy £800 worth, but if you buy shares you might buy 750 shares.

Gilt-edged securities these days are issued for a fixed period of time and at a fixed rate of interest. They can be regarded as an absolutely safe investment, because the holder knows that the Government will pay him £100 on the day that the security matures. The trouble is that inflation will have eroded the value of £100 over the life of the security: £100 will buy less in 1984 than it would have bought in 1970 (see Section 10.3(b)).

(e) Other Securities

Local authorities, overseas governments, and foreign companies also issue securities which can be held by investors, but these are hardly significant compared with the other types of security.

13.5   The Role of the Stock Exchange

The Stock Exchange is not the place where securities are actually issued. It is simply a highly organized market for the purchase and sale of second-hand quoted securities. (Quoted securities are those which the Stock Exchange Council has agreed may be sold on the Exchange (see Section 13.6).) It would be difficult for companies to raise long term capital if there were no organized market enabling investors to exchange their shares for cash. The Stock Exchange provides this facility: it brings together those who want to dispose of

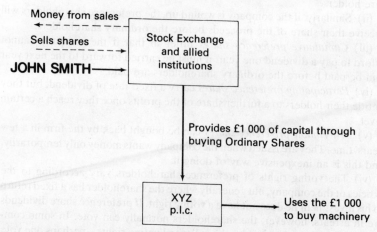

Fig. 13.2 *The Stock Exchange is a market for the sale of second-hand shares. John Smith cannot sell the shares back to XYZ p.l.c. directly*

their investment because they need cash, and those who want to invest because they have surplus cash available. Because prices are not fixed, the Stock Exchange does not and indeed cannot guarantee that an investor who sells shares will receive as much as he paid for them but, except in very unusual circumstances, the investor knows that he will be able to dispose of his holding. On the other hand, the company that issued the securities knows that the money raised is permanently at its disposal, and that people can sell their stocks or shares without affecting the company at all.

In Sections 13.6–13.9 we shall examine the structure of the Stock Exchange and its methods of operation, before looking at the ways in which shares are issued.

13.6   Organization of the Stock Exchange

(a) The Stock Exchange Council

The Stock Exchange is governed by the *Stock Exchange Council*, which is elected by members of the Exchange. The functions of the Council, which has 36 members, are:

(i) **To ensure that the rules of the Stock Exchange are observed by its members.** Enormous sums of money are involved in the transactions that take place on the Exchange, and it is most important that members honour any obligations into which they enter.

(ii) **To protect the investing public**. We have seen that much of the investing is undertaken by large institutions, but there are also over two and a half million individual investors. There are many ways in which they could be misled or even defrauded by members of the Exchange, and the Council tries to ensure that this does not occur.

(iii) **To approve the quotation of new shares**. The Stock Exchange cannot deal in the shares of a company without the approval of the Council. Again the highest standards are demanded, and if there is any doubt about the integrity of the directors of a company, or the soundness of the company itself, a quotation will not be approved. Sometimes, a quotation is suspended, if the behaviour of a company's directors has been questioned.

(b) The Members

The Members of the Stock Exchange, who have to pay substantial membership fees and annual subscriptions, are divided into two groups, stockbrokers and stockjobbers.

(i) **Stockbrokers** are the agents of the investing public. They act on behalf of investors and must follow their instructions. If you want to buy or sell shares on the Stock Exchange you must get a broker to act for you, and you will have to pay him a commission according to a fixed scale of charges.

In practice stockbrokers may be more than agents: they are usually ready to advise their principals (clients) of what action to take. The brokers are in close daily contact with the market and may be aware of important changes of which they are able to inform their clients. In this respect stockbrokers assume the role of investment consultants. They may also buy and sell shares on their own account.

(ii) **Stockjobbers** do not deal with the general public, but operate on their own behalf, aiming to make a profit (called the *jobber's turn*) by buying shares at a low price and selling at a high price. Jobbers are similar to wholesalers in that they hold various quantities of shares that they are willing to sell to brokers in large or small amounts. They normally specialize in a fairly narrow range of securities and, of course, they develop a detailed knowledge of them.

(c) Markets

The groups of securities in which the jobbers specialize are known as markets, and jobbers dealing in particular markets are all to be found at their own *pitch* in the Exchange or *House*, as it is called. If you look at the financial pages of most newspapers they will contain a list of share prices, and the shares mentioned there will normally be divided into markets: gilt-edged, industrials, plantations and so on.

(d) Prices

There are over 10 000 securities dealt in on the Stock Exchange, and thousands of deals are made every day. For reasons we discuss in Section 13.8, the prices of stocks and shares fluctuate from day to day, and a daily list of prices is compiled and published for the benefit of members of the Exchange and the investing public. The sample of prices that appear in the daily papers is taken from this list.

13.7   Stock Exchange Procedure

Suppose we have 1 000 ordinary shares in the Super Motor Company which we bought for £1 each, and now wish to sell at a profit. We don't know anyone who wants to buy them, so we telephone our stockbroker and instruct him to sell them for us. It is his duty to obtain the best price he can.

He will already have a rough idea of the price he is likely to get, for it is unusual for prices to change much from one day to the next. However, he goes onto the floor of the House and finds the appropriate group of jobbers. He will ask each of them in turn 'Super Motors ordinary?' and in response will get two prices from each of them, the lower being the price at which the jobber is willing to buy, the higher being the price at which he will sell. Let us suppose that our broker obtains quotations from three jobbers as follows: (a) £1.27–£1.32, (b) £1.28–£1.32, (c) £1.27½–£1.32½. Since we have instructed our broker to sell our shares it is the first of each pair of prices that will interest him, though he will give no indication of this to the jobber. He will accordingly return to the second jobber to confirm the price and, providing it remains at £1.28, he will say 'I sell 1 000'. We shall return to this transaction in a moment.

Now that the jobber has undertaken to buy 1 000 shares in Super Motors to add to his existing stock of them, he will probably revise his prices. Should another broker inquire about the same share he will quote perhaps £1.27½–£1.30, showing that he is now rather less anxious to acquire more of these shares but keen to sell some. In this way prices may vary from time to time during the day, but the prices quoted by different jobbers for the same shares will tend to even out as brokers buy from the lowest priced and sell to the highest priced.

There are complications in regard to pricing owing to the fact that the dividends on particular shares are paid only once or twice a year. If the dividend on a share has just been paid or is about to be paid to the existing holder, the price will be quoted *ex div* (without dividend); if the dividend is going to be paid to the buyer the price quoted will be *cum div* (with dividend).

Once a bargain has been struck between the broker and the jobber, as in the case of our shares in Super Motors, the procedure is as follows:

(*a*) They each make a note of the *bargain* (transaction) in their bargain books. No money changes hands at this stage.

(*b*) The broker informs us that he has been able to sell our shares.

(*c*) The Stock Exchange year is divided into 25 *accounts*, two of three weeks and the remainder of two weeks, each ending on a Tuesday. Before the end of the account we will receive from our broker a *contract note*, which is a formal notification of the sale of the shares, giving us the following information:

(i) The price obtained for the shares.
(ii) The broker's commission.
(iii) The stamp duty, if any.
(iv) The day on which the broker will pay us the net amount owing to us.

With the contract note we will receive a *transfer form*, which we must sign and return to the stockbroker to confirm the deal. At the same time we send him the share certificates for 1 000 ordinary shares in Super Motors so that they may be passed on to their new owner.

(*d*) The jobber will hope to sell our shares fairly quickly, so that on settlement day at the end of the account several payments can be made.

(i) The jobber can pay our broker for the shares he bought.
(ii) Our broker can pay us the net amount due to us.
(iii) The new owner of the shares can pay his stockbroker, who in turn can pay the jobber. (If the jobber doesn't sell the shares within the account this last payment will not, of course, be made.)

The transfer form can now be forwarded to the Super Motor Company, so that the company secretary can amend the register of shareholders and pay future dividends to the new owner of the shares.

You should note that the only documents that change hands are between members of the Exchange and outsiders. Undertakings between members are verbal agreements only, but they are regarded as absolutely binding by the parties concerned. This is a tradition of the Stock Exchange, which has the motto, 'Dictum Meum Pactum' – 'My word is my bond'.

13.8 Share Prices

We have already seen that jobbers alter their prices according to whether their holding of a particular share is increasing or decreasing. This follows simply from the operation of the economic principles of supply and demand. But the changes in supply and demand only reflect deeper influences on the prices of shares. We can divide these influences into three groups.

(a) Influences Affecting a Particular Share's Price

(i) Much depends on the recent performance of the company that issued the share. If profits have been good and are expected to be buoyant, share prices are likely to be high, as many people will try to acquire them. Poor profits will encourage shareholders to dispose of their holdings.

(ii) The possibility of a merger with another company may cause the share price to change, and although the movement will normally be upwards, the amount of change will depend on the view that shareholders in general take of the proposed merger.

(iii) The development of new products or techniques by a company may lead to optimism and higher share prices. Likewise, new developments by competitors may lead to a fall in the price of the share.

(iv) Government policies aimed at a particular industry may affect share prices of companies in that industry. For example if restrictions on the hire purchase of motor vehicles are intensified the shares of car manufacturers may well fall in price.

(b) Factors Affecting Share Prices in General

(i) The general economic atmosphere affects all share prices. Sometimes the Government does all it can to persuade people to spend money: this will normally mean a period of rising profits and many investors will instruct their stockbrokers to buy shares, causing a general rise in share prices. At other times the Government takes steps to reduce the level of spending: in this case lower profits are expected and share prices fall.

The reasons for changes in Government policy are complex and you can study them more fully in *Success in Economics*. We need only note here that the Stock Exchange is extremely sensitive to changes in economic policy.

(ii) Political factors may also be important. The prospect of a change of

Government often makes the Stock Exchange very jittery; the assassination of a foreign political leader has a similar effect.

(c) Speculation on the Stock Exchange

By speculation we mean the practice of trying to make a quick profit by anticipating changes in the prices of shares. There are three ways in which this can be done.

(i) If a share is priced at £1 today and you have reason to think that by next week it will be worth £1.25, you could buy 1 000 shares today for £1 000 and, if your speculation is correct, sell them next week for £1 250, making a quick £250 profit. People who speculate in this way, expecting a rise in price, are referred to as *bulls*. They may buy shares even if they have no money, hoping to pay at the end of the account out of the proceeds of the sale.

(ii) On the other hand if you own 1 000 shares priced at 50 pence today and you think that they will be worth only 40 pence next week, you could sell them today for £500 and, if your speculation is correct, buy them back for £400 next week, leaving yourself with £100 profit. Speculators of this kind are called *bears*. They may even sell shares they do not own, hoping to be able to buy them back at the lower price before the end of the account. Both bulls and bears are likely to operate on much narrower margins than those indicated, and often over a much shorter period of time.

(iii) It has often happened in the past that newly issued shares have risen in price quite rapidly, since the price of the share may be low compared to the expected dividend that will be paid on it. Accordingly some speculators make a practice of buying new shares, hoping to sell them very quickly at a profit. Such speculators are called *stags*.

Bulls, bears and stags are names applied to speculators who behave in these ways at particular times, whether they are Stock Exchange members or not. They are not labels applied forever to individuals. An investor may behave in a 'bullish' way one day, but be 'bearish' the next. And, of course, it does not follow that speculators always make a profit. If prices move in the opposite direction to the one they expect, they may be in financial difficulties.

The bear jobber expects the price of XYZ shares to fall during the next few days. Although he does not own any of these shares he undertakes to sell some of them at today's price of 50 pence each. He hopes that before he has to honour his commitment the price of the shares will fall so that he can buy them at perhaps 40 pence and sell them for 50 pence.

If XYZ shares do not fall in price he is faced with the choice of buying them at a high and perhaps unprofitable price in order to honour his commitment, or of paying a fee to his client for postponing settlement. This fee is known as *backwardation*, and applies when prices have not fallen as anticipated.

Bulls, on the other hand, expect the price of XYZ shares to rise. They therefore agree to buy some at today's price so that they can sell them at a higher price in a few days' time. The proceeds of this sale would be used to settle the debt they incurred when they agreed to buy the shares. If the price rise does not occur they may persuade the original seller of the shares to postpone settlement in exchange for a payment known this time as *contango*.

There are, then, many influences on share prices. It is sometimes helpful to be able to assess the general feeling of the Exchange and the general movement of share prices. A *share index* is constructed to make this possible. A cross-section of shares is chosen by the compilers of the index, and their average price is called 100. Subsequent changes in the average price of the shares are related to 100. So if the average price of the shares rises by 75 per cent, the value of the index is 175. The most widely consulted indices in this country are those compiled by the *Financial Times*, and you will find it an interesting exercise to follow them for a few weeks.

13.9   The Importance of the Stock Exchange

The Stock Exchange is a rather remote institution to most people, but it serves several very important functions in the commercial and economic life of the country. We have already seen some of these, but there are others which are not so obvious.

(*a*) Although no one can actually raise capital on the Stock Exchange, it would be impossible to raise long term capital without it. Investors are not prepared to commit their money permanently to a company, but the company needs it permanently. It is only through the Stock Exchange that this conflict is overcome and investors are able to turn their shares into cash.

(*b*) We have seen that the Stock Exchange offers protection to investors by insisting on the highest standards of behaviour from members, and by closely examining companies before allowing a quotation. If this did not happen it would be much more difficult for industry, and indeed the Government, to raise the money they need.

(*c*) Pension funds and insurance companies are able to offer a better service to their clients because of the existence of the Stock Exchange, which gives them a profitable outlet for their funds.

(*d*) By providing a ready market in gilt-edged securities, the Stock Exchange allows the Government to implement the various aspects of monetary policy which depend upon the sale and purchase of Government securities.

(*e*) The administration of some taxation depends upon Stock Exchange prices. The capital gains tax is levied to a large extent on the profits made by buying and selling shares. The information provided on the contract notes enables the Inland Revenue to ensure that the right amount of tax is being paid. Similarly the valuation of stocks and shares for capital transfer tax purposes relies heavily upon their Stock Exchange valuation.

(*f*) The Stock Exchange is an important economic indicator. Stock Exchange prices reflect the underlying economic conditions in the country and within particular industries. Low prices reflect pessimism and a grim outlook, high prices, optimism. Potential investors can assess the various possibilities open to them by studying the achievements of different securities as shown in the share indices. However, the Exchange does tend towards extremes of optimism or pessimism, which exaggerate the actual trends.

13.10 The New Issues Market

As we have seen, the Stock Exchange is a market for second-hand securities only. The issue of *new* securities is the concern of the part of the capital market known as the *new issues market*. As the prospects of a firm improve, it may need extra money to exploit the opportunities that arise. Some of the extra funds may be obtained by ploughing profits back into the business, but the planned expansion will frequently need much more capital than can be obtained in this way. If the company is already a public one, an issue of capital can be arranged quite easily, but if it is a private company it must first *go public*.

The company must already have a good trading record for this to be worth while: the Stock Exchange Council needs to see evidence of the firm's good record and current standing before it will grant a quotation. In addition, a great deal of money is needed because the process of issuing capital is expensive in itself. The company must have a market value of at least £500 000 before a quotation is allowed. It is a further requirement that a single category of shares must have a value of £200 000 before dealings can begin. The number of firms in a position to apply for a quotation is thus very limited.

Once a firm has decided to make a new issue, whether it is for the first time or the issue of additional stock it will consult a merchant bank (see Section 12.3) for advice about the timing and method of issue. The merchant banks that specialize in new issues are known as *Issuing Houses*, and many of them are the Accepting Houses we saw in Unit 12, performing a different job. As Issuing Houses they undertake the whole job of issuing the securities for their client and ultimately of delivering to him the capital that has been raised. There are five main methods of issuing new shares.

(a) By Prospectus

This amounts to an invitation to the general public to subscribe capital. The prospectus contains full details of the company's history and future plans, and an application form for shares. Normally applications are opened on the stipulated issue day and it is hoped that all the shares will be disposed of that day. Whether or not they are sold depends upon the view taken by the investing public of the potential of the company in relation to the price of the shares. To allow time for these assessments, the prospectus must appear at least three days before issue day.

(b) By Offer for Sale

This is similar to issue by prospectus except that initially all the shares are taken up by the Issuing House. Subsequently, the Issuing Houses offer them for sale to the public, giving the same details as are set out in the prospectus. The advantage to the company is that they do not have to worry about selling all the shares. That responsibility is taken over by the Issuing House.

In both these methods of issue the public has not only the detailed information presented by the Issuing House, but also the views of the financial press, for most new issues are discussed in their columns.

(c) By Placing

The Issuing House will recommend this method of issue when it knows that it can place the shares with a few large institutional investors. Details of the company do not have to be so widely advertised so the expenses are lower than with other methods. A *private placing* is likely to be more difficult than a public placing because it is for a company which is not quoted on the Stock Exchange and whose shares are less marketable than those of a quoted company. Some of the very large institutions are only interested in dealing in blocks of shares worth hundreds of thousands of pounds, and for them a public placing is an ideal way of obtaining shares.

(d) By Tender

When shares are issued by the methods discussed above they are frequently resold by their initial holders at a premium (i.e. at a price higher than their nominal value) because of the high demand for them. The stags then make a quick profit. To reduce the possibility of this the shares may be issued *by tender*: details of the company and its prospects are again set out in the press, and tenders are invited above a certain price. When all bids have been received the shares are issued at a price that just disposes of all the shares. Those who bid below this 'striking price' receive no shares, and those bidding above the price receive a cash rebate. In this way the company hopes to reduce the profits available to stags, and to increase the capital it raises for itself.

(e) By Issue to Existing Shareholders

When the amount of capital to be raised is not very large, it is sometimes possible to raise it from existing shareholders, by making a *rights* issue. This means that shareholders have the right to buy one new share for every ten, let us say, that they already hold. Sometimes the rights issue is part of a larger issue to the public, with existing shareholders having the right to buy shares on more favourable terms than the public.

At other times an *open offer* may be made to existing shareholders, enabling them to subscribe for new shares but imposing no limit on the number that they may buy. Both methods have the advantage of being very economical to the company.

A *bonus issue* should not be confused with a rights issue. In a bonus issue the shareholder receives the new shares free. This usually occurs when the real value of the company is much in excess of the nominal value of the shares.

13.11   The Unlisted Securities Market

The expense of a full public issue and Stock Exchange quotation has always prevented medium-sized firms from acquiring capital from independent investors. In 1980, however, the Stock Exchange established a second tier market known as the *unlisted securities market*. The requirements for companies entering this market are less stringent than for those seeking a full quotation, but they provide adequate safeguards for investors.

Although initially there were doubts about the wisdom of this development, by the end of 1982 well over 100 companies had taken advantage of the opportunity of raising new capital, mainly by private placing (see Section 13.10(c)), with no untoward results. It is likely that the unlisted securities market will become an important stepping stone towards a full quotation on the Stock Exchange in due course.

13.12   Other Sources of Capital

There are certain circumstances in which a firm might be unwilling or unable to issue new shares, but still need a large amount of capital. Since 1973, an organization called *Finance for Industry* has provided funds through two of its subsidiaries.

(a) **The Industrial and Commercial Finance Corporation** provides medium and long-term finance to small and medium-sized firms. The normal loan varies from £5 000 to £2 million for 7–20 years. ICFC has investments of over £380 million in over 3 300 companies.

(b) **The Finance Corporation for Industry** is prepared to lend much larger sums to larger firms. It will lend £2 million or more on a medium term basis. By 1978, it had committed almost £325 million to 40 different companies.

In 1976, **Equity Capital for Industry** was established. It is jointly owned by Insurance Companies and Finance for Industry, and provides long-term capital to industry, often by means of a shareholding.

(c) **Factoring**, although not concerned with long-term finance, is an increasingly important method for firms to economize on capital. What happens is that the *factors* (often the subsidiary of a bank) take over the firm's debtors. When goods are sold on credit, a copy of the invoice is sent to the factor, who will have agreed in advance to settle the debt within a stated period. It is then the factor's responsibility to obtain payment from the purchaser of the goods.

The agreement that is made between the company and the factor will take account of the average value of debtors, the average period of credit and the proportion of bad debts. In the light of these it is determined how promptly the factor will pay the company and the rate of commission that the factor will charge in order to make his profit. The advantage to the firm is that the system economizes on the amount of capital tied up with debtors.

13.13 Summary: Sources of Finance

Finance is essential to any business. The larger a business grows, the wider the sources of finance available to it. The short term finance it needs may come from the following sources:

(*a*) Trade credit (see Section 6.3).
(*b*) Bank overdrafts and bank loans (see Section 11.11).
(*c*) Hire purchase or other credit arrangements (see Section 6.4).

Long term finance may be obtained through the following methods:

(*a*) By ploughing back profits.
(*b*) The issue of debentures.
(*c*) The issue of preference or ordinary shares.
(*d*) By borrowing from one of a number of special institutions.

13.14 Questions and Exercises

(*a*) **Short Answers**

1. Give two meanings of the word *capital*.
2. Why do people and institutions want capital?
3. Who provides capital?
4. Which financial institutions are important intermediaries in the capital market?
5. Distinguish between unit trusts and investment trusts.
6. What use do the insurance companies make of their funds?
7. Why is the Stock Exchange sometimes called 'a market for second-hand securities'?
8. Distinguish between stockbrokers and stockjobbers.
9. Distinguish between bulls, bears and stags in the Stock Exchange.

(*b*) **Essay Answers**

1. Describe the procedures by which Mrs Jones may sell 1 000 shares she owns in a public limited company quoted on the Stock Exchange.
2. The XYZ Manufacturing p.l.c. wants to issue an extra £1 million of shares. Explain and comment upon the various methods open to the company.
3. Why do share prices fluctuate? Examine the main influences on the price of an individual share.

(*c*) **Projects and Assignments**

1. Build up as much information about the capital market as you can, by visiting the Stock Exchange and other financial institutions.
2. Make a detailed examination of the advantages and disadvantages of six different channels through which you could invest £200 of savings.

Unit Fourteen

The Arithmetic of Business

14.1 Introduction

At the end of a *trading period*, which is normally a year, the owner (or owners) of a business will review its performance. The owner will want to know how much profit he has made. Would he have been better off by investing his money in a building society or a unit trust? He will also want to know how much the business is worth. In a large limited company the calculations required are very complicated, but in a small business they are reasonably straightforward. For a detailed study of this subject you should consult *Success in Principles of Accounting*, but this Unit will enable you to understand the basic principles.

14.2 The Capital of the Business

In Unit 8 we saw that the capital of a limited company can mean the shares issued by that company. That is one way of measuring capital, but there are also several others. Let us consider the proprietor about to open a small retail business. He will have to set aside from his savings a sum of money with which to start the business. Perhaps he decides that he needs £6 000, and puts this into a special bank account. This is the initial capital of the business, and it is also one of its *liabilities*: a liability is any money owed by the business to someone outside it. So even the initial capital of a business is a liability, because it is owed to the owner. In a large company the same principle applies: the capital is owed to the shareholders.

As the business gets under way some of the capital has to be spent. The proprietor needs business premises from which to work, and perhaps a van for collecting and delivering goods. If he were a manufacturer, he would need stocks of raw materials to work with, as well as stocks of finished products to sell. Wages have to be paid to employees and there may be bills for stationery, gas, electricity, and so on. Already the initial capital is being divided up and put to different uses.

(a) Fixed Capital
Suppose he starts by buying a small shop for £3 000, some shop fittings for £1 200, and a second-hand van for £300. Things belonging to the firm are its *assets*, and the shop, shop fittings and van are called *fixed assets*, because they will

probably remain in the business for many years, being used over and over again to help make a profit. Our proprietor has now spent £4 500 of the firm's capital on fixed assets. The *capital* of the firm, however, remains at £6 000, having simply assumed a different form: instead of holding all the capital in the form of cash, the firm now holds only £1 500 in that form, and the rest as fixed capital.

(b) Working Capital

Next the proprietor buys stocks of goods for resale. They cost him £1 000 and, since this is a new business, he may well have to pay cash until his suppliers know him to be reliable. Again the nature of his capital has changed, leaving him with only £500 in cash. However, the purchase of stock is different from the purchase of the shop and other fixed assets: the object is to sell the stock as quickly as possible at a profit, thereby raising the cash to buy more stock for sale. Capital used like this for the day-to-day running of the business is known as *working capital*.

To see how much the firm has, let us examine the balance sheet after it has been trading for a few months. The balance sheet shows the position of the firm at a particular moment in time rather like a photograph. Suppose that after three months our firm's balance sheet looks like Table 14.1.

Table 14.1   A balance sheet

Assets	£	Liabilities	£
Shop	3 000	Capital	6 000
Shop fittings	1 200	Bank loan	400
Van	300	Creditors	600
Stock	1 300		
Debtors	900		
Cash at bank	150		
Cash in till	150		
	7 000		7 000

The formula for establishing working capital is *current assets minus current liabilities*. 'Current' here means short term, usually a year, so current assets and liabilities are those whose nature may be expected to change shortly. The current assets shown in the balance sheet are stock, debtors (people to whom he has supplied goods, but who have not yet paid for them), cash at the bank, and cash in the till, making a total of £2 500. The current liabilities are a bank loan of £400, and £600 that he owes to creditors for goods supplied but not yet paid for. The working capital is therefore

$$£2 500-£1 000=£1 500.$$

Working capital is important for two reasons. First, every time cash is spent on stock and the stock is sold for cash, at a profit, the business should be making a profit and this, after all, is the purpose of running a business. Secondly, any short term liabilities have to be paid for out of working capital, so the ratio of current assets to current liabilities should be adequate. In our example it is 2 500/1 000 = $2\frac{1}{2}$, which means that the firm could easily meet any bills that arrive. If its current liabilities were £2 500 and its current assets £1 000, the firm would be in a much more precarious position.

(c) Liquid Capital

Liquid capital is capital in the form of cash, or capital that can easily be turned into cash. This is one respect in which our firm is *not* in a strong position: it has very little liquid capital in relation to its liabilities. If we exclude debtors, since we don't know how soon they will pay, the firm has only £300 liquid capital, half at the bank and half in the till, and would be in difficulty if all the creditors wanted payment tomorrow. Perhaps the owner is carrying too much stock for safety.

(d) Capital Employed

This is another measure of capital that is sometimes used, and means the sum of the assets the firm is using, whether borrowed or not. In this example the capital employed is £6 100, consisting of the total assets minus the debts owing. This is not to be confused with the *net worth* of the business, which is its value to the owner, and is still £6 000.

14.3 Adding to Capital

In our example the net worth of the business has remained at £6 000, even after three months' trading. While it is possible for this to happen, it is unusual: it implies either that no profits have been made in the period or that they have all been withdrawn by the proprietor for his personal use. In fact there are several ways in which the capital employed in the business can be increased.

(a) By leaving some of the profits in the business.

(b) By borrowing from banks or elsewhere.

(c) By obtaining credit from suppliers, which really means using their capital to run the business.

(d) By converting the business into a larger unit, either by bringing in a partner or by forming a limited company.

(e) By issuing shares to the public, although this can only be done by a public limited company.

It is also possible for the capital employed in a business to *fall*. The proprietor may withdraw too much money for his own use, for example, or creditors may insist on repayment.

Whether capital is increasing or decreasing, the important thing is to be able to understand from the balance sheet whether the firm is in a strong or a weak position to continue trading. Potential suppliers, customers, and shareholders can learn a lot about a company by studying its balance sheet.

14.4 Profit

The purpose of business activity is to make a profit by supplying goods and services to consumers. This is done by buying goods at one price and selling them at a higher price, often after changing their condition. A rough indication of profits can be obtained by subtracting the cost of the goods from the money received from selling them, but we must be more precise. There are several aspects to consider.

(a) Turnover

The turnover of a business is another word for its sales. *Gross turnover* is the total value of goods sold, but the *net turnover* is more significant. This is the gross turnover minus the value of any goods returned by customers. The turnover of a business is important because if the firm doesn't sell anything (i.e. has a zero turnover) it cannot make a profit. If turnover is high the profits are likely to be high, but it does not follow that profits rise in direct proportion to turnover.

(b) Cost of Goods Sold

This can be obtained from the invoices received during the year. It does not include all the firm's purchases, however, because some of them, like the van and the shop fittings, are not intended for resale.

(c) Gross Profit

Gross profit is the difference between turnover and the cost of the goods sold. If during the year the firm sells goods for £50 000 which cost £40 000 to buy, the gross profit is £10 000.

(d) Net Profit

In selling goods for £50 000 the proprietor of the business will have incurred some expenses. Wages, fuel, power and rates will all have been paid during the year. If these amount to £4 000, the firm will have made a net profit of £6 000 at the end of the year.

Whether or not the profit figures of £10 000 and £6 000 are satisfactory to the proprietor depends partly on the kind of business he is running and partly on his own needs. In order that different kinds of businesses can be compared, or that the proprietor can easily compare one year with another, it is often useful to quote gross and net profit as a percentage of turnover.

(*e*) **Percentage Profit**

This is obtained by the formula

$$\text{Percentage profit} = \frac{\text{Profit}}{\text{Turnover}} \times 100$$

Of the £50 000 turnover, £10 000 was gross profit, so the *gross* profit percentage was

$$\frac{£10\ 000}{£50\ 000} \times 100 = 20 \text{ per cent}$$

20 per cent would be considered reasonable in most businesses. The *net* profit percentage was

$$\frac{£6\ 000}{£50\ 000} \times 100 = 12 \text{ per cent}$$

The use of percentages in accounting makes the comparison of different firms much easier. For example, suppose we are given the figures in Table 14.2 for two different firms.

Table 14.2   Comparison of profits (£)

	Firm A	Firm B
Turnover	50 000	30 000
Cost of goods sold	40 000	22 500
Expenses	4 000	2 000
Gross profit	10 000	7 500
Net profit	6 000	5 500

If we look only at the profit figures, A seems to have had a better year than B, though the difference between their net profits is less than that between their gross profits, because B has kept his expenses down. The percentage profit figures on the other hand give a different picture. A's gross percentage profit is 20 per cent and B's is 25 per cent, while their net percentage profits are 12 per cent and 18.3 per cent respectively. B has had much the more satisfactory year, in relation to turnover.

(*f*) **Level of Profits**

The proprietor will examine the annual profit figures in detail. (Indeed he will probably want half-yearly or even quarterly profit figures calculated so that he can keep a close watch on the firm's performance.) If profits are significantly lower than expected, he must investigate the causes.

(i) If *gross* profits are up to normal but *net* profits lower than usual, some of the expenses must be higher than expected. Perhaps too many staff are being employed, or electricity is being wasted? Some staff may be using the firm's vehicles outside working hours at the firm's expense. Perhaps wage rises or other increases have not been passed on to the customer.

(ii) A reduction in the *gross* profit percentage is more serious, and the cause may be more difficult to trace. It could be that money or stock is being stolen: either has the effect of reducing turnover while not reducing costs. In some businesses stock may be wasted. For example, bakers, grocers and other food retailers may find themselves throwing stock away if they have over-estimated the demand for their goods. In other businesses a change of fashion, break- ages, or gradual deterioration of goods may cause goods to be disposed of or sold off at very low prices. The firm probably needs to tighten up on its activities and make sure that it does not carry more stock than it needs. There may, of course, be a simpler explanation: perhaps the firm is paying more for its stock, or selling at lower prices.

This raises the question of the rate at which the stock is sold, which is dealt with in Section 14.5.

(g) Profits and Capital

Profit figures in relation to turnover convey important information about a business. But the proprietor will also be interested in his profits in relation to the capital he put into the business at the beginning. After all, we suggested in Section 14.1 that he might be better off by putting money in a building society or unit trust. Suppose the firm whose balance sheet we looked at in Table 14.1 made a net profit of £1 200 in the first year. The return on capital invested is obtained by the following formula.

$$\text{Return} = \frac{\text{Net profit}}{\text{Capital}} \times 100$$

$$= \frac{£1\ 200}{£6\ 000} \times 100 = 20 \text{ per cent}$$

This is more than he could have earned by investing in a building society or unit trust, but you must remember that he is not necessarily better off. If he had put his £6 000 in a building society, he could withdraw it intact at the end of the year. As it is he has invested much of his money in shop fittings and a van, and there is no guarantee that he would be able to sell these for the same amount that he paid for them. That is one of the risks of business. In addition he has contributed a year's work to the firm. He will probably compare his profits with what he could have earned by working for somebody else.

14.5   The Rate of Turnover

We saw in Section 14.4 that every time goods are sold the firm expects to add to its gross profit, and that firms should try to ensure that stocks are not left on their hands for too long. These two points come together when we consider the *rate of turnover* (also known as the *rate of stock-turn*) which means the number of times that a firm sells its stock each year. To calculate the rate of turnover we need to know the average stock that the firm carried through the year and the amount of stock sold. However, since the stock will be valued at cost price, and the stock sold will be valued at selling price, we must first reduce them to the same terms. We can do this if we know the gross profit percentage on goods. For example, if we know that sales are £15 000 and that there is a gross profit of 33$^1/_3$ per cent, then the cost of goods sold is £10 000.

Once we know the cost of goods sold, we then need to work out the average stock held, which is given by the formula:

$$(\text{Stock held on 1 January} + \text{Stock held on 31 December}) \div 2$$

Finally we are ready to calculate the rate of turnover, for which the formula is

$$\text{Rate of turnover} = \frac{\text{Cost of stock sold}}{\text{Cost of average stock}}$$

Thus, if a trader has a turnover of £36 000, with a gross profit of 25 per cent, and his opening stock was bought for £2 000 and his closing stock for £3 000, the rate of turnover is calculated as follows

$$\text{Cost of stock sold} = £36\,000 - \left(\frac{£36\,000 \times 25}{100} \right)$$

$$= £36\,000 - £9\,000$$
$$= £27\,000$$

$$\text{Cost of average stock} = \frac{£2\,000 + £3\,000}{2}$$

$$= £2\,500$$

$$\text{Rate of turnover} = \frac{27\,000}{2\,500}$$

$$= 10.8$$

This means that the average stock has been sold 10.8 times during the year. (The rate of turnover is always expressed as a number.) However, we cannot tell whether a rate of 10.8 represents a good or bad performance unless we know what kind of business it is. A fishmonger, for example, makes a profit of only a few pence on each fish, and therefore needs to sell a lot of fish to make a living (i.e. have a high rate of turnover). A car dealer on the other hand may make hundreds of pounds on each sale, and can survive with a much lower rate of turnover.

One way of increasing net profits is to increase the rate of turnover. If the average stock is sold twelve times during the year rather than ten, we will expect profits to rise. The supermarkets provide the best example of firms which make huge profits by a high rate of turnover. We saw in Unit 3 that they have many advantages over traditional shops, but one of the most important is their much higher rate of turnover. However, this does not always happen, for it may be that various expenses have increased also. If the increase in expenses is greater than the increase in gross profit, the result will be a reduction in net profit. Or if the increase in the rate of turnover is achieved by reducing prices, the level of net profit may again be reduced.

14.6   Questions and Exercises

(a) Short Answers

1. What is meant by saying that capital is a liability of a business?
2. Distinguish between fixed capital and working capital.
3. What is liquid capital?
4. Name four ways in which the capital of a business may be increased.
5. Distinguish between gross profit and net profit.
6. Give another name for the *turnover* of a business.
7. Show how you would calculate the rate of stock-turn of a business.
8. Why would a newsagent expect to have a higher rate of turnover than the owner of a furniture store?
9. Does a high rate of turnover necessarily imply a high level of profits? Explain your answer.
10. By what means could a retail grocer increase his profits?

(b) Essay Answers

1. Explain the various meanings of the word *capital* in commerce, giving examples to illustrate your answer.
2. How is (a) the gross profit, (b) the net profit of a business calculated? What factors might cause a reduction in the level of net profit?
3. Explain why the rate of turnover is important to a trader, showing the relationship between the rate of turnover and the level of profit.
4. Show why each of the following is important to a trader: (a) capital, (b) fixed capital, (c) working capital, (d) liquid assets.
5. Give examples to show how the following may be calculated: (a) net profit, (b) capital employed, (c) working capital, (d) rate of turnover.

Unit Fifteen

Communications: the Post Office and British Telecom

15.1 Introduction

Commerce can only flourish when there is contact between all the individuals and institutions involved. This contact may take a number of forms.

(*a*) The earliest kind of contact was physical: early traders would *travel* in order to conduct their business. Businessmen still travel a great deal but it is not so essential to do so now.

(*b*) The specialist trader must not only be able to send goods to consumers, but he must also establish a market for the goods in the first place. This is the role of *advertising*. The methods of advertising and the problems it creates are the subject of Unit 16.

(*c*) Businessmen need written confirmation of the transactions they are involved in, and frequently they need to be in immediate contact with each other by telephone. It is here that the Post Office and British Telecom are important. (Until October 1981 the two organizations were both within the Post Office, but now they are separate organizations. We shall deal with them both in this Unit, since together they provide the main communications network in the United Kingdom.)

The two organizations offer a wide variety of services. British Telecom is responsible for the telecommunications services: the Post Office retains its traditional mail services as well as providing facilities for the settlement of debts. Full details of the services can be found in the *Post Office Guide* or from the local Telecom offices. Here we shall examine the principal services, bearing in mind particularly the ways in which communication services are important to commercial life.

15.2 Postal Services

(*a*) Letter Post

This is the principal service offered by the Post Office, which deals with 26 million letters every day. They are divided into two groups, first class and second class, the intention being that first class letters should receive priority and be delivered the day after posting, while second class letters should normally take a day longer. Surveys conducted by the Post Office suggest that 94 per cent of first class and 90 per cent of second class letters are delivered on time.

The delivery of letters is an immense task, and the two-tier system is an attempt to ease the daily burden by spreading it out over the working day. There are other ways, too, in which the Post Office tries to streamline the operation.

(i) **Postcodes** have been introduced to allow the automatic sorting of letters. By means of a code of letters and numbers, each letter can be sorted down to the final stage for the postman to put them into the right order. Automatic sorting has not yet been introduced in all areas, but where it is in operation letters carrying the postcode arrive more quickly than those without it.

Fig. 15.1   Operating a postcoding machine

(ii) **Standard sized envelopes**. The use of standard sized envelopes is also being encouraged by the Post Office. This is helpful in the process of *facing* the letters, that is, stacking them so that the stamps are all in the top right-hand corner and can be automatically cancelled.

The service has deficiencies for large businesses and for urgent communication, and the Post Office offers a number of refinements which are available to all customers but are primarily designed for businessmen.

(b) **Certificates of Posting**
For a small charge, the Post Office will issue a certificate providing proof that you have posted a parcel to a particular address.

(c) **Recorded Delivery Service**
This service provides proof that you not only posted a letter but, more important, that it was delivered. A nominal charge is made for the service, and the Post Office clerk gives the sender a slip of paper proving that the letter has been sent. When it is delivered, the letter has to be signed for, preferably by the addressee. In the event of non-delivery, a limited amount of compensation is payable. For an additional fee the Post Office will inform the sender when delivery has been made, though no extra care is taken of letters under this service.

The recorded delivery service is often used by traders who want to ensure that debtors receive their bills, and by solicitors sending important documents by post. Compensation of up to £18 will be paid for loss of documents. It should not be used for sending cash or anything which is of any value since no compensation will be offered. Where valuable items are concerned, the registered post system should be used (see Section 15.4*(c)*).

(d) **Franking Machines**
It is no trouble for us as individuals to buy stamps and stick them on our letters as we send them. But some large companies dispatch several thousand letters from their head office every day, and it would be laborious and time-wasting to have to stick stamps on each one. To avoid this the Post Office allows customers with a heavy outward mail to use a franking machine, which prints the postage payable on each envelope. The machine contains a meter which records the total postage payable on the letters passed through it, and the amount is payable to the Post Office periodically, normally in advance.

This system is time-saving, not only for the businesses but also for the Post Office, because it saves them cancelling stamps on the letters when they arrive at the sorting office. The only drawback is that the users may try to defraud the Post Office by franking letters with a lower amount than is strictly payable, but this is discouraged by a system of spot-checks.

(e) **Business Reply Service**
This service enables members of the public to send short replies to businesses without having to pay for a stamp. It is used mainly by traders who are advertising their goods and are anxious to encourage replies from the public. Before the service can be used, a licence must be obtained from the Post Office and a deposit paid to cover the likely costs of delivering the letters. When they are delivered the letters are subject to a small surcharge over the ordinary letter rate.

(f) **Freepost**
A variation of the business reply service is the freepost system. With approval

from the Post Office and an advance deposit to cover the cost, a company may invite its customers or potential customers to address letters as follows

> Thurays Sports Limited
> *Freepost*
> High Street
> Graybury

Letters will be delivered by second class mail, though again the Post Office imposes a small surcharge on the usual second class rate.

(g) Express Services

Where it is urgent to send a letter or package more quickly than the ordinary postal service can deal with it, the letter may be delivered *express post* by a special Post Office messenger. Alternatively it may be sent as a *railway letter*, whereby the Post Office undertakes to dispatch the letter by the first available train to the station specified by the sender.

Either of these systems could be used if, for example, a supplier insists on having an order in writing before he dispatches goods and the trader has forgotten to order on time. They are expensive services since they often involve the Post Office in heavy costs.

(h) Datapost

Datapost is a special service originally developed to ensure that computer data collected from contracted customers one day would be delivered the following morning. Now all kinds of documents and other small items such as spare parts are handled. In 1981 about 4 million packets were sent by Datapost.

The Post Office lost its monopoly over some postal services in 1981. It is likely that competition will be restricted to services such as express delivery and Datapost.

(i) Air Mail Service

Both personal and business letters are regularly sent overseas by air mail, when the sender wants to be sure that they arrive in days rather than weeks. Bills of lading (see Section 19.6) are always forwarded by air, so that they arrive before the goods to which they relate.

(j) Parcel Post

The Post Office operates a parcel delivery service for parcels up to 10 kg weight. Although this is not an economic way of sending large consignments of goods, the Post Office parcels service handles 180 million parcels a year, and at Christmas as many as a million a day.

(k) Cash on Delivery

An additional service which is useful to traders is that of cash on delivery. The Post Office undertakes to collect payment for the goods being delivered before they are actually handed over. The sender of the goods pays for the service, though of course the cost is generally included in the price paid by the consumer. Cash on delivery provides a safeguard to sellers and buyers: sellers do not have money tied up in bad debts and do not have to keep sending reminders to debtors. Also mail order customers do not have to send off money in advance to possibly obscure companies which may take months to deliver the goods.

As you can see, the Post Office provides a comprehensive service for the transmission of documents and goods between people and firms. Business could not be conducted satisfactorily without its services for, as we saw in Unit 5, documentary evidence of orders, bills and payments is essential. Sometimes, however, businessmen need a more immediate form of communication. To meet this requirement British Telecom provides a range of *telecommunication services*.

15.3   Telecommunications

While the mail services provided by the Post Office grow steadily, the most direct and immediate communication is provided by the various telecommunication services of British Telecom. Some of these services have the additional advantage of giving the recipient a typewritten or printed record of the communication.

(a) The Telephone

Business life today would be inconceivable without the telephone. The service was first provided by the Post Office in 1912, and in 1980 there were 20 million subscribers to the service who made 20 000 million calls. Charges are made by a combination of a fixed quarterly rental and payments proportionate to the number and length of the calls and the distance over which they are made.

The majority of subscribers are now linked to the *Subscriber Trunk Dialling* (STD) system, which enables one subscriber to dial direct to any other on the system. This is much cheaper than making calls via the operator, although the chances of misdialling are greater.

Speed is the immediate advantage of the telephone. A trader, for example, can place an order for goods or get a quotation for them much more rapidly by telephone than by letter. Moreover, there may be details of the job or consignment to be discussed, and this can be achieved more efficiently in a five-minute telephone conversation than by the exchange of three or four letters.

It is important, however, that agreements made by telephone are confirmed in writing as soon as possible, for two reasons. Without written confirmation there would be no evidence of a contract between the two parties, and it is easy to imagine the difficulties to which this could lead; also words can easily be misheard over the telephone, and a written follow-up avoids any confusion. It is even a good idea to spell out vital words when making an important business call.

To ensure that the best use is made of the telephone system, British Telecom provides a number of ancillary services for subscribers, though not all of them are designed for businessmen. These extra services include:

(i) **Directories**. In addition to the basic directories containing an alphabetical list of the subscribers in a given area, classified trade directories are also available. Indeed the best known of these, the *Yellow Pages*, are issued to all subscribers. Most of the other classified directories are published privately (some of them charging excessive rates in view of the small circulation they enjoy).

The advantages of the *Yellow Pages* are that the subscriber can readily obtain the telephone number of, for example, a plumber, because all the local plumbers will be listed in the same place in the directory. Thus plumbers and other businesses enjoy a quiet and inexpensive kind of advertising, and British Telecom enjoys extra revenue from the more intensive use of the system.

(ii) **Directory inquiries services** provide assistance to callers unable to trace the number of the person they wish to call. (Sometimes a subscriber deliberately chooses to have his number excluded from the directory, because he does not want it to be available to everyone. In such cases Directory Inquiries will be unable to help.)

(iii) **Redirected calls.** Sometimes it may be inconvenient for a person to accept calls on his normal number. In this case British Telecom can intercept the calls and redirect them to a number where they can be dealt with. This service operates when people have to change their number or when, as happens with family doctors, they are temporarily off duty.

(iv) **Miscellaneous services** provided by British Telecom include such things as alarm calls, where you can arrange for the telephone operator to ring until you answer, recorded weather forecasts, the time, and the latest score in a Test Match in progress. In 1980 over 600 million calls were made to recorded information services including nearly 450 million to the speaking clock. There is also a *freefone* service on the pattern of the freepost service described earlier.

(b) Telex

Teleprinters have been described as a cross between the telephone and the typewriter.

Subscribers to this service have a teleprinter installed in their office and are given a number in the same way as telephone users. Messages can then be sent to other subscribers: the telex operator types the message out and it is automatically printed at the recipient's office, even if there is no one there to receive it. The main advantage of this system is that messages can be received at any time of the day or night, so when offices open in the morning in London, written information is already to hand about price changes or other developments that have occurred in Tokyo during the night. Likewise, information can be transmitted onward to New York, and so on. Telex users in Britain can contact 155 countries direct. Firms with offices in different places make heavy use of the telex to maintain contact, using codes where confidential material is being transmitted.

Fig. 15.2 Goonhilly Downs Radio Station

(c) Telemessages

These have replaced telegrams as a means of communicating quickly with people within the United Kingdom without a telephone or telex. The message that you wish to send is dictated over the telephone to the operator (minimum charge £3.00 for 50 words, plus VAT). The message is then transmitted by telex to the office nearest to the addressee and British Telecom guarantee that it will be delivered with the first class post the following morning. This is not so efficient as the former telegram service which normally provided same day delivery. The overseas telegram service still remains.

(d) Radio and Television

The development and refinement of radio and television has brought about immense improvements in business communications. The launching of space satellites has been the main source of improvement, because they can carry thousands of telephone conversations, or several television programmes simultaneously. The satellite high above the earth's surface receives messages transmitted from one centre, and bounces them back to other centres. In 1964 the International Consortium for Satellite Telecommunications, Intelsat, was set up to supervise the development of the system. Now over 70 countries subscribe to Intelsat, and 17 to Eutelsat, its European counterpart.

(e) Prestel

Prestel is a system which allows a subscriber to have information extracted from a computer through the telephone network displayed on an adapted television set. The subscriber can 'dial' into any of 150 000 'pages' of information on a wide range of subjects. Many of these deal with current events and are constantly updated, thereby providing businessmen with immediate checks on such things as commodity prices and interest rates.

The importance of rapid and efficient communications in business cannot be exaggerated. As commerce and trade become more competitive and complex, the need of up-to-date information grows. Decisions about buying, production and marketing may commit a company to thousands of pounds of expenditure: the better and more complete the information available to the firm, the less chance there is of wrong decisions being made. For this reason and many others, the search for improvements in the system of communications will continue.

Major developments include DATEL, the transmission of computer information via the telephone and telegraph systems, and the provision of the data processing services for commerce and industry through National Data Processing, British Telecom's computer bureau.

15.4 Payment through the Post Office

The Post Office offers a number of facilities for the settlement of debts, the most important for businesses being those operated by National Girobank, which we shall deal with in Section 15.5. There are other less formal methods of payment which should not be overlooked.

(a) Postal Orders
Postal orders are issued for any amount from 25 pence to £10, on payment of a *fee*, which is 20 pence for postal orders up to £1 in value and 26 pence for those of greater value.

Postal orders are a convenient way of making payments if you do not have many to make. Their disadvantage is that you have to go to the Post Office to get them because they are not issued in books like cheques. The payee's name also has to be filled in because postal orders are not negotiable: only the payee can collect the money from the Post Office.

Postal orders can be crossed in the same way as cheques to ensure that they are paid into a bank account. As they are not negotiable it is advisable to check that the payee does have a bank account before crossing an order.

(b) Money Orders
These have not been issued since 1973, when the upper limit for postal orders was increased to £10. However, when money has to be sent urgently, an Inland Telegraph Payment Order can be purchased for amounts of up to £100, for a fee of £3.50. Instructions are then telegraphed to the Post Office nearest the payee to make the payment. If necessary a message can be included at extra cost.

Overseas money orders and overseas telegraph money orders are still available for people wishing to make small payments abroad, for example to members of the armed forces or merchant navy. Again it is possible to include a message, for which an extra charge is made.

(c) Registered Post
On the rare occasions when cash has to be sent through the post, the safest way to send it is by registered letter. This must be handed in to the Post Office (not put in the letter-box) and a receipt obtained. A fee is payable in addition to the first class letter rate. The fee varies according to the value of the contents of the packet, the minimum being £1, which provides for up to £500 in compensation, and the maximum £1.20, for up to £1 750. Naturally the Post Office takes special care of registered packets and it is very unusual for one to go astray.

15.5 National Girobank

Girobank is the main way in which the Post Office competes with the Clearing Banks in the settlement of debts. All accounts are held centrally at a computer centre in Bootle: money can be cheaply and efficiently transferred from one account to another, or deposited from outside the system, or indeed paid outside the system.

The facilities provided are similar but not identical to those of the banks, as you will see.

(a) Methods of Payment

These vary according to whether the payment is to another Girobank account holder or to someone outside the system. Payment to another account holder is made by filling in a *transfer form* with details of the payment. There is room on the form for a message explaining the payment if the drawer wants to write one. The form is sent to the Girobank centre, where the payment is made. It is then forwarded to the payee, as notice that the money has been paid.

If an account holder wants to make a payment to someone without a Girobank account, or wants to withdraw cash, he does so by completing a *cheque*, which can be presented by the payee at his Clearing Bank and cleared in the usual way. If it is necessary to pay cash to someone, the cheque must be authenticated at the Girobank centre before being forwarded to the payee, who can then cash it at his local Post Office. The reason for this is that overdrafts are not allowed in Girobank.

Account holders are generally allowed to draw up to £50 in cash on alternate days at two named Post Offices, but not on consecutive days. However, customers are allowed to draw up to £50 at any Post Office, provided they have held an account for six months and have been issued with a *cheque card* by Girobank.

Girobank affords the same facility for *standing order payments* as the Clearing Banks. This allows regular commitments to be met punctually. Where the bills are not of the same amount each month, the *automatic debit transfer* system allows the payee to request payment from Girobank (as long as a pre-arranged limit is not exceeded).

(b) Paying In

Paying money into a Girobank account is quite straightforward: a deposit form is completed and handed in at any Post Office with the money. If cheques are being paid in they will not be credited to a Girobank account until they have been cleared.

If someone without a Girobank account wants to pay money into an account, he completes a *transcash* form or one specially prepared by the payee and hands the form and the cash into the Post Office, who make a nominal charge for the service.

(c) Advantages of Girobank

The relative merits of the National Girobank and the Clearing Banks are debatable. There are several points which should be borne in mind.

(i) Payments between Girobank account holders are usually quicker than those between customers of different bank branches. Once the Girobank transfer form reaches the computer the transaction is complete. The bank cheque has a longer journey to make.

(ii) There is very little difference in cost as long as the bank account remains in credit. Girobank account holders make a limited payment for stationery which is all printed with their name on. On the other hand they are provided with pre-paid first class envelopes for their remittances through the Girobank centre.

(iii) Post Offices are more convenient than banks in that they are open not only for longer hours, but also on Saturdays.

(iv) Girobank sends frequent statements showing the position of the account. Business customers can receive them whenever the balance in the account changes, while other customers receive statements whenever money is paid into their accounts (and sometimes more often still). The banks do not normally send statements this often, although special arrangements can be made for individual customers.

(d) Disadvantages of Girobank

However, the Girobank system has its disadvantages, and there are several ways in which it compares unfavourably with the banks.

(i) One advantage that the banks have over Girobank is the overdraft facilities which they provide. We have seen that overdrafts are not allowed within the Girobank system. (However, Girobank customers are able to arrange loans on comparable terms to the customers of the Clearing Banks.)

(ii) All in all, the banks provide a much more comprehensive range of financial services than Girobank. In the long run this may count against Girobank because people sometimes need advice on matters outside its scope.

(iii) No interest is payable on Girobank deposits since the Girobank account corresponds to a current account at a bank. However, Girobank account holders can use the savings facilities provided by the Post Office, which are outlined in Section 15.6.

(iv) A minor disadvantage of Girobank is that Post Offices have all kinds of other business to contract. It may be frustrating to the account holder to have to queue up behind several people wanting to renew their television licences or inquire about the postage rates to Australia.

15.6   Saving at the Post Office

We do not intend to examine savings institutions in general in this Unit, but we shall look briefly at the savings facilities provided by the Post Office.

(a) The National Savings Bank

(i) **Ordinary accounts** are primarily intended for small savings and interest of 5 per cent is paid on deposits.

(ii) **Investment accounts.** These pay a much higher rate of interest (13 per cent in 1981); the exact rate changes from time to time as interest rates generally fluctuate.

(b) Savings Certificates

These are issued for different amounts and on different terms from year to year. They are fairly liquid in that they can be cashed at about a week's notice, but they have to be held until they mature to provide a reasonable income. They are free of income tax.

It is now possible to save by making a contract to pay in regular instalments. The *Save As You Earn* scheme, as it is called, allows subscribers to pay in 60 equal monthly instalments (maximum £50 per month). The 1981 issue of this savings contract was *index-linked*: at the end of the period the repayment will purchase as much as the original contributions.

(c) Premium Bonds

These have proved a very popular form of saving, even though the holder receives no interest. Each bond qualifies you for a stake in the draw for cash prizes. These prizes, some of them worth thousands of pounds, replace the normal system of interest payments as the incentive for people to invest. The money which would be used to pay the interest if the Government borrowed from the public in the ordinary way is used to pay the prizewinners. Subscribers must purchase a minimum of £5 of bonds, and there is a maximum holding of £10 000.

15.7   Questions and Exercises

(a) Short Answers

1. Explain the difference between the recorded delivery service and the registered post.
2. What are the advantages of freepost and the business reply service?
3. How does the cash on delivery service help traders?
4. How does the cash on delivery service help consumers?
5. What methods of payment are offered by the Post Office?
6. Name four ways in which the National Girobank differs from the Clearing Banks.
7. What is the two-tier postal system?
8. What is the purpose of postcodes?
9. What is the advantage of holding an investment account at the Post Office?

(b) Essay Answers

1. Examine the services available to the businessman under the headings (a) postal services, (b) telecommunications.
2. Describe the operation of National Girobank, showing its advantages over the Clearing Banks.
3. Describe the services offered by the Post Office for the payment of debts.
4. What means of communication are offered by the Post Office and British Telecom?

5.   Explain the savings facilities offered by the Post Office. Compare them with the facilities offered by two other financial institutions.

(c) Projects and Assignments

1.   Make a collection of news cuttings and photographs of matters affecting the Post Office, and use it to describe the problems facing the Post Office.
2.   Make a detailed survey of the National Girobank and the services it offers.
3.   Use the current *Post Office Guide* to draw up a report on *either* United Kingdom subsidiary postal services (i.e. services other than the main letter and parcel post) *or* making payments through the Post Office. Show how the customer benefits from these services.

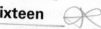

Communications: Advertising and Marketing

16.1 Introduction

We have seen that one of the effects of the division of labour is that each manufacturer produces more goods than he can use himself. To dispose of them a market must be found, and it is the function of the *marketing department* of the firm to establish a market for its products. We shall take a general look at the work of the marketing department at the end of this Unit, but for most of it we shall concentrate on one aspect of marketing, *advertising*, in its various forms.

Advertising is used for so many different purposes that it can only be loosely defined as the spreading of information or awareness. This covers, for instance, the Government's efforts to reduce cigarette smoking and encourage road safety. In the context of commerce, however, the main object of advertising is specifically to increase, or at least maintain, the sales of a product or service. Before we look at the different types of advertising, let us first consider the aims of advertisers in more detail.

16.2 The Aims of Advertising

(a) Higher Sales

The main purpose of any business is to make a profit, and in general the more goods a firm sells, the higher its profits. Indeed profits should rise at a higher rate than sales because some of the costs of production do not increase with output. In commercial terms, as sales increase, the *cost per unit of production* is reduced. The cost per unit can be calculated by dividing the total costs by the number of units. Let us take an example.

Suppose that the annual cost of producing plastic trays can be divided as follows

Cost of machinery	£8 000
Rent of factory	£2 000
Cost of labour and materials	£100 per thousand units

and that sales have been running at 10 000 units per year.

Total costs are £8 000 + £2 000 + £1 000 (the cost of labour and materials for 10 000 units). Therefore the cost per unit will be

$$\frac{£11\ 000}{10\ 000} = £1.10$$

The producer now tries to increase his sales by *advertising*, at a cost of £2 000. The effect of the campaign is to increase his sales by 25 per cent, so that he sells 12 500 units. His costs will now be

Machinery and rent	£10 000
Advertising	£2 000
Labour and materials	£1 250
	£13 250

The cost per unit will therefore have fallen to £13 250/12 500 = £1.06. The overall cost of production is lower, even though the advertising has cost £2 000. If sales had increased by more than 25 per cent, the reduction in costs per unit would have been even more significant.

If you study advertisements on television and in the press you will find that, while their basic purpose is to increase sales, some of them have more specific aims.

(b) New Products
These have to be brought to the attention of the public if they are to catch on. One area where advertising has virtually created a demand in recent years is that of men's toiletries, which are now generally accepted. Large amounts of capital are spent on developing new products. Many of them fail because they don't immediately appeal to consumers, often because the advertising is inappropriate.

(c) Information
Many advertisements are designed to inform consumers of changes in the nature of the product. You have probably noticed how many products are described as *new* or *new formula* in advertisements.

(d) Branded Goods
Manufacturers' and retailers' branded goods are often advertised to keep the brand name in the public eye. Sometimes only the brand name is mentioned in the advertisement, and there is no reference to particular goods.

(e) Retail Outlets
Some advertising is restricted to the trade press, in an attempt to get more retailers to sell the product. Broadening the market in this way should result in higher sales.

(f) The Company's Image

Businesses generally want to project a favourable image of themselves to the public: they like to be known for the reliability or high quality of their products, for giving value for money, for putting the customer first and so on. Many advertisements are designed purely to project the desired image, and do not attempt to 'sell' goods directly.

(g) Other Objectives

The list above is by no means exhaustive. There may be many other objectives, for example, the opening up of overseas markets. But whatever objective receives the heaviest emphasis in a commercial advertisement, the overriding aim, in the short run or the long run, is always to increase sales.

16.3 Types of Advertising

We can divide advertising into different categories, according to its approach or attitude or according to its medium. We consider the medium used for advertising in Section 16.5. Here we identify the various types of advertising.

(a) Persuasive or Competitive Advertising

This type is aimed solely at consumers, and is the kind you see most of on television: it tries to persuade you to buy the advertiser's product rather than his competitor's by assuring you that it is better. Perhaps the best examples are provided by the manufacturers of household detergents who all produce virtually the same product but try to persuade the housewife that their own particular brand is outstanding. It is this kind of advertising that is most frequently criticized as being wasteful. However, in a competitive field it is essential for the individual firm to keep the public familiar with the names of its products if it is to maintain its share of the market.

(b) Informative Advertising

All advertising is informative to some extent, in that it is informing people that a product exists or an event is taking place. But the term informative advertising is normally reserved for the following goods and services.

(i) **Advertising in technical and trade journals**. Such advertisements usually contain technical details of products and invite inquiries from interested parties.

(ii) **Advertising of particular events**, such as trade fairs, exhibitions, concerts and sporting activities. It is true that the advertisers hope to attract people to attend the event, but on the whole they do this by stating facts rather than by making persuasive claims.

(iii) **Advertising of employment opportunities**. Again you could argue that the advertiser is hoping to persuade people to offer their services, but these advertisements are more informative than persuasive.

It is frequently difficult to draw the line between persuasive and informative advertising, for many advertisements contain elements of both. Nevertheless, it is useful to be able to detect persuasive bias in advertisements.

(c) Generic Advertising

When all the producers in one industry combine to advertise the product in general rather than their own particular brands, we call the result generic advertising. Advertisements which exhort you to 'Join the tea-set' or 'Drink more beer' are familiar examples. Such advertisements belong to a special kind of persuasive advertising, and are normally financed by the *trade association* to which firms in the industry belong. (A trade association is a body representing the interests of all the firms in an industry; in addition to this kind of joint advertising, the trade association might make itself responsible for research, information, and negotiation with the Government or the trade unions.)

16.4   Advertising Agents

If you have a second-hand car or washing machine to sell, you can draft an advertisement setting out the details and the price required and insert it in the local newspaper or shop window. Newspaper columns also provide a convenient means of advertising both for retailers and for employers wanting to attract staff. But a national campaign to advertise a new brand of chocolate or a new model of car needs rather more care if sales are to be won. Most manufacturers do not possess the particular skills that are needed to devise, make and place such advertisements. The advertiser normally consults advertising agents and selects one of them to run the campaign for him. Since the advertising agent handles campaigns for many advertisers, he can afford to employ specialists in many fields, a luxury which individual manufacturers could not afford for themselves. The advertising agent has five main functions.

(a)   Creating the Advertisement

This is done on the basis of information provided by the advertiser about the nature of the product, its strengths and weaknesses, and the market at which it is aimed. The amount that the advertiser is prepared to spend is also relevant, of course. The agency's work on behalf of each client is the responsibility of an *account executive*: he organizes the campaign but does not actually create the advertisement itself. This job is done by *copywriters*: they are the people who think up the advertisements you see on television and in the newspapers.

(b)   Producing the Advertisement

The agency's production department then goes to work on putting the ideas of the copywriter into practice: artists produce drafts of posters and the film department produces films in the agent's own studio or on location. The finished advertisement can then be shown to the client for his approval and, if he wants changes, amendments can be made.

(c) Placing the Advertisement

It will have been agreed in advance which advertising media are to be used for the campaign (see Section 16.5). The agency normally books advertising time on television or space in the press in advance of its requirements, and then places its advertisements as necessary. The agency receives a commission from the television or newspaper company for the advertisements that it places with them and, of course, the advertiser pays the television or newspaper company. The commission that the agency receives from the media owners frequently enables it to make these arrangements without any extra charge to large advertisers.

Those are the three main functions of the advertising agent. Nowadays, however, they offer other services to those clients who once again don't want to employ specialists on a full-time basis.

(d) Market Research

Market research can be defined as investigation of all the factors influencing the distribution of the product from the producer to the final consumer. Its purpose is to provide manufacturers with as much information as possible about the market for their products, often before the creation of the advertising campaign, so that they know exactly who they are aiming at. They may conduct such investigations for themselves, they may employ a firm specializing in market research, or they may use their advertising agent.

The research is normally undertaken by means of carefully drafted questionnaires. They are designed to obtain details of the number of potential customers, their location, their tastes, as shown by their reactions to rival products, and the ways in which tastes may be changing. Many refinements can be included, such as the effectiveness of different kinds of packaging or different methods of selling, but the basic idea remains the same – to find out more about the market, so that more goods can be sold and more profits made.

(e) Advice

Since the success or failure of a new product can depend upon the way in which it is presented to the public, it is important that the advertising agent is consulted in the early stages of the product's life. Agencies develop a sense of what will and what will not sell a product, and will normally be able to offer useful advice about, for example, the name of a new product or its packaging. They can certainly advise about the best media for advertising the product.

16.5   Advertising Media

An advertising medium is a means or vehicle for advertising: television and the press have already been mentioned, but there are many other ways in which goods can be advertised, some of which are suitable for small and highly localized markets while others are more suitable for goods sold on a national or even international scale. We shall look briefly at each of them in turn.

(a) Television

Television is probably the best medium for advertising consumer goods. It has the advantage of providing a combination of sound and vision and, if necessary, of giving a national coverage, though it is unusual for an advertiser to buy time from all the independent television companies at once. A further advantage of television advertising is the fact that advertisements can be shown at times appropriate to the market for the goods: for example, children's sweets and toys can be promoted between children's programmes, and household goods later in the evening when adults are more likely to be watching television.

Some people argue that television advertising has the advantage of a relaxed and therefore receptive audience but, on the other hand, some viewers find advertisements an unnecessary intrusion into their entertainment, and find other things to do during commercial breaks.

Television advertising is expensive, but few doubt its effectiveness: when a sporting event is televised, many advertisers pay to place posters in places where they will catch the eye of the television camera. When football matches from Europe are shown on television, you will often see advertising hoardings around the ground, aimed specifically at British viewers.

(b) The National Press

The importance of the national press as an advertising medium has declined since commercial television began in 1955, but it is still widely used. As papers are published every day, they are very suitable for advertising 'topical' products: 'Congratulations to John Smith who won yesterday's Grand Prix using Whiz Petrol.' Another advantage is that advertisements can be placed in appropriate places in the newspaper: sports equipment on the sports pages, dresses on the fashion pages and so on. Magazines which specialize in particular subjects are also useful to advertisers.

One disadvantage is that the producer's advertisements may be submerged in a large number of others, unless he pays a higher rate to have it isolated. Also, except in the colour supplements, the poor quality of the paper often prevents good reproduction of advertisements.

To the newspaper proprietor, however, advertising is essential. The price we pay for our newspapers only goes about halfway towards giving producers a fair profit. The difference is made up by revenue from advertising.

(c) The Local Press

This has not been affected by commercial television in the same way as the national press, though local radio has taken over some papers' informative advertising. Local papers are very important to local advertisers: since they often have a monopoly in their area, the advertiser can be sure of reaching almost every household, and weekly papers are usually around the house for several days, so their advertisements are more likely to be seen by potential customers. Once again, advertising revenue is of enormous importance to the newspaper proprietor: sometimes over 40 per cent of a paper is given over to advertisements.

(d) Posters

For some producers posters provide a more economical form of advertising. Posters have to be carefully designed and located if they are to deliver their message to the customer, but once in position they do not need much attention. Their effect comes from repetition, as many of the people who pass them do so every day. They tend to rely on visual effect rather than written information.

Similar considerations apply to the advertisements we see in trains and buses, except that here the advertiser has a temporarily captive audience. Many passengers have nothing to do but study the advertisements.

(e) The Cinema

Producers and traders may ask their advertising agent to produce a short commercial for them to circulate to cinemas. In general these have the same advantages and disadvantages as television commercials, but they lack the cumulative impact of frequent repetition, since few people visit the cinema more than once a week.

(f) Other Media

The methods above are the main means of advertising, but small traders may use other methods to keep their name before the public.

(i) They may carry an advertisement on their van.

(ii) They may advertise on the paper bags that they provide to customers.

(iii) They may have circulars delivered to local households.

(iv) They may use some of the methods of sales promotion we discuss in Section 16.9.

16.6   The Case for Advertising

Advertising is the subject of much heated debate between those who see it as a waste of valuable resources and those who see it as essential to the survival of our economic system. As usual the truth lies somewhere between the two extremes, and in this Section and the next we shall consider the arguments for and against advertising. These are seven main arguments in favour of advertising.

(a) Advertising leads to higher profits, which the producer can either retain, or share with his customers by charging lower prices. In a very competitive industry he will probably do the latter.

(b) Without advertising it would be almost impossible to launch new products. Consumers would only know about them when they saw them in the shops or when other people spoke about them. Producers would never be prepared to invest vast sums in new products.

(c) Consumers can be better informed of the goods available and of their relative merits through advertising. This is often true, even of competitive advertising.

(d) Many would argue that, by introducing new products to consumers, advertising improves the standard of living.

(e) Some people argue that advertised goods are of a higher quality than other goods, because the producer needs to establish or protect his reputation. Shoddy goods will cause his subsequent advertisements to be ignored.

(f) An indirect benefit of advertising is that it keeps the price of newspapers at a reasonable level, and without advertising there would, of course, be no commercial television at all.

(g) On a broader scale, advertising may help to keep people employed. If a firm can sell more goods as a result of advertising, the labour force will almost certainly increase to meet the extra demand.

16.7 The Case against Advertising

There are not many people who would want to abolish all advertising. The classified advertisements in local and national newspapers are an important source of information about houses, second-hand cars and many other things for sale. The same is true of display advertisements for jobs. But there are several criticisms which are justified.

(a) Advertising can be very expensive. Altogether over £2 500 million is spent on advertising each year in the UK alone. A full-page advertisement in the national press costs several thousand pounds, and 30 seconds of television time may cost several hundred pounds. The manufacturer may find his capital severely stretched to meet the costs.

(b) The cost of advertising may lead to higher prices for consumers if sales do not increase sufficiently to cover the cost of the advertising.

(c) Advertising uses scarce resources which could be better employed elsewhere. This is really an economic argument, but it is worth looking at here. The people employed in drafting and making advertisements are often very talented. Some of the advertisements they produce are not designed to introduce new products or increase sales, but merely to maintain the advertiser's share of the market. Advertisements for bread and detergents, for example, are not likely to increase total sales. The people employed in the advertising industry might therefore make a greater contribution to our economic life if they worked in other occupations.

(d) Advertising is the main form of non-price competition, as in the sale of detergents. Consumers might be better off if there were less advertising and more competition over prices. (This argument must, of course, be balanced against the possibility that extra sales cover the cost of the advertisement and lead to lower prices.)

(e) The most serious criticisms of advertising are directed at the persuasive kind. Advertising may persuade consumers to buy things they do not really want and cannot afford. You may find that difficult to believe, but it is true. Extremely subtle techniques can be employed to persuade consumers that they should not be without the latest household appliance. For centuries people managed without deep freezers: now many people regard them as a necessity. You can probably think of many other examples where advertising seems to create needs that were not there before.

(f) When people cannot afford the goods being advertised, they may be tempted to live beyond their means, by buying the goods on credit or by hire purchase.

(g) Some people criticize advertising on ethical rather than economic grounds. They point out that it often exploits people suggesting, for example, that only by using a certain product can they really give their family the treatment they deserve. Other advertisements exploit sex by implying strongly that girls who wear the advertisers' products will be surrounded by the most desirable men. Yet others suggest that the consumption of alcohol and tobacco is the symbol of maturity without emphasizing the dangers associated with these products.

(h) There have been cases in the past of advertisements misleading the public. Today the Trade Descriptions Act offers some protection, and more detailed guidance is given by the Advertising Standards Authority (see Section 16.8), but the danger remains.

(i) A minor criticism that can be made of television advertising is that it interrupts programmes (though you may sometimes consider that to be an advantage).

There is, therefore, much to be said on both sides. It must be left to the individual to judge for himself the desirability of heavy advertising, but we can safely conclude that advertising is generally worth while for producers.

16.8   Protecting the Consumer

As we saw in Unit 7, the object of producers is to increase their profits, and there is a danger that they will deceive consumers in their efforts to increase sales. We saw that the Trade Descriptions Act exercises legal controls over the contents of advertisements.

In addition, the advertising industry itself has established the Advertising Standards Authority, to maintain standards within the industry. The Authority, representing a large number of bodies, supervises a *Code of Advertising Practice* first drawn up in 1962. The Code is a very detailed document setting out general principles to which advertisers and advertising agents should adhere. It is a voluntary code, but much more detailed in its requirements than the Trade Descriptions Act. There is provision for complaints made by the public about advertisements to be investigated, and for the Authority to make recommendations where appropriate.

16.9   Sales Promotions

Advertising is just one of the ways in which producers try to increase sales. Other methods of winning the attention of the public belong to the general category of sales promotions. The aims are of course the same as with advertising, but promotion schemes tend to demand more of the consumer than just watching or reading an advertisement. You are probably familiar with some of the schemes.

(a)   Free Samples

The best way of introducing consumers to a product is to let them try it out free. It is a very expensive method of promoting sales, especially where a sample is sent to every household. Accordingly it is a method reserved for things that are cheap and have a national sale. Often the distribution of free samples is linked with a fairly extensive back-up advertising programme. Sometimes free samples are given at particular shops. This has the effect of persuading people to do their shopping there, and increasing the retailer's sales.

(b)   Price Reductions

These are so widely used that they are no longer regarded as special promotional activities. Housewives have been conditioned to expect that household detergents will be offered at '2 pence off' the recommended price, and the cartons are often printed with the price reduction.

Sometimes the price reductions are indirect or conditional. Some manufacturers distribute coupons to householders which can be used in part payment for their goods; others allow a price reduction in exchange for the label from the previous packet bought. In either case the retailer, who is involved in extra work, redeems the labels for cash from the manufacturer or his representative.

(c)   Competitions

Sometimes producers organize competitions. A condition of entry is the purchase of perhaps six packets of the producer's goods. This achieves an immediate boost in sales, which the producer hopes will be sustained, as new customers become regular buyers.

(d)   Free Gifts

Petrol stations try to increase their sales by giving glasses, footballs or cups away when a certain amount of petrol is bought. Cigarette manufacturers have a variation of this: they sometimes include coupons in their packets, which can be redeemed for a free packet of cigarettes at a later date or used in part payment for another packet of the same brand. Since the aim is to win the loyalty of the consumer and retain his custom, the former scheme requiring him to collect, say, 10 coupons is generally preferred.

16.10   The Marketing Department

Many large firms have marketing departments, which are responsible for the organization of advertising and sales promotions. We shall conclude this Unit with a summary of the work of such a department.

Once goods have been produced they have to be sold. To be sold they have to appeal to the public – they have to have a good image. The creation of this image is the responsibility of the *brand manager*, and there are a number of things for which he is accountable.

(a) Packaging
One way to distinguish your product from its competitors is to provide it with attractive packaging. This may result in higher sales, but it may also lead to higher prices for consumers. You will find it interesting to examine some of the articles you buy and to consider the packaging. Many items have three or four different layers of packaging on them; this is especially true of articles sold *gift-wrapped* at Christmas.

(b) Advertising and Sales Promotion
Each product has a budget allocated to it, in which a stated amount of money is set aside for publicity. The brand manager must decide how this money is to be spent.

(c) Market Research
If the manager is to make the correct decisions, he must have detailed information about the product and its market. He will therefore initiate research to obtain the information he wants.

(d) Sales
He may also be responsible for a team of salesmen, or representatives, who visit retailers to introduce the product and provide display material and free samples. They also deal with complaints and queries, and generally maintain the link between the company and its customers.

16.11   Questions and Exercises

(a) Short Answers
1. What is the main aim of commercial advertising?
2. Briefly explain the three different kinds of advertising.
3. What is the function of the copywriter in an advertising agency?
4. Why do firms engage in market research?
5. What is meant by the term *advertising media*? What are the main media in the United Kingdom?

6. Show by means of an example how advertising may reduce prices.
7. Show by means of an example how advertising may increase prices.
8. Why is the *Code of Advertising Practice* necessary?
9. Make a list of the methods currently being used by firms to promote the sales of their goods.
10. Why do advertisers need a thorough knowledge of the Trade Descriptions Act?

(b) Essay Answers

1. Distinguish between informative and persuasive advertising. Give examples of each type.
2. What are the advantages of advertising to (a) producers, (b) consumers?
3. What advertising media would you recommend for a company about to launch the following products (a) a new brand of tea, (b) a new electric milk float, (c) new fashion jewellery? Explain why the media you choose are appropriate.
4. 'Since advertising increases prices it should be abolished.' Write an essay arguing against this statement.
5. 'The purpose of advertising is to increase demand.' To what extent do you agree with this statement?

(c) Projects and Assignments

1. Make a collection of advertisements from the local and national press under the headings *informative* and *persuasive*.
2. Make a collection of advertisements to show how advertisers sometimes try to exploit weaknesses in consumers.
3. Obtain a copy of the Advertising Standards Authority's *Code of Advertising Practice*. Examine the requirements of the Code and explain why they are necessary. Give examples of five advertisements, showing how they conform to the Code.
4. Sports sponsorship is a popular method of advertising. Compile a table of such sponsorship showing the sport, the sponsor and the money involved. Examine the implications of sponsorship for the sports concerned.

Unit Seventeen

Communications: Transport

17.1 Introduction

The system of mass production relies on an efficient transport system for its
very existence, because production is *indirect*: by this we mean that enormous
amounts of goods are produced in one place for consumers who live all over
the country or indeed all over the world. Economic activity would be impossible without transport, and our commercial system would collapse.

We must therefore examine the topic in some detail, considering first the
requirements for an efficient transport system, and then how far the different
forms of transport meet these requirements.

17.2 An Efficient Transport System

Every day of the year goods are on the move: products as diverse as newspapers, boxes of matches, generating equipment, aircraft engines, medicine and
bricks are all travelling to their markets. There are many ways in which
consignments can vary. Sometimes the journey is only of a few miles, but on
other occasions the goods may be consigned to the other end of the country or
the other side of the world. Some goods are needed urgently and at very short
notice, while others are needed at regular intervals, and on a continuous basis.
Some goods are extremely valuable in proportion to their size, like diamonds;
others are of low value but great bulk, like coal. Some are fragile, others are
robust. If a transport system is to be efficient, it must be adaptable enough to
deal with every possible kind of consignment.

The accessibility of the *terminal* (where the journey starts or ends) is
another key factor. It was once the practice to build factories and warehouses
close to canals and railway lines, so that large consignments could easily be
delivered. As commercial life has expanded shops and factories have multiplied
and become more widely dispersed, and railways and canals have lost traffic to
the roads, which can usually provide a more direct service. Several factors such
as the development of the motorway network and the use of containers have
added to the advantages of road transport in this respect, and we shall need to
look at them in detail.

An efficient transport system must be *regular* and *punctual*. Most goods are
both produced and consumed in a continuous flow: producers need to be able
to dispose of their output promptly after its manufacture, so that they can keep

their own spending on warehousing to a minimum. At the other end of the distributive chain, retailers require the steady flow of goods that is provided by regular deliveries. Spasmodic and irregular transport is therefore a nuisance both to producers and retailers. It is just as important that goods arrive punctually. In the complex factories of today the whole workforce may be left idle if a batch of components arrives late. This is not the same, of course, as saying that *speed* is necessary: it may not matter if the components are delivered by horse and cart as long as they arrive at the right time. (There may, of course, be other reasons for not using a horse and cart!)

There are, then, many factors to be taken into account when assessing the efficiency of the transport system or the relative merits of different forms of transport. We must now look at the main forms of transport and the advantages that each of them offers to traders. We should also be able to see why some forms of transport win custom at the expense of others.

17.3   Road Transport

There are almost 350 000 miles of roads in the United Kingdom, and they are the most important form of transport in the country. We normally measure the usage of transport in terms of tonne-kilometres. If, for example, a load of 50 tonnes is carried 100 kilometres, the journey represents 5 000 tonne-kilometres. Table 17.1 shows the extent to which road transport dominates other forms of inland transport (the figures represent tonne-kilometres in thousands of millions).

Table 17.1   Inland transport in the United Kingdom

| | 000 million tonne-kilometres | | | |
	1971	%	1981	%
Road	85.9	64.7	94.4	63.6
Rail	21.8	16.4	17.5	11.8
Inland waterways and coastal shipping	21.5	16.2	27.1	18.3
Pipelines	3.6	2.7	9.3	6.3
Total	132.8		148.3	

Even if all the freight carried by the railways were transferred to the roads it would represent only 20 per cent increase in road transport. But many people advocate that goods should be shifted from the roads to the railways: it is clear that a 20 per cent reduction in road transport would require an enormous increase in railway investment to cope with traffic that had almost doubled. Why is it that such a large proportion of total inland freight is carried by road?

(a) Advantages of Road Transport

(i) **Flexibility**. Road transport firms can provide a door-to-door service. Goods can be loaded at the factory and delivered straight to the customer. There is no problem of changing from one form of transport to another, with all the extra handling that this involves. Remote places may be inaccessible to the railways, but can nearly always be reached by road.

Fig. 17.1 Road transport can accommodate exceptional loads

The frequency of road journeys can easily be adjusted. The nature of a railway system requires that train journeys be carefully timetabled. If a trader has an urgent consignment he cannot expect railway timetables to be amended to accommodate the goods: he must wait for the next appropriate train. On the other hand, it is quite likely that he can find a road transport company to help him at fairly short notice.

Special facilities can be provided by road hauliers to deal with exceptional loads. The height and width regulations which necessarily restrict the loads that can be carried by rail are not so severe for road transport.

(ii) **Economy**. The road haulage industry is very competitive, consisting of both large and small firms. This competition is an incentive to efficiency and economy, often resulting in lower charges for customers. *Return loads* exemplify this: once a driver has delivered a consignment he has to make a return journey, and his employer has to meet the costs of this journey. If the driver can find a return load to take with him it reduces the overall costs to the employer, even if the load is taken at a cheaper rate than normal.

(iii) **Innovations**. Post-war developments have accelerated the growth of road freight transport. The major change has been the development of the motorway network. These roads facilitate the rapid movement of goods between the main industrial areas of the country. Huge lorries are now able to provide a shuttle service, so that raw materials, components and finished articles can be delivered in a continuous flow.

More recently the development of containerization has given road haulage a further boost by increasing its efficiency (see Section 17.8).

(b) Disadvantages of Road Transport
Although these and other advantages have contributed to the growth of road transport, there are a number of disadvantages which also ought to be mentioned.

(i) **Bulk**. Road haulage is not suitable for transporting goods of great bulk for long distances. It would be hopelessly uneconomic, for example, to transport coal from South Wales to London by road, when the railways can carry so much more on a single journey. Labour and fuel costs put the road hauliers at a considerable disadvantage here. Even so, many bulk commodities *are* taken by road because of the convenience it provides, and because lorries will have to be used in any case once the rail journey is complete. When this happens businessmen may pay more than is strictly necessary for transport, which means that the final consumer pays more.

(ii) **Congestion and delays**. Road transport may be subject to delays which do not trouble the railways. Road congestion becomes more severe each year. One of the benefits of the motorways is that they bypass congested town centres, but even they do not entirely overcome the problem. Most road journeys begin and end in heavily industrialized urban areas. The existing housing and other buildings make the construction of new roads very difficult, so the road transport of the 1980s is frequently delayed by the roads of the 1920s.

(iii) **The social costs** of road transport are very great. When the road haulier works out his rates for a consignment, he will only be interested in what we may call the *private costs* – the costs to him of making the journey and delivering the goods. Such things as the driver's wages, fuel, depreciation on the lorry, tax and insurance will enter into his calculations, so that he can be sure of making a profit. He does not, however, take into account such things as the cost to other people of traffic congestion, atmospheric pollution and noise, the expense of keeping up the roads and the road signalling system, or the burdens caused by accidents. These all have to be met by society as a whole, and are the *social costs* of road transport. There are, of course, social costs involved in journeys by rail too, but it is unlikely that they are as high as those involved in road transport. It is for this reason that the Government makes efforts from time to time to divert freight traffic from the roads to the railways. Inevitably they have little success, because the convenience of road transport to its users outweighs its disadvantages to society.

(iv) **Longer journeys**. Goods travelling by road may spend longer on the journey than goods travelling by rail. Speed limits are normally less restrictive on the railways, and there are fewer traffic jams. However, this disadvantage is more than made up for by the flexibility of road transport in providing a door-to-door service, without the transhipment that is necessary for most goods sent by rail.

17.4   Rail Transport

As we saw in Unit 9, the railways in the United Kingdom are a nationalized industry. Nationalization was necessary in 1947 owing to the weak condition of the industry, which had been deprived of capital investment for many years. Since nationalization, the system has been extensively modernized; diesel and electric trains have replaced steam, many uneconomic lines have been closed down, and new services have been introduced to meet the needs of commerce and industry. Indeed the rail system offers several advantages over other forms of transport.

(*a*)   Advantages of Rail Transport

(i) **Speed between two points**. Once the journey has begun, rail transport between, say, London and Manchester is undoubtedly faster than road transport. The difficulties occur at either end of the journey: in getting goods to the London terminal through heavily congested streets, and in dispatching them from the Manchester station. In the competition for passengers between the railways and the airlines, on the other hand, the delays caused by road traffic congestion favour the railways. An airport is bound to be outside the city centre, while a railway passenger terminal is usually in the heart of the city. Therefore the speed advantage enjoyed by the airlines over medium distances is partly eroded by the problems of access to and from the city centres.

The planned introduction of faster trains with speeds of up to 150 mph will increase the time advantage and the benefits can be expected to extend to freight transport in due course.

(ii) **Economy in the use of labour.** This would seem to be one of the great advantages of the railways. While every lorry has a driver and sometimes a driver's mate, it only takes two men – a driver and a guard – to run a train with 50 or 60 trucks. The wage bills for the two systems will obviously be very different. But the advantage to the railways may not be as great as these figures suggest: the railways require a larger team behind the scenes to programme trains and maintain the network.

(iii) **Access to ports.** Railways have direct and easy access to ports, so they offer a distinct advantage for exporting, especially where manufacturers have their own railway sidings.

(iv) **Containerization** has been helpful to the railways as well as to the road haulage industry. One of the main problems of the railways is that of the repeated handling of the goods. A consignment usually has to be loaded into a lorry at the factory and then unloaded, before being transferred to the train. At the other end it has to be taken off the train, loaded onto a lorry and finally unloaded again. In such circumstances delays, breakages and theft are difficult to avoid. Containers overcome most of these problems. Goods are packed into the container, which is then loaded on to a lorry, mechanically transferred from the lorry to the train and later back to a lorry for final delivery. Only then is the container opened. British Rail have developed their own container system – Freightliner – with their own lorries, to exploit the advantages as fully as possible.

(v) **Special facilities** are provided for industrial customers. Bulk deliveries of oil, cement, coal and motor cars, for instance, are often carried in the producer's own rolling-stock, painted with his own livery.

(*b*) **Difficulties of Rail Transport**
If the railways can offer these advantages, why do they find it so difficult to compete with road hauliers? We have already partly answered this question in looking at the advantages of the road transport industry, but you should also remember the following difficulties that the railways face.

(i) **The problem of transhipment.** Only a few industrial customers have their own sidings. For the others lorries are necessary for at least part of the journey, and in this case many customers decide to use lorries for the whole journey.

(ii) **Damage and delays.** Transhipment means extra handling, which, as we have seen, adds to the risk of damage or theft. It also means long delays in shunting yards while a full load is assembled. Such delays may be expensive to customers, because goods held up in this way represent extra capital tied up in stock.

(iii) **Size of overheads.** It is very difficult to estimate the cost of delivering a given consignment of goods by railway. The reason for this is the enormous range of overhead costs that the railways have to bear: the capital costs of the track, signalling, rolling-stock, terminals and managerial staff. (The problem is much less severe for the road haulier.) The very size of the railway industry is a disadvantage in some ways: contact with customers is necessarily remote, with the result that the industry is very difficult to run effectively.

(iv) **Short journeys** by rail usually waste time and money, particularly where the consignments are small. Only where bulk loads are carried on a continuous basis does the railway have a real advantage.

(v) **Rigidity.** Timetables impose a rigidity on the railways which the road

Fig. 17.2 Freightliner terminal, Glasgow. Note the integration of road and rail transport

hauliers do not suffer from. The greatest flexibility is enjoyed by the manufacturer who operates his own fleet of lorries, and can programme them exactly to his own requirements.

17.5   Other Inland Transport

As we saw in Table 17.1, the bulk of inland freight is carried by road and rail. The other forms of inland transport are relatively unimportant. In the UK the *airways* are hardly used at all for freight transport, owing to the short distances involved. In countries like Australia and the United States of America, however, they play a more important part. International air freight is increasing, as we shall see in Section 17.7. However, the airways are still primarily concerned with international passenger transport.

Inland waterways are important in some countries, but have mostly fallen into disuse in the United Kingdom. They provided a cheap but slow form of transport, which was largely superseded by the railways in the nineteenth century. Now only a small minority of bulk consignments are carried by canal.

Pipelines are frequently used for transporting oil and gas over long distances. They involve heavy capital costs, but once installed can make a considerable savings for producers.

17.6   Sea Transport

Road and rail transport carry the bulk of inland consignments, but most of our international trade relies on sea transport, though an increasing amount is being carried by air. There are several types of sea transport available.

(a) Liners
Liners run on fixed routes to a fixed timetable. They carry passengers and general or mixed cargo. The liner operators belong to *shipping conferences*, which determine the fares, the freight charges and the frequency of journeys.

(b) Tramp Ships
These ships do not have fixed routes or timetables and do not normally carry passengers. They go where business takes them, and may be *chartered* (contracted to a user) at the Baltic Exchange in London (see Section 4.5), either for a specific period (*time charter*) or for a specific voyage (*voyage charter*). Their rates are likely to be highly competitive, for their owners need to keep them working at all times.

(c) Coastal Shipping
This is really an alternative to inland transport for bulk trade. It may be more economical to send coal or timber, for example, round the coast rather than inland. Also, large ocean-going tankers cannot gain access to some refineries, so their cargo may be discharged into coasters to complete its journey. Refined oil is often distributed in this way.

(d) **Bulk Carriers**

These are designed for special purposes. Oil tankers are the best example, though ships are also built specially to accommodate other minerals or timber. Refrigerated vessels are available for transporting perishables over long distances.

It would be difficult to underestimate the importance of sea transport to the United Kingdom. Because Britain is an island lacking in indigenous raw materials and farming land, we need to import an enormous amount from abroad. Millions of tonnes of minerals, timber, grain and wheat have to be brought into the country; equally, large quantities of manufactured goods are exported to help pay for these imports. All these goods must be carried by sea or air, and the quantities involved almost always call for sea transport.

The great advantage of sea transport is that tens or even hundreds of thousands of tonnes can be carried at one time. Bulk oil carriers can deliver three or four hundred thousand tonnes in a single journey. As you can imagine, there are considerable economies of scale in this, for the size of the crew and the amount of fuel required by the vessel do not increase in proportion to the capacity of the ship.

Sea transport also offers considerable flexibility. Every week vessels leave the major ports for all parts of the world, and an exporter can usually find accommodation for his cargo fairly easily. Of course the goods will not be delivered as quickly as they would by air, but speed is not necessarily the most

Fig. 17.3 A large tanker discharging its cargo of crude oil

important consideration. Punctuality is normally more significant. A manufacturer in this country does not usually want his raw materials delivered from Australia in 36 hours, but he does want them to arrive at regular intervals, so that production is not held up by shortages.

Specially built vessels give sea transport an added advantage. Perishable goods can be carried round the world and arrive in perfect condition, thanks to refrigerated vessels, and raw materials can be specially dealt with. Ships and terminal facilities are now often designed together, so that sophisticated loading and discharging methods can be used: for example, grain cargoes are now *pumped* ashore at main terminals. The growth of containerization has been accompanied by the building of special container vessels, with special facilities to deal with them at the ports (see Section 17.8).

17.7   Air Transport

Sea transport continues to dominate international trade and will do so for the foreseeable future, but an increasing amount of the world's trade is being carried by air. There are a number of factors that account for this.

(a) Technological Progress
This has led to larger aircraft, which are capable of carrying greater loads.

(b) Speed
Speed of delivery is important for some consignments. Mail, newspapers, medical supplies and other emergency requirements come into this category. An even more important factor in the growth of air transport is the need for machinery and components to be available at short notice. Office machinery, computer components and vehicle spares can now be rushed quickly from one side of the world to the other.

The speed of air transport may also prevent hold-ups in production, and thus save expensive capital assets from standing idle. By having components delivered by air in small consignments rather than by sea in large consignments, it may be possible to economize on warehousing facilities, thereby releasing capital and space for more productive uses.

(c) Cost
Although the rate per tonne is higher by air than by sea, the cost of transport must be related to the value of the goods being delivered. If the goods are of low bulk and high value they can absorb the cost of air freight without a large increase in their price. Many United Kingdom exports, such as electrical machinery, belong to this category. On the other hand the price of iron ore would increase significantly if it were sent by air.

(d) Incidental Expenses
Expenses associated with exporting are often lower when goods are sent by air.

For example, when sea transport is used, goods may have to be well packed to protect them against the effects of weather or corrosion by sea water; less elaborate precautions are normally needed for goods sent by air. Moreover, since the goods are in transit for a shorter period, insurance charges are usually lower.

It is the newness of air transport that is responsible for its main disadvantage: history has dictated that many industrial concentrations are close to the major ports, so that goods delivered by sea can quickly reach their final destinations, and exports can quickly begin their journey. For this reason major steel works and oil refineries are almost all situated on the coast. Airports are constructed away from the main industrial sites, and although in time they exert their own magnetic pull on industries, the fact remains that a long secondary journey may be necessary for many goods arriving by air.

Another important limitation of air freight is the size of the loads that can be carried. Even the largest aircraft cannot compete economically with sea transport when the cargoes are of great bulk.

17.8　Containers

The outstanding feature of post-war transport has been the increasing use of containers. Freight is now packed in containers at the point of manufacture, and the container is sealed and not opened again until it reaches its final destination. Special cranes lift the containers on and off lorries and ships, taking a matter of hours rather than days to load and unload the vessel. Heavy initial capital expenditure is required to buy the containers, vehicles and handling equipment but considerable economies result from containerization. Nor are the benefits only economic. The goods are safer in sealed containers, protected both from the weather and from pilfering. Also, they are sealed with the authority of the customs, which reduces formalities at the port of arrival.

One of the disadvantages of containers is that they are only suitable for large consignments: the small exporter may have difficulty in finding accommodation for his goods on container ships. For this, however, he can use the services of a freight forwarding agent (see Section 19.12).

We have seen that there is considerable variety in the transport facilities available to traders. The methods adopted by any single trader will depend upon a number of factors, the most important of which will be the value and bulk of the consignment, and the degree of urgency with which it must be delivered. However, the important point is that our industrial and economic system could not exist without transport to bring about the physical transfer of goods from their place of production to their place of consumption.

17.9　Questions and Exercises

(a) **Short Answers**

1.　Why does mass production require an efficient transport system?

2. What is meant by the *terminal* in transport? Why is it important?
3. Which form of inland transport in the United Kingdom carries most goods?
4. Give four reasons for this.
5. Which form of transport carries most of the United Kingdom imports?
6. Give four reasons for this.
7. What is the difference between private costs and social costs?
8. Give three examples of the social costs of a road journey.
9. What is meant by *containerization*?
10. What methods of transport would be most suitable for the following consignments: (*a*) a human kidney from London to Geneva, (*b*) 100 tonnes of coal from South Wales to London, (*c*) a 25 tonne electricity generator from Birmingham to Norwich, (*d*) a diamond ring from South Africa to London?

(*b*) Essay Answers

1. What factors would be considered by a producer before he decided on the means of transport for his goods?
2. Compare the advantages and disadvantages of road and rail transport.
3. What benefits have resulted from containerization? What disadvantages does the system have?
4. Air transport is taking an increasing amount of United Kingdom exports. How do you account for this?
5. 'The great advantage of road transport is that it offers door-to-door delivery.' What other reasons are there for the growth of road transport at the expense of the railways?

(*c*) Projects and Assignments

1. Make a collection of news cuttings about transport. Use them to describe the difficulties faced by (*a*) road hauliers, (*b*) railways, (*c*) airlines.
2. Compile a scrapbook to show the importance of containerization.
3. Discover all you can about traffic in towns. Examine and comment upon the possible solutions to urban traffic congestion.
4. Make a collection of news cuttings over three or four months, and use them as the basis of a report on the major transport problems facing the United Kingdom.

Unit Eighteen

Business Risks: Insurance

18.1 Introduction

The insurance industry today is very big business, providing a vital service, primarily to commerce and industry, but also to millions of individuals. Most of us are covered by some kind of insurance policy, to protect our financial interests in case of some accident or misfortune. In this Unit we are going to examine the principles underlying insurance, the services that are offered, and the structure of the industry itself.

18.2 Insurance Risks

All businessmen take risks. They are an inherent part of our economic system. The risks taken differ in nature and, in this context, may be divided into two groups, *insurable risks* and *non-insurable risks*. The insurance companies will be prepared to safeguard you against insurable risks but not against non-insurable risks.

The difference between these two types is that insurable risks are calculable, while non-insurable risks are not. Insurable risks occur regularly enough for the insurance company to calculate with some accuracy the likelihood of their occurring during the period of insurance. They can make this prediction on the basis of past statistics. If, on the other hand, no statistics are available, the necessary calculations cannot be made and insurance cannot be undertaken. Some examples will help to show you the difference.

A retailer can insure against his premises being burnt to the ground, because there are statistics which tell the insurance company how susceptible retail premises are to fire. Statistics will also show what sort of shops are most likely to catch fire, and in what areas the risk is greatest. On the other hand, a retailer may hold a stock of girls' dresses worth several hundred pounds, which he hopes to sell over the next few weeks. He cannot insure against the possibility that he will not sell them because of a change in fashion, or simply because he has misjudged the demand for them. There are no records which show how quickly these particular dresses will go out of fashion, or how competent the retailer is at judging demand. These, therefore, are non-insurable risks.

You sometimes hear it said that you cannot insure against an 'act of God'. This phrase is used to describe various natural disasters, such as floods and earthquakes. In fact the insurance companies can predict fairly accurately the likelihood of a particular building being damaged by a flood or an earthquake, and they are normally prepared to offer insurance in respect of them.

18.3   The Pooling of Risks

The reason why risks must be calculable before they can be insurable is that insurance is a pooling of risks. A large number of people wishing to insure their property against theft contribute money to a central pool supervised by the insurance company. Neither the company nor anyone else can say for certain that any given house will be burgled, but they can predict on the basis of the experience of previous years that perhaps 3 per cent of insured houses will be burgled. If they are confident of this, and if they know the number of people subscribing to the pool, they can calculate the *premium* that each subscriber should pay. If the likelihood of the event occurring is not known, then the company cannot offer protection.

Suppose that the company knows that, for every £1 000 of personal property it insures against theft, 3 per cent of it will be stolen so that the company will have to compensate the owners. Suppose also that the company is insuring £4 million of property and, for the sake of convenience, has no charges or costs to meet other than the compensation. The compensation will amount to £4 000 000 × 3/100 = £120 000, and this is the income it must obtain from premiums.

Therefore every time someone insures property worth £1 000 they will have to pay a premium of £30. The normal way of expressing this is to say that the premium is £3 per cent. In practice, of course, the insurance company will incur expenses in administering the pool, and will want to make a profit, so the premium would be calculated at something more than £3 per cent.

The important thing is that the premiums should be high enough to ensure that those who suffer from theft can be properly compensated, the fortunate who do not lose property coming to the aid of the unfortunate.

18.4   Types of Insurance

It is customary to divide insurance into four main groups: marine insurance, fire insurance, life insurance and accident insurance. The last one includes all insurance policies not included in the other groups.

(a) Marine Insurance

Marine insurance existed in Italy as early as the twelfth century, and was introduced to Britain by Italian merchants in the thirteenth century. Italian merchants engaged in overseas trade were faced with large losses if one of their vessels was lost at sea. They therefore pooled their risks, so that if one of them lost a vessel, the loss was borne by the group as a whole.

Today marine insurance is more or less monopolized by Lloyd's of London, and it is a very sophisticated business. A variety of policies are available to shipowners and traders to compensate them in the event of loss.

(i) **Hull insurance**. This covers the vessel itself, including all its fixtures. If it is lost at sea, or damaged by adverse weather conditions or by other vessels, compensation is paid to the owners. Hull policies may be divided into *time policies*, which cover the vessel for a set period, usually twelve months, and *voyage policies*, which cover it for a specific voyage, however long it may take.

(ii) **Cargo insurance**. We shall see in Unit 19 that the holder of the *bill of lading* is the owner of the goods. Unless the cargo is insured, the importer will be unwilling to accept the bill of lading, and no one will be interested in any bill of exchange drawn in respect of the cargo. This is because the goods may be lost or damaged at sea. Thus international trade would be almost non-existent without cargo insurance. The cargo is normally insured for its full value, but the responsibility for payment of the premium depends upon the terms on which the goods are being sold – Cost, Insurance and Freight, where the seller pays, or Free on Board, where the buyer pays (see Unit 20).

Rather than negotiate a separate insurance cover for each cargo, some shipping companies prefer to take out a *floating policy* to cover the likely value of their cargo for the following six or twelve months. The insurers are notified of the value of each cargo, and when the total value of these equals the value insured on the floating policy, a new premium is paid to cover a further period.

(iii) **Freight insurance**. Freight is not a synonym for cargo in this context. It is the charge levied by the shipowner for carrying the goods. It is usually paid to the shipowner in advance, even though he is not strictly entitled to it until the cargo is safely delivered to its destination. If the goods are not delivered for some reason, the owner may face a claim for repayment of the freight. It is customary for an insurance policy to be taken out against this possibility.

(iv) **Shipowner's liability**. This phrase covers a multitude of events which may be the fault of the shipowner or his employees: collisions with other vessels or dock installations, injury to passengers, crew or dock workers, pollution of the water or beaches, and so on. Substantial sums may be claimed by third parties in compensation for damage or injury in these circumstances, so the shipowners carry a further insurance to cover them against this risk.

(b) Fire Insurance

The Fire of London in 1666 led to the introduction of fire insurance in Britain. Traders and property owners who suffered from the disaster sought ways of protecting themselves against further losses, and in 1680 the first fire insurance policies were drawn up. The early fire insurance groups, anxious to keep the claims against them as small as possible, established their own fire brigades to put out fires which affected their properties. This job has long since been taken over by local government bodies, of course.

The Fire Offices, as these insurance companies are called, have diversified considerably in response to the needs of policy holders, for it is not only fire that threatens property: storms, floods and extremes of temperature may also cause damage, or houses may be burgled. A general *household policy* provides cover against all these risks.

Losses through fire cost the nation hundreds of millions of pounds each year, and the insurance companies seek to minimize the loss by allowing preferential premiums to policy holders who install special fire-prevention devices, and by charging extra to those who can be shown to constitute a higher risk. They also participate in research programmes to make fire prevention more effective.

Businessmen find it necessary to insure against more than the actual cost of repairing fire damage. Just as special policies have been devised to help householders, so the insurance companies offer special policies to business-men who suffer from fires. The most important of these is a policy for *consequential loss*. If the premises are badly damaged the proprietor may be unable to carry on his business for some months; as a consequence he will lose the profits that he would otherwise have made in this time. A policy for consequential loss covers him against this, and by enabling him to meet any fixed costs that may fall due, allows the business to remain in existence until the damage has been repaired.

(c) Life Assurance

The term *assurance* is used when a claim will definitely be made under the policy. We say life assurance, for example, because everyone dies sometime. (In the other branches of insurance there is no certainty that a claim will ever be made.)

Normally the aim of insurance is to compensate the person for some loss or damage. The aims of life assurance are somewhat different in that the person himself cannot be compensated. The aims also vary, which is why several types of life assurance policy are available.

(i) **Whole life policies** are payable on the death of the insured. The sum assured may simply be enough to pay for the funeral, or it may be much larger to give some benefit to dependants.

(ii) **Term policies** provide benefit only if death occurs during a specified period. *Mortgage guarantee policies* are of this type. When a couple are buying a house on a mortgage, the building society normally requires the man to take out a life assurance policy for the duration of the mortgage. In the event of his death the proceeds of the policy are used to pay off the mortgage.

(iii) **Endowment policies** guarantee that a fixed sum will be payable on a specified date or at death, whichever is earlier. They are therefore a means of saving as well as a form of insurance. Some endowment policies are *with profits*, in which case the policy holder receives a share of the profits made by the insurance company from investing his savings. Such policies require a slightly higher premium than policies without profits.

It is quite common for endowment policies to be arranged to coincide with an important event in the policy holder's life. Some people take out policies which mature at about the time their children are likely to get married; others choose to receive a lump sum when they retire. A common practice is to take out a policy which matures at your retirement, and then immediately use the proceeds to finance an *annuity*. (This means that in return for a lump sum payment the insurance company undertakes to make weekly or monthly payments to the policy holder for a specified period.) In this way you can arrange to have a regular income for the rest of your life.

(iv) **Family income policies**. If the policy holder dies, the dependants will be paid an agreed sum at regular intervals (e.g. £40 a month) until an agreed date (usually 15–30 years after the policy was taken out). Obviously this would be an important policy for a man with a young family.

(v) **Special policies** have been developed by the insurance companies to meet particular requirements. *Group policies* provide cover for the employees of a small firm; *house purchase policies* link the proceeds of an endowment policy to the purchase of a particular house; *unit linked policies* permit investment in a unit trust as well as giving ordinary life cover.

Thus the life assurance companies offer a broad choice to their clients, and we can see that the purpose of taking out a life assurance policy may be to provide a lump sum for dependants, to provide a regular income for dependants, or to save for one's retirement or some special occasion.

Where the premiums are paid weekly or monthly, the term *industrial life assurance* is used. This is because the practice of collecting premiums regularly began in industrial areas in the nineteenth century.

(d) Accident Insurance

There are several different forms of accident insurance, covering many situations.

(i) **Personal accident insurance** covers the insured against partial or total disability arising from accidental causes. Sportsmen often take out an accident insurance in case they sustain an injury which prevents them from working for a period. Aircraft passengers can obtain short term policies to cover them for the duration of a flight. Most motor insurance provides cover for injuries received in an accident.

(ii) **Liability insurance** constitutes a broad field. If someone receives an injury on your property he may well have a claim against you. To cover yourself you should have a public liability policy to compensate the unfortunate person; if you are an employer you must also carry an employer's liability policy, in case any of your staff are injured while at work.

You will often hear motorists talk about *third party insurance*. This is a reference to the three parties involved in a contract of accident insurance. The contract is made between the *first party* (the insured person) and the *second party* (the insurer) in respect of the *third party*, which refers to anyone who makes a claim against the first party. All motorists are required by law to hold a third party insurance policy, so that injured people can obtain some compensation.

(iii) **Property insurance** is another form of accident insurance. Most motorists insure their car against accidental damage, though they are not obliged to by law. Manufacturers insure their stock and machinery, farmers their animals and householders their personal valuables. The cover provided is normally for accident and theft, and for householders such cover will often be provided as part of a general household policy. The same policy may also cover them against public liability, but it is important for the policy holder to examine the policy carefully to find out the extent of his protection.

(iv) **Miscellaneous insurance** policies which come under the heading of accident insurance include such things as *fidelity guarantees*, which provide compensation to an employer if one of his staff is found guilty of embezzlement of the firm's funds, and *pluvius policies* which insure the organizers of garden parties and other outdoor events against loss of takings owing to rain. You can also insure your holiday against rain.

(e) Aviation Insurance
There is a growing market in aviation insurance, shared between Lloyds and the insurance companies. A variety of policies is available but there are three main categories.

(i) **Comprehensive policies** cover accidental damage to the plane, injury to passengers or loss of their property, and injury to other people.

(ii) **Personal insurance** is taken out by airlines to cover their employees, or by individual passengers to cover themselves for the duration of a flight.

(iii) **Cargo insurance** may relate to individual consignments or to a series of consignments up to a stated value during a prescribed period.

There are all kinds of policies to meet all kinds of contingencies. Even where there are no standard policies an insurance company may be able to offer cover – as long as there is some basis on which to calculate the premium, and as long as the policy adheres to the principles of insurance.

18.5 The Principles of Insurance
The basis on which insurance operates – the pooling of risks – would be open to abuse if certain fundamental principles were not observed in each contract of

insurance. Policy holders would be able to defraud the insurance companies and destroy the operation of the pool without these basic principles. We must examine them in some detail.

(a) Utmost Good Faith (Uberrima Fides)

If you wish to take out an insurance policy you must answer all the questions that the company asks you. You must also give them any additional information that is relevant to your application, so that the company can make an accurate assessment of the risk and calculate the premium that you should pay.

Suppose I apply for insurance for my motor car. One of the questions I am asked is 'Have you been convicted of any motoring offences in the last three years?' If I have had no convictions during the last three years I can quite truthfully answer 'No' to this question. However, if I am expecting to appear in court next week on a charge of dangerous driving, I must declare this to the insurance company, as it will affect the size of the premium they wish to charge.

The principle applies to all kinds of insurance: when applying for life insurance, for example, you must disclose your correct age and any chronic illnesses that have occurred in your family. The contract is invalid if any of the material facts are withheld from the company and subsequently come to light, and there is no obligation on the company to meet any claim arising under the policy.

It is also important for the company to show utmost good faith, by explaining to their prospective clients the terms of the insurance and the exact cover being provided. In fact they normally do this by including all the details on the policy: it is hardly their fault if policy holders fail to read the details, however small the print.

(b) Insurable Interest

You are only permitted to insure against a risk if you have an insurable interest in that event not occurring: that is to say, if the event does occur, *you* must suffer some kind of loss or incur some kind of liability. If your car is stolen or damaged you would suffer a loss, and are therefore entitled to insure it against theft or damage; if *my* car is stolen or damaged you would not be affected and you cannot, therefore, insure it. Similarly if people are injured in my shop I may have to compensate them; if they are injured in your shop I won't have to compensate them; thus I can insure against the former but not the latter. I can insure my life or my wife's life but not the life of my neighbour, unless he happens to be my business partner.

The reason for this principle is that you are not allowed to make a profit from insurance. You would do so if you collected money when your neighbour's car was damaged – and you might even be tempted to damage it yourself. However, it is the third principle of insurance that specifically prevents profit-making.

(c) Indemnity

The object of all insurance (except for life insurance and personal accident insurance) is to restore the insured to the position he was in before a stipulated event occurred. If your six-year-old car is damaged so badly in an accident that it cannot be repaired you cannot expect the insurance company to give you the money for a brand new car; the company will pay you sufficient to buy a six-year-old car of a similar model. If they bought you a new car you would be making a profit, and there would be an epidemic of people deliberately damaging their cars. If, on the other hand, the company give you only half the car's present value, you would be making a loss. They must try to compensate the insured precisely.

The insured person might think that he can get round this principle of insurance by accepting the money payment made in exact compensation by the company and then selling the wrecked vehicle to the local scrap dealer. This is prevented by the doctrine of *subrogation*, which assigns all the rights over the car to the company settling the claim. Any money raised through the sale of the car belongs to the insurance company, not the insured.

The dishonest might not yet be satisfied: they might insure the car with two different insurance companies and claim from both of them when the vehicle is damaged. The doctrine of *contribution* determines that each company pays a proportion of the cost, and that no profit is made by the insured.

Although the principle of indemnity is meant to put the insured in the position he was in just prior to the accident, a limit to the compensation is set by the policy itself. If I insured the contents of my house for £1 500 in 1977, £1 500 is the maximum compensation I can expect from the insurance company in the event of a claim being made. Suppose that the contents are now worth £2 500, and a fire destroys £2 000 of them. Clearly the insurance company cannot pay me £2 000 when my contribution to the pool has been geared to a maximum payment of £1 500. If the policy does not include an *average clause*, I can claim and expect to be paid the full amount insured – £1 500. It is more likely that the average clause is included, and then the insurance company can justifiably argue that they are liable for only a proportion of the damage: 1 500/2 500 of it in fact. They will maintain that the balance of the risk is carried by the insured person.

Thus, I can only expect to receive £2 000 × 1 500/2 500 = £1 200. Just as the principle of indemnity prevents you from gaining from *over*-insurance, the average clause prevents you from making a profit from *under*-insurance. It is obviously important to keep the value of insurance policies closely linked to the value of property, especially in times of inflation.

(d) Proximate Cause

Before the insurer pays out on a claim he will want to satisfy himself that the event is within the precise terms of the policy. You might insure the food in your deep-freeze against the effects of a failure in the electricity supply, but the policy will usually exclude a failure caused by a strike of workers at the power station. If there is a power failure caused by such a strike, the insurance company will not pay out because the doctrine of proximate cause has not been met. If, on the other hand, the failure results from accidental damage to the power line, the company will pay out, because this cause has not been excluded from the policy.

Similarly, if you insure yourself against death by accident when flying but die from a heart attack during a flight, the insurer will not be required to meet any claim made under the policy.

18.6 The Premium

We have seen that the premium is the payment made into the central pool by each policy holder. The payment is not the same for all policy holders, so we must now look closely at what determines the size of the premium paid. The calculation of accident insurance premiums is particularly complicated. Let us consider some of the factors that are taken into account before a policy for motor insurance is issued. The insurer will need the following information.

(a) The age of the driver. Statistics show that drivers under 25 or over 65 are more likely to make claims than other people.

(b) The type of car. There is a greater chance of an accident if he is driving a 3 000 cc sports car than if he is driving a 1 200 cc family saloon.

(c) The cost of repair. The cost of repairing damage to a Rolls-Royce is likely to be greater than the cost of repairing a cheaper car.

(d) The area where the driver lives. Accidents are more likely to occur in densely populated areas than in remote and underpopulated rural areas.

(e) The driver's record. If he has a long history of colliding with telegraph poles or other motorists, the company will think carefully before fixing the premium. Likewise, if he has recently been convicted of motoring offences his premium will be higher.

(f) The driver's occupation. Racing drivers are sometimes unable to adjust their driving to ordinary road conditions, and can therefore expect high premiums. Company representatives who cover huge distances each year, often under great pressure, may also expect to pay a high premium. Students are viewed with some suspicion by insurance companies, but teachers, for example, normally receive a discount on the basic premium, since the insurance companies' statistics show that they are involved in accidents less frequently than many other groups.

In addition to these factors the insurer will have to take into account the size of the average claim he has received, so that the pool can be large enough to meet claims in the year to come. Not surprisingly, insurance companies keep volumes of statistics of past events, on which to base their calculations. If the statistics show that an event is likely to occur, the premium will be high; if the event only occurs rarely, it will be lower.

18.7   The Insurance Market

Householders, businessmen and also the Government need insurance cover against all kinds of contingencies. There are two groups of insurers to cater for them – the insurance companies and Lloyd's of London.

(a) The Insurance Companies

Some of these are nationally known organizations offering the whole range of insurance cover; others specialize in, for example, motor insurance. Industrial Life offices deal primarily in life assurance, their branch offices collecting the premiums on a weekly or monthly basis. Most of the companies belong to the British Insurance Association, a body which lays down standards of behaviour for the companies.

If you want to obtain insurance cover from one of the companies, you can either visit one of their branch offices or arrange for one of their agents to call on you. Alternatively you can consult an *insurance broker*, whose job it is to provide a link between the companies and members of the public wishing to buy insurance. He is paid by the companies on a commission basis.

We have already seen the range of services provided by insurance companies, in Section 18.4.

(b) Lloyd's of London

Lloyd's began as a coffee-house near the Tower of London. It was there that merchants engaged in international trade became involved in insurance, by agreeing to share the losses should a vessel be lost. When the first insurance policies were drawn up, the merchants used to write their names under one another, indicating the amount of the risk they were prepared to accept. It was for this reason that they became known as *underwriters*. Edward Lloyd, the owner of the coffee-house, encouraged the merchants by providing them with pens and stationery. After Lloyd's death in 1713 the business of insurance grew, and Lloyd's was the centre of it.

In 1771 Lloyd's moved to new premises, and in 1871 the Corporation of Lloyd's was set up by Act of Parliament. The Corporation is governed by a Committee of Members who administer the rules to ensure that the integrity of Lloyd's is maintained, and that only people of the highest financial and personal standards can deal there. It is important to remember that Lloyd's does not itself offer insurance; it provides the facilities and the buildings through which the members can offer insurance. The members may be divided into underwriters and brokers.

(i) **Underwriters** are the only people allowed to accept insurance at Lloyd's. Each underwriter must be nominated by one member, supported by five others, and then elected unanimously by all the members. He must be able to show considerable financial resources and deposit a large sum with the Corporation before he can start trading. This is because any claims that have to be met on a Lloyd's policy are met from the personal resources of members.

It was once possible for a shipowner to find perhaps half a dozen underwriters who would insure his vessel between them. Today an ocean-going vessel and its cargo may be worth several million pounds, and it might take several days to obtain insurance cover if each underwriter had to be contacted individually. To overcome this problem underwriters have formed themselves into groups known as *syndicates*, which may involve a couple of hundred underwriters or a couple of dozen. The syndicate is represented at Lloyd's by an underwriting agent who, when he accepts insurance, does so on behalf of the whole syndicate. In this way the vessel and its cargo can quickly be covered.

Like most institutions Lloyd's has adapted itself over the years and now offers cover on much more than marine insurance. Fire and accident policies are also issued there, but ordinary life assurance policies are not available through Lloyd's. Short term life policies are issued, however, to cover a particular journey or expedition.

(ii) **Brokers**. Members of the public are not allowed to deal directly with underwriters. They must deal through one of the authorized Lloyd's brokers. The broker's job is to obtain the best policy he can for his client – the member of the public requiring insurance.

When a Lloyd's broker receives instructions to obtain insurance he makes out a *slip* – a sheet of paper setting out the details of the cover required. He must then find underwriters who specialize in underwriting this kind of risk, and obtain quotations from them. The broker accepts the most favourable, and the underwriter writes down the amount of the risk he is prepared to accept and the rate at which the premium is charged. He initials the slip, and all concerned will regard this as binding. The broker then takes the slip round to other underwriters to get them to accept some of the risk, until eventually the whole risk is covered. It is the first underwriter who sets the premium, because all the others will accept the rate he has quoted. If a claim later arises that has to be settled, it will be met by the underwriters in proportion to the amount they have agreed. For example if the owners of the ocean tanker *Spillit* want insurance cover for £3 million, their broker will approach several underwriters specializing in this area of insurance. Perhaps he obtains a quotation for cover for £500 000 at a premium of 1 per cent. This means that the underwriter will cover damage or loss up to the value of £500 000 for a premium of £5 000. If this quotation is acceptable the broker will then have to find other underwriters willing to accept part of the risk at the same rate, until the whole £3 million is covered.

If the vessel is subsequently lost, the first underwriter (or his syndicate) will have to pay £500 000; if the vessel suffers £600 000 of damage this underwriter, because he has covered 1/6 of the total risk, will have to pay £100 000 to the shipping company.

Once the whole of the risk is covered, the policy can be prepared. It is then sent to Lloyd's Policy Signing Office, where it is checked and then signed by members of the appropriate syndicates. It can now be sent to the client by the brokers.

While insurance remains the most important service provided at Lloyd's, the Corporation's long association with ships and shipping has given rise to some ancillary activities. The Corporation maintains a network of overseas agents who supply Lloyd's with information of shipping movements throughout their areas. These reports form the basis of two important daily publications: *Lloyd's List and Shipping Gazette* and *Lloyd's Shipping Index*, each containing a mass of information on shipping movements. Both are consulted regularly by shipowners and merchants.

18.8 Business and Insurance

While insurance is important to us all, it is perhaps most important to those in business. Insurance makes trading easier, by eliminating certain risks. Who would export thousands of pounds worth of goods without insurance cover? Who could afford to hold large stocks of goods if there were no insurance against fire and theft? In this Section we summarize the policies that a small trader would find it advisable to carry.

(*a*) Fire: his premises and his stock should be covered.

(*b*) Theft: his stock needs to be covered.

(*c*) Accidental damage: he needs to insure his property against accidental damage, and he might have a separate policy to cover plate-glass windows or other fixtures particularly liable to damage.

(*d*) Consequential loss: each of the above policies may contain a clause covering him against consequential loss.

(*e*) Motor insurance: he will have to insure any motor vehicles he owns.

(*f*) Employer's liability and public liability: these cover him in case of an injury on his premises.

(*g*) Fidelity guarantee: he would be well advised to insure against his employees embezzling the takings.

This insurance cover would remove a large number of risks from his shoulders, and the businessman could then concentrate on running the business, hoping that uninsurable risks could be avoided.

18.9 Questions and Exercises

(*a*) **Short Answers**

1. Give examples of insurable risks and non-insurable risks.
2. What is meant by the pooling of risks?
3. Why is an insurance policy a contract of 'utmost good faith'?
4. Explain precisely what is meant by insurable interest.
5. What risks would you expect a shopkeeper to insure against?
6. What are the advantages of endowment policies?

7. What is meant by third party insurance?
8. Give an example to show how insurance premiums are calculated.
9. Explain what is meant by (a) indemnity, (b) subrogation, (c) contribution.
10. What are the functions of (a) Lloyd's brokers, (b) Lloyd's underwriters?

(b) Essay Answers

1. What are the principles of insurance? Give examples to show their importance.
2. What are the main risks undertaken by businessmen? Show what insurance cover is needed by the owner of a factory.
3. Show how the principles of insurance apply in the case of a man (a) insuring his factory against fire, (b) making a claim under the policy.
4. Describe in full the services offered by Lloyd's of London.
5. Explain what is meant by the pooling of risks. Give examples to show how the pool operates.

(c) Projects and Assignments

1. Obtain the annual reports of three insurance companies, so that you can compare their profits and the ways in which they invest their money.
2. Examine the main institutions of the British Insurance Market and explain their functions.
3. Obtain details of the general household insurance offered by any of the main insurance companies. Show how the policy depends upon the basic principles of insurance.
4. Obtain statistics for: (a) the number of cars and motor cycles, (b) the number of accidents, (c) the cost of living, in the United Kingdom in recent years. Show why insurance premiums have increased, and why premiums for different groups vary.

Unit Nineteen

International Trade: Exporting

19.1 Introduction

No country produces all the goods required by its inhabitants. The United Kingdom exports about £60 000 million of goods each year and in a good year imports a similar amount. There are several reasons for the large volume of international trade.

(a) Different agricultural products require different climates if they are to be grown successfully. It is possible to grow tropical fruit in Britain, but only under expensive artificial conditions, so it is cheaper for us to import this type of fruit.

(b) Similarly, basic raw materials can only be produced by those countries fortunate enough to have them. Other nations have to import them.

(c) Many goods can only be produced by very sophisticated equipment, and only the advanced industrial nations own such equipment. A large amount of international trade consists of these industrial nations exporting their manufactured goods in exchange for the food and raw materials of the less developed countries.

(d) An increasing proportion of international trade, however, is between the industrial nations themselves. In 1980 the United Kingdom manufactured 1 300 000 cars and exported 505 000; at the same time we imported 550 000 cars from other countries. There are many reasons for this: consumers have different tastes, foreign cars may be better than ours in some respects; or they may be more easily available at the time people are buying cars.

Whatever the reasons for a particular batch of imports or exports, the total amount of goods moving in each direction is watched carefully by the Government, since it affects the *Balance of Payments* (see Unit 22), and may influence the whole economic life of the country.

For this reason we must examine the place of exports and imports in commercial life, looking not only at their volume and value but also at the problems which exporters and importers face.

19.2 The Volume of Exports

Fig. 19.1 shows the structure of United Kingdom exports in 1982, both by the destination of the goods and the type of goods exported.

The main points to note are as follows.

(a) The overwhelming majority of our exports are manufactured or semi-manufactured goods.

(b) The main market for our exports was Europe, although the USA was the single most important customer. At one time the Commonwealth was the main market, but the development of the European Free Trade Area and especially the European Economic Community (see Section 19.10) has provided very good opportunities for British exporters.

Our exports normally increase each year, but the global figures for exports conceal the performances of individual industries. As time goes by new products are developed, overseas customers begin to produce their own substitutes for our goods, old products become redundant and the structure of our trade changes.

19.3   Methods of Exporting

There are a number of methods open to the firm wishing to enter the export market. It may organize the whole project itself with its own employees doing all the work, either from head office or by going abroad; or it may hand over some or all of the work to an outside organization, called an Export House.

(a) Export Houses

This term covers several types of firm offering services in the export trade. Their functions may include any or all of the following:

(i) They may act as *merchants*, obtaining orders from abroad and then bringing the goods from the manufacturer in this country. In this way the home producer avoids many of the difficulties of exporting for he simply sells his goods to the home-based merchant. The merchant has full responsibility for the goods he handles. If prices fall after he has bought the goods he may make a loss.

(ii) Alternatively, they may be *agents*, looking for customers on behalf of manufacturers wishing to sell in export markets. There are two kinds of agents: *factors* and *brokers*, both of whom are paid on a commission basis.

The *factor* has possession of the goods for which he is finding a buyer; he can sell the goods in his own name and at the price *he* thinks best; and he is empowered to receive payment for the goods from the buyer. None of these characteristics belong to *brokers*, with whom factors are often confused. Brokers merely bring buyers and sellers together without taking possession of the goods.

(b) Overseas Agents

While a large amount of export business is conducted by merchants and agents based in the United Kingdom, it will often be preferable to employ an agent

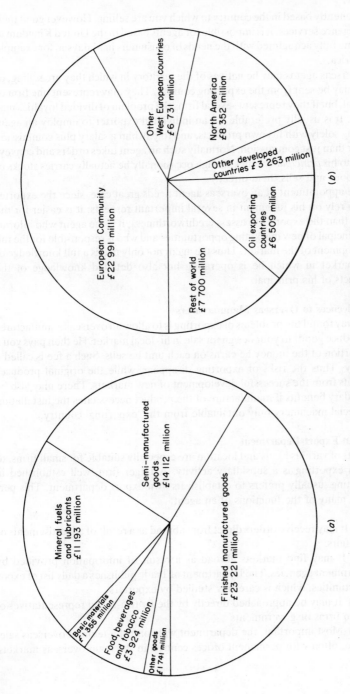

Fig. 19.1 The structure of United Kingdom exports, 1982 (£55 546 million): (a) type of exports; (b) main destination of exports

(a)

Finished manufactured goods
£23 221 million

Semi-manufactured goods
£14 112 million

Mineral fuels and lubricants
£11 193 million

Basic materials
£1 355 million

Food, beverages and tobacco
£3 924 million

Other goods
£1 741 million

(b)

European Community
£22 991 million

Other West European countries
£6 731 million

North America
£8 352 million

Other developed countries £3 263 million

Oil exporting countries
£6 509 million

Rest of world
£7 700 million

permanently based in the country to which you are selling. However good their intelligence services, it is impossible for agents based in the United Kingdom to become fully acquainted with the needs of consumers in Malaysia, for example, or Africa.

Overseas agents may be natives of the territory in which they are selling, or they may be sent from the exporting country. They may represent one firm or several, but if they represent several firms the problem of divided loyalties may occur. It is usually preferable for an individual exporter to employ an agent dealing solely with his own products, and to pay him a salary plus commission rather than just commission. Normally such an agent takes orders and conveys them to his *principal* (client), though occasionally he actually carries stocks of the goods and sells them direct.

The appointment of an overseas agent needs great care, since the exporter has to rely on his judgment in several important respects: it is easier for the agent than the exporter to assess creditworthiness; it is the agent who informs his principal of new marketing opportunities and who is responsible for the full development of the market. Thus the agent not only needs a full knowledge of the market in which he is operating but also detailed knowledge of the products of his principal.

(c) Licences to Overseas Manufacturers

One way round the problems of exporting is to allow an overseas manufacturer to produce goods to your design for sale in his local market. He then pays you a proportion of the money he earns on each unit he sells. Such a fee is called a *royalty*. Thus the risks of exporting disappear, while the original producer benefits from the successful development of new markets. There may also be secondary benefits if manufacture of the product necessitates the installation of special machinery only obtainable from the 'exporting' country.

(d) An Export Department

Agents of various kinds and location are especially suitable for small firms, to whom exporting is a subsidiary activity. A larger firm, well established in exporting, usually prefers to establish its own export department. This performs many of the functions of an agent.

(i) It may receive orders direct from abroad as a result of advertisements or trade fairs.

(ii) It may find markets abroad as a result of information provided by Government agencies. The Department of Trade publishes a daily list of export opportunities, which is carefully studied by exporters.

(iii) It may be approached directly by the British-based representatives of foreign firms or governments.

(iv) Most important, the department will control a team of overseas sales people, often with permanent offices centred in the main overseas markets.

These salesmen will be full time employees of the firm and will be expensive to keep in the field. But export markets are increasingly competitive, and there is no doubt that the volume and value of the exports of a particular firm depend very much on the effort that it puts into selling its goods. This is why an increasing number of firms establish their own export departments with permanent representatives overseas, charged solely with selling the company's products. It is generally best for the overseas representative to be a native of the area, for then he will be more aware of the exact needs of local customers.

(e) Manufacturing Abroad

In very highly developed export trades, there is another possibility, which is to set up manufacturing plant in the overseas market. This, of course, is only possible for very wealthy firms like Shell and Ford, and may not be in the interests of the exporting country, because it reduces the amount of actual exporting done. But to the firm it carries the considerable advantage of bringing it nearer to its market and, since it will be employing local labour, of making its products more acceptable in the host country. Companies who develop their overseas sales in this way are known as *multinational companies*. A fuller discussion of their role can be found in *Success in Economics*.

19.4 Obtaining Payment for Exports

The trader who sells goods in the home market has relatively few problems when it comes to collecting his money. The highly developed banking system not only facilitates payment, but also provides the trader with an assessment of the creditworthiness of a potential customer (see Section 11.12). When the overseas buyer has to pay for goods he has imported from Britain he cannot normally just write a cheque to settle the account. There are a number of methods of payment possible, and the one used for a particular transaction will depend upon the type of goods involved, the length of credit required (if any), and the creditworthiness of the customer. These are the main methods of payment currently in use.

(a) Open Account Transactions

This method is nearest to that operating in home trade, and is only used when the exporter is selling to an established customer whom he trusts. All the main British banks have branches in the leading overseas centres, and where they do not they appoint a bank to represent them. The importer pays the money into his local branch of the exporter's bank, from where it can be transferred rapidly by cable transfer to the exporter's account.

There is the risk that the importer will default on his debt or that payment will be unduly delayed. To safeguard himself against this the exporter can take out an insurance policy with the Export Credits Guarantee Department, which has a variety of schemes designed to cover this danger (see Section 19.11).

(b) Bills of Exchange

'A bill of exchange is an unconditional order in writing, addressed by one person to another, signed by the person giving it, requiring the person to whom it is addressed to pay on demand or at fixed or determinable future time, a sum certain in money to or to the order of a specified person, or to bearer.' This is the definition of a bill of exchange to be found in the Bills of Exchange Act 1882. We will examine the details of this definition shortly.

For centuries the bill of exchange has played an important part in the commercial life of the country. The need for it arises in two sets of circumstances.

(i) Where the buyer of goods needs a period of credit before paying, so that he can work upon raw materials he has bought and sell them, but where the seller cannot afford to give credit as it ties up his own capital.

(ii) Where the distance between the supplier and the buyer is so large that there is a delay of perhaps several weeks between the dispatch and the arrival of the goods.

The bill of exchange can overcome both problems, of which the former is more likely to arise in domestic trade, the latter in exporting.

Suppose that John Smith Ltd. have dispatched goods worth £5 000, by sea, to James Head in Brazil. It will be some time before they arrive, and Smith does not want his capital tied up in credit. On the other hand, Head will not be very anxious to pay for the goods until they actually arrive in good condition. Smith therefore draws up a bill of exchange like the one shown in Fig. 19.2.

£5 000	31 Any Road
	Somewhere
30 November 19. .	England

90 days after sight pay John Smith Ltd
five thousand pounds at National
Westminster Bank, Somewhere.

| To: J. Head | Signed: J. Smith |
| Rio, Brazil | Director |

Fig. 19.2 A bill of exchange

Note that

(i) The bill *instructs* J. Head to pay the appropriate sum at a particular time.
(ii) The drawer of the bill is J. Smith, a director of the exporting firm.
(iii) The drawee is J. Head, the importer.

Once the bill has been drawn up it is sent to the importer who signs on it 'accepted', to acknowledge his debt and to signify his agreement to the terms of the bill. He will not be willing to accept the bill until he is sure that the goods are on their way to him. It will therefore be accompanied by a copy of the *bill of lading*, which is signed by the ship's master and proves that the goods are on their way (see Section 19.6). A copy of the insurance policy covering the goods will also accompany the bill of exchange, as will any invoices in connexion with the deal.

In practice it is usually unnecessary to send the bill of exchange and the shipping documents to the head office in Brazil. Because of the distance involved the bill of exchange (now a *documentary bill* because it is accompanied by the shipping documents such as the bill of lading and the insurance policy) will be accepted by J. Head's London agent and returned to the exporter. As long as the agent is one of the leading accepting houses, J. Smith can now *discount* the bill: it is passed on to a bank (negotiated), for a sum slightly less than its face value. J. Smith Ltd now have their money, and the bank makes a profit by collecting £5 000 in a few weeks' time. J. Head meanwhile receives the documents relating to the transaction, which will permit him to claim the goods when they arrive. He will then arrange for the £5 000 to be handed over on the due date.

Once again there is a danger that the importer will default. This no longer worries the exporter, as the bill has been accepted by an Accepting House, which has thereby guaranteed payment on the due date. But the Accepting House must take precautions to ensure that it does not accept bills on which it will be called to meet its guarantee.

Letters of credit were devised to facilitate the use and acceptance of bills of exchange in international trade. In the case we examined above J. Head would have instructed his bank in Rio to instruct their London branch to issue a letter of credit to J. Smith Ltd, stating that £5 000 would be paid to the company in exchange for the documentary bill. The letter of credit can be *revocable* or *irrevocable*: if it is revocable it is liable to cancellation by the importer, but if it is irrevocable it can only be withdrawn with the permission of the exporter. Consequently the second type is much safer for the exporter. Where documentary credits are involved the bill of exchange will normally be a 'sight bill', i.e. payable when presented.

19.5   The Finance of Trade

In the previous Section we dealt with the basic means of securing payment for exports. We saw in passing that exporters often cannot afford to give extensive credit, and that importers cannot always afford to pay cash for their goods. In these circumstances it is common for finance to be provided by third parties.

(a)   The Clearing Banks

As we have seen, the banks provide loans and overdrafts for all kinds of purposes, and they are normally prepared to lend to exporters who have supplied goods on credit. The bank usually needs some kind of security, and an Export Credits Guarantee Department insurance policy is usually adequate (see Section 19.11). Then, if the importer does not pay up in time, the bank can be repaid from the proceeds of the insurance policy.

(*b*) **Self-financing**
Many of the larger exporters undertake to finance themselves. They are prepared to see their capital tied up in debts, but of course they are likely to include the cost of credit in the price of their goods.

(*c*) **Other Methods**
Where the bill of exchange is used, short term finance is provided by anyone discounting the bill. Also, some finance companies specialize in advancing money against the debts owing to exporters and then assuming responsibility for collecting the money due.

19.6   The Documentation Involved in Exporting

One of the obstacles confronting an exporter is the documentation involved, which is extensive for a number of reasons.

(i)   A written record is essential, as in all business transactions.

(ii)   The Government needs to be kept informed of the level of exports and imports.

(iii)   There are a large number of intermediaries, and often several thousand miles, between exporters and importers. Detailed documentation of transactions helps to keep track of goods.

(iv)   There are many legal requirements to comply with. As we shall see in Unit 20, importing countries are often very strict about the goods they allow into the country, and they demand written evidence of their nature and origin.

The main documents needed to ensure that a consignment of exports reaches its destination safely are as follows.

(*a*) **Bill of Lading**
This is perhaps the most important document in international trade. It contains the names of the consignor (sender) of the goods and the consignee (recipient), full details of the goods themselves, their destination and the name of the ship. The markings on the crates are also given. No goods can be exported by sea without the bill of lading being properly drawn up, usually in triplicate. One copy is kept by the ship's master, one copy is retained by the consignor, and one copy is sent on, usually by air, to the consignee.

When the goods are delivered to the ship, the bill of lading is signed by the ship's master, and serves as a receipt for the goods. If the goods arrive at the ship damaged the bill is endorsed accordingly, and is known as a *dirty bill*; otherwise it is a *clean bill*. Once signed, the bill of lading is evidence of a contract between the consignor and the shipping company for the carriage of goods to their destination, in keeping with the terms of the bill.

Most important, the bill of lading is the *document of title* to the goods. The holder of the bill of lading is entitled to claim the goods from the ship's master when the vessel reaches its destination. This is why the consignee's copy is normally sent ahead of the vessel carrying the goods. Without his copy he cannot take possession of the goods or remove them from the ship.

In legal terms the bill of lading is a 'quasi-negotiable instrument': this means that the holder of the bill can transfer his title by endorsing it in favour of someone else.

(b) Airway Bill

This corresponds to the bill of lading but is used only when goods are sent by air. It is made out in triplicate: one copy is retained by the consignor, another by the airline, and one is carried *with the goods* for the consignee. The airway bill differs from the bill of lading in that it is not a document of title, and therefore not quasi-negotiable.

(c) Consular Invoice

When goods are imported into a country, customs duties are often levied on them, and these are normally calculated from the price of the goods as stated on the invoice. Obviously it would be possible to reduce the duty payable by falsifying the price on the invoice. A consular or certified invoice prevents this, because the prices on it are certified as correct by the consul or other representative of the importing country resident in the exporting country.

(d) Certificate of Insurance

A certificate of insurance is usually enclosed which, together with the other documents, assures interested parties that the goods have been properly insured.

(e) Shipping Note

When the goods are delivered to the docks, they are accompanied by a formal request to the port authorities, known as a shipping note. It tells the authorities what goods are involved, their port of destination and the ship they are to be sent in. A copy of the note is signed by port authorities and retained by the exporter as proof of delivery to the port. It is then referred to as a *dock receipt*.

(f) Mate's Receipt

Sometimes the cargo is delivered direct to the ship and put aboard. In this case a mate's receipt is issued by the ship's mate.

(g) Certificate of Origin

The duty that an importing country imposes on goods varies according to the country from which they have come. Members of the European Free Trade

Area are each allowed to impose their own tariffs on goods imported from non-members, but impose no tariffs on goods imported from members. Non-members could therefore be tempted to send all their exports via the country with the lowest tariff against them, and they could then be re-exported from there duty-free to the other members. This practice is prevented by the use of certificates of origin which usually accompany duty-free goods to confirm that they were produced, or largely produced, in the exporting country.

There are, as you might expect, many other documents used in exporting, but we have now seen the most important of them.

19.7   The Government and Exporting

The Government is interested in exporting for several reasons. Most important, it must ensure that the nation exports enough to pay for its imports (see Unit 21), and it therefore takes special steps to encourage exporters. The Government itself provides a wide range of services to promote the growth of exports: it sometimes establishes autonomous bodies to facilitate trade, and it negotiates continuously for the reduction of tariff barriers against exports. These activities are considered in the next four Sections.

In a few special cases, it is true, a Government may want to *discourage* the export of certain goods, either because they are in short supply at home or because the Government wants to prevent foreign countries acquiring them. Control of this sort is usually achieved through a system of export licences.

19.8   The Department of Trade

This is the Government department with the main responsibility for exporting. It provides several services to encourage exporters.

(a) The British Overseas Trade Board
Attached to the Department of Trade is the British Overseas Trade Board, which has the general task of supervising export promotion. It consists mainly of businessmen, with representatives from the Department of Trade and the Foreign Office. The board has an advisory rather than an executive role, but many promotional schemes benefit directly from its advice.

(b) Trade Fairs and Promotions
There is a special division of the Department of Trade which supports trade fairs and other promotions, though it does not normally organize them. The Department often rents space at large international trade fairs and sublets it at a very economic rate to British companies wishing to expand in the areas concerned. More intensive promotions of exports take the form of *British weeks*, where local shops in foreign cities are given every incentive to sell British goods. These are organized by the Department and wherever possible a programme of sporting and social events is held to boost the image of British goods.

(*c*) **Export Intelligence**

Among the special problems facing exporters is the difficulty of learning about opportunities. The Department of Trade's Export Intelligence Service provides an efficient and economical way of overcoming this problem. For a small annual subscription the service provides information about a variety of topics including specific exporting opportunities, conditions in particular markets, import regulations in overseas countries, trade fairs and British weeks. The information is collected by the commercial staff of British Embassies overseas and is processed through the Department's own computer, so that subscribers to the system usually receive the relevant information within 48 hours of its arriving in London.

More general information is provided in *Trade and Industry*, the weekly magazine published by the Department of Trade and the Department of Industry. The potential exporter can find details of changes in foreign tariffs and export opportunities.

The individual firm hoping to enter the export market for the first time can approach the Department of Trade for an assessment of the prospects. If the firm provides a detailed specification of its products, the Department will report back on the most likely market for the goods, perhaps suggesting modifications that could be made to meet local requirements in a particular area.

19.9   The Central Office of Information

The Central Office of Information provides publicity services for British exporters. Although commercial advertising is not accepted, any newsworthy item, such as the details of new products or the execution of an important export order, may well be incorporated in a newsletter, broadcast or film produced by the COI for the benefit of businessmen and consumers overseas.

Translation of documents written in a foreign language sometimes poses a problem to exporters. Similarly it is important that publicity material that is to appear in foreign countries is properly translated from the English. The Central Office of Information is normally able to suggest a suitable translator. (There are, in fact, several non-Government bodies such as the Institute of Linguists that provide a similar service.)

19.10   Tariff Barriers

A tariff is a tax imposed on goods entering a country. (Some countries also impose a tariff on goods leaving the country, but these are exceptional and we shall not pursue them here.) There are a number of reasons for imposing tariffs or customs duties on other countries' exports.

(*a*) The need to protect home industry from foreign competition.

(*b*) The need to protect the Balance of Payments (see Unit 21).

(*c*) The need to maintain full employment in home industries.

(*d*) The need for the Government to raise revenue (e.g. from tobacco).

Whatever the reason for imposing the tariff, the existence of tariffs has three effects.

(a) They reduce the total benefit from international trade, and in extreme circumstances thay can stop trade altogether.

(b) They make it more difficult for exporters to sell goods since, like all taxes, they increase prices.

(c) They complicate the process of international trade, since the customs authorities require documentation to make sure that the correct amount of duty is paid.

To alleviate the first two, if not the third, of these problems, Governments seek to reduce tariff barriers between countries. This may be done in a number of ways.

(a) Bilateral negotiations between two countries which impose tariffs on each other's exports.

(b) Multilateral negotiations between countries, usually organized by a body such as the General Agreement on Tariffs and Trade (GATT), whose object is to secure the abolition of all tariffs and other obstacles to trade. At conferences organized by GATT, attempts are made to encourage all members to adopt a more open policy towards other countries.

(c) The establishment of trading blocs. The two European examples are the European Free Trade Association and European Economic Community. Members of EFTA (founded in 1959) undertook to eliminate tariffs against fellow members by 1970, in respect of industrial goods, and this target has been achieved. Individual members deal with non-members as they wish: if they want to impose tariffs against them there is no EFTA rule to prevent it.

The EEC, also known as the Common Market, was founded in 1957, and Britain joined it in 1973. Here too members undertook to eliminate trade barriers within the EEC, and this has been achieved. Since 1977 Britain, Denmark and Ireland have traded on equal terms with the original six members, France, Germany, Italy, Belgium, the Netherlands and Luxemburg. In 1981 the Market was further enlarged by the admission of Greece. Beyond the abolition of tariff barriers between themselves, the members of the EEC also undertook to establish a *Common External Tariff* against non-members. If outsiders export to the EEC, the tariff payable on their goods is the same whichever EEC country they enter although, of course, different goods are taxed at different rates. Members of the EEC also strive to establish common policies for agriculture, taxation and transport among other things, and it is altogether a more cohesive organization than EFTA.

There may well be important economic benefits to be derived from membership of the EEC, but it is important to realize that its effect on trade is liberalizing only from the point of view of members. For non-members it may have the effect of increasing the barriers to trade. Members of the British Commonwealth, for example, now find it more difficult to sell goods in Britain than they did before Britain joined the EEC.

19.11   The Export Credits Guarantee Department

This is dealt with separately here, even though it is under the direction of the Department of Trade, for the ECGD enjoys considerable autonomy and is run as a commercial enterprise and not as a Government department.

Exporters often send goods to brokers they don't know, in countries where political conditions are unstable and from where it may be difficult to secure payment. Large sums of money may be tied up in an export order and, without insurance, the danger of non-payment would deter many potential exporters from entering the export trade. The bulk of export insurance is provided through the ECGD. The usual principles of insurance apply and the main policies offered by the department are these.

(a) Comprehensive Policies

With a comprehensive policy the exporting firm insures all its exports to all markets for one year against non-payment for any of the following reasons: because the buyer does not want to pay; because he is prevented from paying by his Government, who cannot afford the foreign currency (see Unit 21); because of war; or because the import licence has been cancelled by the Government before the goods are delivered.

The period covered varies from six months for consumer goods to five years for expensive investment goods. The premiums vary according to the period of time involved and the markets to which the trader is exporting.

(b) Specific Policies

A basic principle of the ECGD is that a client must insure all his exports. This enables the ECGD to pool the risks in the normal way. However, the Department does issue specific policies for large 'once and for all' transactions, such as the sale of expensive generating equipment for a power station. Because the risks to the ECGD are greater, the premiums are higher.

(c) Investment Insurance

A new departure for the ECGD has been the attempt to encourage overseas investment, especially in developing countries. Some of these countries are subject to quite rapid political changes which can result in an expensive investment being nationalized, with no compensation to the owner. The ECGD scheme normally offers up to 90 per cent compensation for a period of up to 15 years.

19.12   The Difficulties Facing Exporters

It should be clear by now that the exporter faces difficulties which are often unknown to the home trader. We have already examined some of them but we will conclude this Unit by listing the difficulties and some of the ways in which they may be overcome.

(a) Distance

For British exporters the distance involved in exporting is always greater than in domestic trade, which may complicate *negotiations* and necessitate the appointment of representatives overseas. It also makes *transport* more complicated: British exporters have to use sea or air transport, but of course this does not always apply to exporters in other countries.

(b) Language Differences

These may mean that *communications* with overseas traders must be carefully translated, while publicity material and instructions which accompany goods must be prepared in several languages.

(c) Cultural Differences and Local Requirements

These factors must be taken into account when exporting, which makes *market research* more complicated (see Section 16.4). We have seen how this is overcome to some extent by the intelligence services of the Departments of Trade and Industry.

(d) Technical Differences

Different Governments may have different technical specifications for goods sold in their country. The exporter dealing with several overseas countries may have to produce half a dozen or more different specifications for electrical equipment. One of the benefits of EEC membership is the establishment of uniform technical specifications and requirements in member countries.

(e) Tariff Barriers

Tariffs are a considerable obstacle to trade, and they can only be avoided by not exporting to those countries which impose them. Governments are continually negotiating for their abolition.

(f) Customs Regulations

These have to be obeyed, and they create more work for the exporter.

(g) Documentation

Documentation is much more complicated in exporting than in home trade, and involves the exporter in more work. However, much of this can be handed over to a *freight forwarder*, who specializes in making all the arrangements in connexion with the export of goods, from advising on packing to collecting payment.

(h) Payment

Payment poses an additional problem, because the exporter uses a different currency from his customer. Currency must, therefore, be exchanged in the foreign exchange market. As we shall see in Unit 21, the exporter can never be certain how much he will be able to obtain in the market.

(i) Insurance

Insurance is also more complicated for the exporter, because the risks are greater. Again, the Government makes every effort to overcome the problem.

Exporting is only one side of international trade. Importing is the other. We have already seen something of the importer's role but there are many aspects of importing that deserve special attention. We turn to these in Unit 20.

19.13 Questions and Exercises

(a) Short Answers
1. What are the main markets for British exports?
2. Name four institutions which assist in exporting.
3. Explain the important role of bills of exchange in international trade.
4. What is a letter of credit?
5. What are the functions of a bill of lading?
6. What is the purpose of a consular invoice?
7. What are the functions of the British Overseas Trade Board?
8. Why is the Export Credits Guarantee Department important to exporters?
9. Make a list of the difficulties facing exporters which do not affect those involved only in domestic trade.
10. Why is it important to export?

(b) Essay Answers
1. Describe the problems facing a manufacturer entering the export market for the first time. How are the problems overcome?
2. Describe the main means by which an exporter may secure payment for his goods.
3. Describe the functions of the Export Credits Guarantee Department.
4. What assistance is given to exporters by the Government?
5. What obstacles do foreign governments place in the way of United Kingdom exports? Why is this done?

(c) Projects and Assignments
1. Make a collection of news cuttings about British exports.
2. Banks are of great assistance to firms engaged in exporting. Show, with examples, the ways in which this help is given.

Unit Twenty

International Trade: Importing

20.1 Introduction

Importers, like exporters, are faced with problems that don't arise in domestic trade. Many of them are identical to those we discussed in relation to exporting – language, distance, payment and so on – and there is no need to repeat them here. But some of the importer's problems are different from the exporter's, in particular those of documentation. The importer is more closely involved with the customs authorities than the exporter, since imports are more strictly controlled than exports.

The import procedures that are necessary to meet customs regulations are the subject of most of this Unit, but first we can learn much about the nature of our economy by studying the structure of our imports.

20.2 The Structure of United Kingdom Imports

As you can see in Fig. 20.1(a), over two-thirds of the United Kingdom imports are now manufactured or semi-manufactured goods. This has not always been so. The traditional pattern was for over half of Britain's imports to consist of food and basic materials. Now international trade consists increasingly of the exchange of manufactured goods between industrial nations. This is reflected in Fig. 20.1(b) where you can see how the main sources of British imports are now the industrial countries. The significance of UK trade with less developed countries has declined relatively. While it is true that more food and raw materials are imported now, these have not expanded as rapidly as imports in general. There seem to be two reasons for this: as the wealth of the UK has risen, the demand for food has not expanded in proportion to income; and modern science has developed artificial substitutes for many of the raw materials that were once imported. Accordingly, imports of primary products have not kept up with the overall rate of expansion. (However, recent rises in the price of these commodities will alter the balance of the UK's import bill quite considerably.)

20.3 Intermediaries in Importing

Those firms wishing to import goods from abroad may organize the whole process for themselves, but only the largest are likely to do so. Other firms use the services provided by a number of agents and merchants in order to obtain

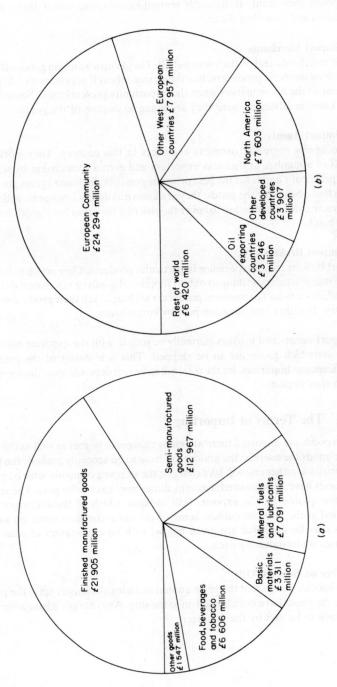

Fig. 20.1 The structure of United Kingdom imports, 1982 (£53 427 million)
(a) type of imports; (b) main sources of British imports

(a)

Other goods £1 547 million

Finished manufactured goods £21 905 million

Semi-manufactured goods £12 967 million

Mineral fuels and lubricants £7 091 million

Basic materials £3 311 million

Food, beverages and tobacco £6 606 million

(b)

European Community £24 294 million

Other West European countries £7 957 million

North America £7 603 million

Other developed countries £3 907 million

Oil exporting countries £3 246 million

Rest of world £6 420 million

the goods they want. It is worth reminding ourselves about these inter-mediaries and how they differ.

(a) Import Merchants

These merchants deal on their own behalf. They keep a watch on goods offered for sale by overseas producers, buy them, store them if necessary and dispose of them on the home market when the opportunity presents itself. Sometimes they know in advance where they are going to dispose of the goods.

(b) Import Agents

These agents represent overseas exporters in this country. They work on behalf of a number of overseas exporters and earn a commission by selling their principal's goods for the best price they can obtain. Some agents guarantee to find a buyer for the goods: they are known as *del credere* agents and they receive an extra commission to cover the risk that they may have goods left on their hands.

(c) Import Brokers

Import brokers usually specialize in particular products. They act on behalf of home manufacturers wishing to obtain supplies of goods or raw materials from abroad, or on behalf of overseas producers wishing to sell their produce in this country. In either case they are paid by commission.

Import agents and brokers normally negotiate with the exporter over the *terms* on which goods are to be shipped. This is a matter of the greatest significance to importers, for the total bill to be met depends upon the terms on which they import.

20.4   The Terms of Importing

When goods are imported there are many charges to be met as well as the cost of the goods themselves: the goods may have to be specially packed; the port authorities at either end will levy charges; the shipping company must be paid; the goods have to be insured; customs duties may have to be paid. The terms that are quoted by the exporter will indicate which of these charges are included in the price he quotes. Some of the more common terms on which goods may be imported are given below, with an explanation of what the importer understands by each.

(a) Free on Board (FOB)

The importer knows that the price quoted includes all charges up to the point where the goods have been loaded on to the ship. Any charges arising after this will have to be met by the importer.

(b) Free Alongside Ship (FAS)

This is not quite so advantageous for the importer, since he has to pay the expenses of loading the goods on to the ship.

(c) Cost, Insurance and Freight (CIF)

Here he knows his commitment quite clearly, for the price quoted includes the cost of the goods, the insurance premium, and the freight or carriage charges levied by the shipping company.

(d) Ex Ship

The importer has to pay for the unloading of the goods from the ship once they have reached the port. All charges up to this point have to be met by the exporter.

(e) Duty Paid

This is not frequently used, but it means that the exporter pays the import duty on the goods as well as all the charges. The importer's calculations are thus much simplified.

There are many other terms on which goods may be exported, but those above are the most widely used and serve to show how the importer's expenses vary according to the terms quoted. When the goods have reached the importer, the agent or merchant will send him a bill setting out the details: it will show the cost of the goods and any other charges, including commission. This bill is known by the technical term *account sales*. The importer may already have received from the exporter a *pro forma invoice*. This is not a demand for payment but a statement showing the goods being sent, their cost and other charges that are going to be made. It serves as an advice note to the importer.

20.5 The Importer and the Customs

Although the transaction between the importer and the exporter is now complete, the importer is not yet free to remove his goods from the port and sell them. First he must satisfy the port authorities of his title to the goods by presenting the bill of lading. (He may also have to show them the other documents relating to the shipment.)

Next he must deal with the customs officers, who check that no import regulations are being broken. They also have to decide how much duty is payable, if any. We shall now look at the importer's dealings with the customs in greater detail.

(a) The Ship's Manifest

The importer can do nothing until this has been delivered. It is a report from the ship's master setting out details of the vessel, its journey and, most important to us, the cargo carried. The report should be delivered to the customs within 24 hours of arrival at the port, and until it has been, no goods can be unloaded from the ship.

(b) The Bill of Entry

The importer then files a *bill of entry* with the customs. This is a document giving details of the goods he is importing. The exact procedure then varies according to whether the goods are duty free or dutiable. In either case the goods cannot be removed without the authority of the customs officers.

(c) Entry of Duty-free Goods

The importer prepares an *entry for duty-free goods* form, setting out the details of the goods he is importing, including the vessel from which they are being discharged. The customs officers can then compare this form with the ship's report to see that the details correspond. If they do, one copy of the form is endorsed by the customs and returned to the importer. This can then be presented to the dock authorities as evidence that the goods can be released.

The purpose of this procedure is to ensure that the goods really are duty free, and to keep a full record of goods entering the country for statistical purposes.

(d) Entry of Dutiable Goods

If the importer wants immediate possession of goods which are dutiable, he must fill in an *entry for home use ex ship* form. This will contain the same details as the entry of duty-free goods, but in addition the importer must state the amount of duty to be paid. This can be determined by reference to the *Customs and Excise Tariff*, which sets out the duty payable on different categories of goods.

The duties may be charged on one of two bases. *Ad valorem duties* are levied according to the *value* of the goods imported, in which case the entry must of course contain the value of the consignment. (It is in connexion with these duties that the consular or certified invoice we mentioned in Section 19.6(c) is necessary.) Alternatively the duty may be *specific*, and levied on the *quantity* of goods to be imported. Again the entry will need to contain the relevant details.

When the entry has been checked by the customs officer and the duty paid, a copy of the form is presented to the dock authority. When the goods are unloaded they are carefully checked by the customs to see that they correspond with the details on the entry. (The customs, of course, have very wide powers to check goods entering the country, to prevent smuggling.) If the details on the entry do not correspond with the consignment, an adjustment is made to the duty payable. The customs interest in the goods is then at an end, and the importer can seek delivery of the goods from the shipping company in the usual way.

It may be that the importer is not in a position to pay the duty on his consignment immediately. Since the customs will not release the goods until the duty has been paid, some provision must be made for them. Special warehouses called *bonded warehouses* (Section 20.6) are established where imports can be stored until the duty has been paid. If the consignment is going to be stored in a bonded warehouse, the importer completes an *entry for warehousing*, very similar to the entry for home use, containing details of the goods but no assessment of the duty payable. The goods are then delivered direct to the bonded warehouse and cannot be released until the duty has been paid.

20.6 Bonded Warehouses

The duty payable on a consignment of tobacco or wine may run into hundreds of thousands of pounds. If this had to be paid as soon as the goods arrived in the United Kingdom, importers would have large amounts of capital tied up, even though they might not want the use of the materials for some time. Bonded warehouses overcome this problem.

(a) They are owned either by importers or independent concerns, not by the customs.

(b) They are normally located at ports, airports or land frontiers, but some large importers have their own bonded warehouses located at their factories. Cigarette manufacturers, for example, who have enormous amounts of duty to pay, do not like to remove tobacco from bond until they are about to use it. Accordingly they need the bonded warehouse to be located as near as possible to the factory.

(c) They are subject to customs supervision. The owner must give a *bond*, which is a written undertaking that goods will be released from the warehouse only in the presence of a customs officer and only when the duty has been paid. Should the regulations be broken the bond stipulates a financial penalty that the owner must pay to the authorities.

(d) Goods may be removed from bond in small lots. This represents a considerable economy to the importer.

(e) While in bond goods may be sampled, packed or blended, but they must not be manufactured. They may be moved from one bonded warehouse to another by *bonded carmen*.

(f) The owner of the goods may sell them while they are in bond, in which case of course the purchaser becomes liable for the customs duty.

(g) Once the duty has been paid on the goods they may be removed on the authority of a *warrant* issued by the customs officers.

(h) Sometimes goods are imported temporarily, the purpose being to re-export them. In this case they can be stored in a bonded warehouse pending re-export without any duty being paid. When Britain dominated world shipping, goods for several European countries would be brought from America to London for reshipment to their eventual destinations. With the expansion of international transport, however, this *entrepot* trade has declined in importance.

If the goods have to be manufactured in some way before they are re-exported, the procedure is different, because, as we have seen, duty must be paid before goods can be manufactured. Duty has to be paid, for example, on imported tobacco. But if the tobacco is made into cigarettes for export, the exporter is entitled to claim repayment of the duty paid on the tobacco. This is known as *customs drawback*.

20.7   The Role of the Customs

It is appropriate at this point to summarize the role of the Customs and Excise authorities in the import and export trade.

(a) Statistics
The customs compile a wide range of statistics showing the pattern of trade and the movement of goods. (They are not responsible for checking the movement of *people*, which is the responsibility of the Home Office and is exercised through the Immigration Department.)

(b) Control
They supervise the movement of goods in and out of the country, ensuring that prohibited goods are not imported or exported.

(c) Revenue
The duty payable on imports (and some exports) is collected by the customs.

(d) Bonded Warehouses
These warehouses are controlled, but not owned, by the customs.

(e) Public Health
The customs have certain functions in connexion with the control of infectious diseases. For example they organize quarantine for animals.

20.8   The Port and Harbour Authorities

While the customs are responsible for the supervisory functions we outlined in the previous Section, the process of importing and exporting in the United Kingdom could not go ahead without the facilities provided by the docks and the bodies controlling them. We shall confine our comments to the docks, even though parallel facilities are provided by the airport authorities for the increasing amount of trade undertaken by the airlines.

In the United Kingdom some docks are privately owned, but the majority of trade is undertaken by the publicly owned docks. The form of ownership is immaterial to the services that have to be provided by these authorities.

(a) Deep Water and Clear Access
These are the first requirements of any port. As the size of ships increases, the deeper the water needs to be. The authority has to spend considerable sums on dredging to keep the channels to the port clear. It also provides pilots, with a detailed knowledge of the approach, to take over the steering of vessels entering and leaving the port.

(b) Wharves

Adequate facilities must be provided for the speedy discharge and loading of vessels: cranes, warehouses and labour should be available to deal with ships as soon as possible. Dock charges are based partly on the time that a dock is occupied, so if the port earns a reputation of being slow in turning ships round it will gradually lose traffic. Recently the development of containerization has speeded up the handling of cargoes, though it has also necessitated the installation of special and very expensive handling equipment (see Unit 18).

(c) Access

A port must be linked to the road and railway networks by a transport system which is capable of dealing with the volume of traffic generated. Without easy access the port will lose business to other centres.

(d) Office Space

Shipping companies, customs officers and other organizations using the port all need office space.

(e) Ship-repair Yards

Repair yards and dry docks should also be provided so that routine maintenance can be effectively carried out. Moreover, provision must be made for ships to refuel and take on any other supplies they need.

(f) Special Facilities

Certain imports, such as timber, grain, coal and oil require special handling. If ports want to attract trade in these goods they must provide the special facilities necessary to deal with them.

20.9 Questions and Exercises

(a) Short Answers
1. What are the main sources of British imports?
2. Why is it important that the terms of importing are clearly stated?
3. Explain the difference between imports FOB and imports CIF.
4. What is the purpose of a pro forma invoice?
5. Distinguish between ad valorem duties and specific duties.
6. What is meant by *bonded* in the term *bonded warehouse*?
7. What is *customs drawback*?
8. What characteristics would you expect of a good port?
9. What are the functions of a port authority?
10. What are the functions of the customs authorities?

(b) Essay Answers
1. Explain the documentation needed for (a) dutiable imports, (b) non-dutiable imports.

2. Describe the methods by which an importer can pay for the goods he receives.
3. What problems face an importer that do not exist if he buys from a local supplier?
4. Describe in detail the functions of the bill of lading in international trade.
5. Explain the functions of (*a*) the customs authority, (*b*) the port authority in monitoring and facilitating importing.

(c) Projects
1. Keep a scrapbook to show the functions of docks and ports in relation to importing.
2. By referring to the *Annual Abstract of Statistics* make a comparison of British imports in 1970 and 1980. What differences are revealed?

Unit Twenty-one

The Balance of Payments

21.1 Introduction

A country's Balance of Payments is a record of all its financial and economic transactions with the rest of the world. Every time someone in the United Kingdom imports or exports goods, takes a holiday overseas or receives interest from abroad, the Balance of Payments is affected.

The essential difference between these transactions and purely domestic transactions is that our domestic transactions can be settled in currency that is familiar to and recognized by all the parties concerned, while our overseas transactions involve two different currencies. The British importer of a £7 000 German car will find that his German supplier will not have much use for 7 000 pound notes. The importer will have to instruct his bank to buy £7 000 worth of Deutsche Marks from the *foreign exchange market* (see Section 21.7), which is the collective name given to the institutions concerned with buying and selling foreign currency. The importer's bank balance will fall by £7 000, but he can now use the Deutsche Marks to pay for his car. Although the importer will go nowhere near the Bank of England this is, in effect, where the Deutsche Marks will come from. The real reason for concern over the Balance of Payments is that if too many people want to buy German cars, or anything else from abroad, the Bank of England's reserves of foreign currency will begin to dwindle.

The Government, in conjunction with the Bank of England, keeps a watchful eye on our trading performance, so that if necessary they can take corrective measures to protect the currency reserves.

21.2 The Structure of the Balance of Payments

It would be possible simply to lump together all the payments received from other countries, and all the payments made to other countries, deduct one from the other and thus determine the Balance of Payments for the year. However, this would not reveal very much about the causes of the surplus or deficit which was revealed. If there were a surplus, we would know only that receipts exceeded payments; if there were a deficit, only that payments exceeded receipts. We can get a much better picture of our performance by classifying the transactions under several different headings.

(a) Visible Trade

We have been dealing with visible trade in Units 19 and 20. The value of goods crossing national boundaries is added together to give the *balance of visible trade*. You already know a good deal about our visible trade, and there is no need to elaborate on it here except to say that we often import goods to a greater value than our exports.

Each month a provisional estimate of the previous month's balance of visible trade is made (the trade figures) and well publicized on television and in the press. The monthly figures, and indeed the annual figures, are almost always amended later owing to the late delivery of some of the appropriate documents to the authorities, but they are accurate enough to indicate the broad pattern of trade.

(b) Invisible Trade

The services which we sell abroad or buy from overseas suppliers are known as invisible trade. As a general rule, where the UK provides the service, the UK Balance of Payments is improved. For example, if an American businessman flies by British Airways, dollars are earned by the corporation and the Balance of Payments is helped; conversely, if a British businessman flies by Pan American, sterling is paid out and the Balance of Payments is harmed. (Of course if the British businessman flies by British Airways the Balance of Payments is not affected.)

There are many services which contribute to the *balance of invisible trade*, and since most of them are commercial it is right that we should give them special attention. This we shall do in Section 21.4. It is a feature of the UK Balance of Payments that the invisible trade balance is always in surplus, though we shall see that some items within it show a deficit.

The payment for many invisible services is often considerably delayed. Bank charges, for example, are paid retrospectively. Accordingly the authorities do not make a monthly estimate of the balance; they publish their figures on a quarterly basis.

Table 21.1   The United Kingdom Balance of Payments on current account, 1976–82 (£m)

	1976	1977	1978	1979	1980	1981	1982
Visible trade	−3 601	−1 744	−1 175	−3 458	+1 178	+3 008	+2 119
Invisible trade	+2 529	+2 115	+1 618	+2 595	+2 028	+3 539	+3 309
Current balance	−1 072	+ 371	+ 443	− 863	+3 206	+6 547	+5 428

(c) The Balance of Payments on Current Account

This is the name given to the visible balance and the invisible balance taken together. Sometimes there is a surplus, sometimes a deficit. The most recent figures are given in Table 21.1.

(d) Investment and Other Capital Flows

Many transactions between countries do not arise directly from the sale of goods, but from investments and loans of various kinds. Any of the following may be found under this heading.

(i) Overseas investment by private individuals or by companies in property or shares. If you buy a villa overseas your payment will appear in this part of the Balance of Payments, and will of course harm the Balance of Payments because money is leaving the country. The take-over of a British firm by an American company, on the other hand, brings money into the country, thereby benefiting the Balance of Payments. However, the benefit will only be temporary, because the profits made by the firm will be sent back to the USA. Such take-overs, therefore, while helping to keep our unemployment down, may ultimately have an adverse effect on our Balance of Payments.

(ii) Overseas investment by the Government or other public sector authorities. The Government may spend money on defence bases overseas; the nationalized industries may raise funds in foreign countries; other countries may build new embassies here. Each will have its affect on the Balance of Payments: if money comes into the country the Balance of Payments improves; if money leaves the country it deteriorates.

(iii) Repayment of loans and investments. While repayments of loans and investments appear in this part of the account, it is important to remember that any interest, dividend or rent resulting from investments appears in the current account as an invisible export. These are all treated as payment for the service provided by the capital.

(iv) Trade credit. If we export investment goods worth £1 million on credit this is equivalent to our lending £1 million to the importing country. It would appear as an outflow of capital in the account, while any credit we received on our imports would appear as an inflow of capital.

Taken together, the *Balance of Payments on current account* and the *investment and other capital flows* should give the overall Balance of Payments surplus or deficit. There is a further section of the accounts which provides a check on this, as we shall now see.

(e) Official Financing

We saw in Section 21.1 that when British residents buy goods from abroad the foreign currency is obtained from the Bank of England. Likewise, any foreign currency that is earned by exporters is deposited there. At the beginning of the year the Bank has a known amount of foreign currency (and gold) in its possession. If there is a Balance of Payments surplus of £100 million during the year the Bank's reserves should increase by £100 million, although they may use some of this money to repay past debts. If there is a deficit of £100 million, the Bank's holding of foreign currency should be reduced by the same amount, although in this case they may cover the deficit by borrowing. Either way, the official figures provide a check on the Balance of Payments surplus or deficit as shown by the first two accounts. There are normally three items which make up the official finance.

(i) **Transactions with the International Monetary Fund**. If we have a deficit we normally obtain some foreign currency from this organization which was established specially for this purpose: if there is a shortage of Deutsche Marks because too many people are buying German cars, we borrow Deutsche Marks from the fund, which are then placed at the disposal of importers needing German currency. In surplus years we are able to repay the Fund.

(ii) **Transactions with the central banks of other countries**. Again, in deficit years we borrow, in surplus years we lend.

(iii) **Changes in the foreign exchange reserves**. If the deficit or surplus is only small, the Government may decide to settle the difference by paying out of, or adding to, the foreign exchange reserves.

It is likely that a combination of all three methods would be used in a normal year and if all transactions were accurately recorded the items in the official finance would exactly balance the surplus or deficit in the other accounts. In practice the two sides do *not* usually balance. But while the official financing figures are known to be accurate, it is acknowledged that mistakes and over-sights sometimes occur in the other two accounts. In order to achieve a balance between the two sides, therefore, a balancing item equal to the difference between them is included. This simply represents the errors and omissions that have occurred.

21.3   The Performance in 1982

Table 21.2 summarizes the United Kingdom Balance of Payments trans-actions for 1982.

(a) There was a visible surplus of £2 119 million, to which was added the surplus on invisible trade of £3 309 million, giving a current account surplus of £5 428 million.

(b) Various kinds of investment in both directions resulted in a net outflow of funds of £2 851 million.

Table 21.2   The United Kingdom Balance of Payments, 1982

	£m	£m
Current account		
Visible exports	+55 546	
Visible imports	−53 427	
Visible balance		+2 119
Invisible exports	+31 724	
Invisible imports	−28 415	
		+3 309
Balance of Payments on current account		+5 428
Balance of investment items		−2 851
Overall Balance of Payments		+2 577
Official financing		
Repayments of loans to overseas central banks		− 137
Reduction in foreign currency reserves		+1 421
Balancing item		−3 861
		−2 577

(c) The current account and investment account together give a surplus of £2 577 million (£5 428 million − £2 851 million). This is the net amount of money flowing into the country as a result of international transactions.

(d) The official financing section of the account is used to show what happens to the surplus funds (or, in a deficit year, how the deficit is financed). To make the account balance we need to arrive at a total of −£2 577 million (in effect we have to cancel out the +£2 577 million). In 1982 £137 million was repaid to the central banks of other countries; this would have been borrowed in a previous deficit year. Normally with such a large surplus we would expect funds to be added to the foreign exchange reserves. However, in 1982 the reserves (for technical reasons which don't concern us) actually fell by £1 421 million. (In this part of the accounts a plus sign indicates a decrease in assets, a minus sign an increase.) Together these figures (+1 421 and −137) give us +1 284. The balancing item of −£3 861 million gives us the total of −£2 577 million. The balancing item is simply an indication of the errors and omissions which have occurred elsewhere in the accounts.

21.4 The Invisible Trade of the United Kingdom

The strongest part of the United Kingdom Balance of Payments is normally the
invisible trade account. As we saw in Section 21.3 it yielded an overall surplus
of £3 309 million in 1982. This disguises the fact that the Government itself
always has a large deficit while the private sector always has a surplus. Of
course the total value of invisible trade in each direction was much greater than
this. Table 21.3 shows the composition of invisible trade.

(a) Interest, Profits and Dividends

One of the most important items was interest, profits and dividends, which
brought £8 204 million into the country. Substantial as this amount is, it was
once much larger in relation to the rest of the Balance of Payments. But the
sale of many overseas investments during the war years naturally ended the
income from them. In other cases the nationalization of assets by overseas
governments has deprived the United Kingdom of income that would otherwise have been available. Frequently the compensation offered was only a
fraction of the true value of the assets seized.

Table 21.3   The United Kingdom invisible trade, 1982 (£m)

	Credits	Debits	Balance
Interest, profits and dividends	10 991	9 414	+1 577
Government services	435	1 239	− 804
Sea and air transport	6 036	5 988	+ 48
Travel	3 184	3 650	− 466
Transfers	3 151	5 263	−2 112
Other services	7 927	2 861	+5 066
	31 724	28 415	+3 309

(b) Government Expenditure

The Government's expenditure on invisible items was £1 239 million, while its
income was only £435 million. The expenditure was largely interest on accumulated borrowing, but also included substantial expenditure on the armed forces
overseas and diplomatic staff.

(c) Transport

This usually shows a modest surplus but does not significantly affect the

Balance of Payments, although large sums are involved. Shipping was once one of our strongest visible exports, but it has declined in importance as other countries have developed their own ocean-going fleets.

(d) Travel
This is an estimate of the amount spent in Britain by visitors from abroad and by United Kingdom residents travelling abroad. Between 60 per cent and 75 per cent of all travel expenditure is by tourists: British expenditure is centred on the Mediterranean countries, but most of our tourist revenue comes from United States citizens.

(e) Other Services
There are a number of services which make an important contribution to our overseas earnings. This item, which reflects the importance of the City of London, includes earnings from banking and insurance as well as the commission earned by brokers and agents acting on behalf of overseas clients. Many overseas residents run bank accounts in London, and many overseas companies hold insurance policies at Lloyd's: these services have to be paid for. Over the years London has built up a high reputation as a financial centre and, despite increasing competition from elsewhere, it continues to flourish, earning large sums of foreign currency in the process.

For many years the vital need to export has been acknowledged, and many Governments have given special incentives to manufacturers in export markets. But it was not until 1966 that the Committee on Invisible Exports was established specifically to consider ways of increasing invisible exports. Since then invisible exports have generally shared in the Government's export promotion schemes.

21.5 The United Kingdom Balance of Payments, 1950–1980

You can see from Fig. 21.1 that the current account balance varies enormously from year to year; however, the invisible account is always in surplus. The reasons for the fluctuations in the overall balance are properly the study of economics and can be pursued in *Success in Economics*.

While it is not appropriate to examine the causes of the fluctuations in the Balance of Payments here, we ought to consider the reaction of the Government to a persistent deficit. How do we turn a deficit into a surplus?

21.6 The Government and the Balance of Payments

We explained the reason for the Government's concern about the Balance of Payments in Section 21.1. It does not want the foreign currency reserves to be exhausted. But this is likely to occur if we persist in importing more than we export. Accordingly, when there is a deficit, the Government takes steps to correct it. There are a number of ways of doing this.

(a) Restricting Imports

The Government may decide that the best way to reduce the deficit is to impose restrictions on imports. Customs duties can be imposed to increase the price and therefore discourage people from buying. An alternative policy is to limit the *quantity* of goods imported, by a system of licensing.

(b) Encouraging Exports

Alternatively, the Government may decide that the main trouble is too few exports. It may intensify the export promotion schemes we discussed in Unit 19, but a more effective method of increasing exports is to *subsidize* exporters. A subsidy is a payment made to a producer to enable him to reduce his costs. By subsidizing exporters, the Government aims to reduce the price of exports and thus encourage their sale overseas.

However, imposing tariffs on imports and subsidizing exports mean that changes have to be made in international agreements, and the Government may prefer to rely on other methods.

(c) Increasing Taxes

If the Government increases the rate of income tax, it reduces the amount of money that each worker has to spend each week (unless, of course, people secure increases in their income to compensate for the extra tax). If people are spending less money, they buy fewer goods. Some of the goods they stop buying will be those produced by other countries, and others will embody raw materials from abroad. Gradually the amount we spend on imports will fall and the Balance of Payments will improve. But the Government hopes that the tax increases will have a more subtle effect. If we are buying fewer goods because we have less money, home producers will have stocks of finished goods left on their hands. They may try to sell them overseas, and if they are successful there will be a further improvement in the Balance of Payments.

There are difficulties about increasing income tax, or any other tax, and it doesn't always work as smoothly as this. Moreover the tax rise may have to be substantial before it has any effect.

(d) Reducing Borrowing

Since much expenditure is financed by various forms of borrowing, another way of reducing the volume of imports is to reduce the level of borrowing. This can be done either by increasing interest rates so that borrowing becomes more expensive, or by issuing instructions to the banks to lend less, or by increasing the restrictions on hire purchase and other credit transactions.

(e) Exchange Control

We saw earlier that if we want to buy goods abroad we must first obtain the appropriate foreign currency through the foreign exchange market. One way to reduce imports is to prevent residents from acquiring foreign currency. For some years after the Second World War it was almost impossible for residents

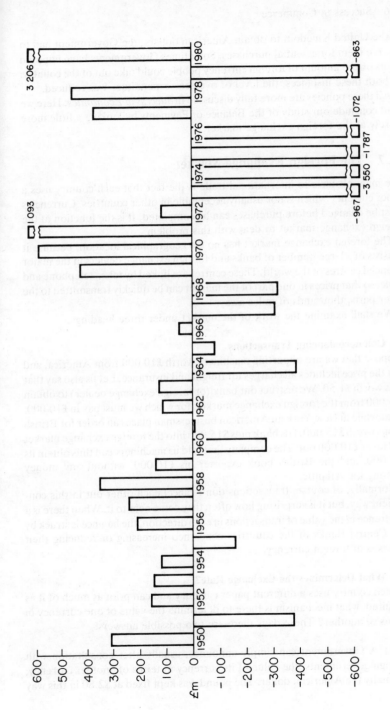

Fig. 21.1 *United Kingdom Balance of Payments on current account, 1950–80*

of the United Kingdom to obtain American dollars; the Government had to reserve them for essential purchases. Sometimes Governments have imposed limits on the amount of foreign currency people could take out of the country. In both these instances, the level of overseas expenditure was reduced.

All these policies are more fully discussed in *Success in Economics*. Here we shall conclude our study of the Balance of Payments by looking a little more closely at the foreign exchange market.

21.7   The Foreign Exchange Market

The main obstacle to international trade is the fact that each country uses a paper currency which is not usually acceptable in other countries. Currencies must be changed before purchases can be completed. It is the function of the foreign exchange market to deal with this problem.

The foreign exchange market has no set geographical location, because it consists of a large number of banks and foreign exchange dealers in the major financial centres of the world. These centres are linked by telex, telephone and cable, so that prices in one part of the market can be quickly transmitted to the other parts, thousands of miles away.

We shall examine the work of the market under three headings.

(a) Counterbalancing Transactions

Suppose that we are importing machinery worth £10 000 from America, and that the price includes all charges for freight and insurance. Let us also say that £1 is worth $1.50. We instruct our bank (or foreign exchange dealer) to obtain $15 000 from the foreign exchange market, for which we must pay in £10 000. Meanwhile in New York an American businessman places an order for British books worth $15 000. His bank puts $15 000 into the foreign exchange market and takes £10 000 out. The company that sold us machinery can thus obtain its $15 000, and the British book exporter his £10 000, without any money crossing the Atlantic.

Normally, of course, transactions don't cancel each other out in this convenient way, but it is surprising how often they come near to it. When there is a difference in the value of transactions in each direction, the balance is struck by the Central Banks of the countries concerned increasing or reducing their reserves of foreign currency.

(b) What Determines the Exchange Rate?

If each country uses a different paper currency and can print as much of it as required, what mechanism is there to determine the value of one currency in terms of another? These days there are two possible answers.

(i) A Government can simply announce, usually after consultation with foreign governments, the value of its currency in terms of another currency, normally the American dollar. The pound was kept fixed at $2.80 in this way from 1949–67. This was known as its *par value*, and the Bank of England had the task of maintaining the rate within very narrow limits on either side of this figure. This was done by the Exchange Equalization Account at the Bank of England which keeps the foreign exchange reserves (see Section 12.6).

If a large number of people wanted pounds to buy British goods, the value of the currency rose towards its permitted upper limit of $2.82. Just before it reached this level the Bank of England would offer to sell sterling at, perhaps $2.81⁷/₈. This would establish a maximum price, since nobody would buy from anyone else at a higher price if they could buy from the Bank of England at this price.

If very *few* people wanted sterling, but many wanted dollars to buy American exports, the price of sterling would fall towards its lower limit of $2.78. The Bank of England could prevent it reaching this level by offering to *buy* sterling at $2.78¹/₈, thereby establishing a minimum price.

How does the Government decide where to fix the exchange rate? Several techniques are used, including the *purchasing power parity theory*: a representative selection of goods is bought in the USA, and then the same selection is bought in Britain; if the goods cost $250 in the USA and £100 in Britain, the rate is fixed at $2.50 = £1. However, this is not as simple as it appears, because it is extremely difficult to produce perfectly corresponding selections of goods in two different countries.

(ii) An alternative to the Government fixing the rate in this way is to allow the forces of supply and demand to take over and determine the rate. This is the system of *floating exchange rates*. The value of a currency is then determined by what dealers are prepared to pay for it. If exports are worth more than imports, the currency will be in demand and will rise in value; if imports are worth more than exports, the currency will fall in value. If British importers put £100 000 into the foreign exchange market to buy dollars, and American importers put in $200 000 to buy pounds, the exchange rate is $2 = £1. A change in the pattern of trade will result in a different exchange rate. Since 1972 the Government has allowed market forces to influence the exchange rate while reserving the right to intervene. In recent years the rate against the US dollar has varied between 1.60 dollars and 2.00 dollars to the pound.

(c) Problems for Traders

We saw in Unit 20 that the existence of different currencies poses problems for exporters and importers which do not exist for those engaged in domestic trade. The difficulty is that the exchange rate may vary from time to time, and traders cannot therefore be sure of precisely how much they are going to receive, or pay, for goods until the actual day of payment.

Suppose that we agree to sell a £3 000 car to an American customer and, knowing that the exchange rate is $1.50=£1, we invoice him for $4 500. By the time the transaction is completed the rate has risen to $1.60=£1, and the $4 500 which the American importer has transferred to the foreign exchange market is now worth $4 500/1.60=£2 812.50. We receive less money than we had expected. (Of course if the rate had changed to $1.40=£1, we would have made an unexpected gain.) We *could* overcome the problem by invoicing the customer in sterling, but this only transfers the risk to him: if the rate rises to $1.60=£1, he must pay more than $4 500 to buy the car.

This kind of risk is greater during a period of floating exchange rates when the rate may *depreciate* (fall) or *appreciate* (rise) quite significantly in a matter of days. It also exists when rates are fixed by Governments, for they have the right to alter the par value without notice: a reduction in value is then known as *devaluation*, and an increase as *revaluation*.

Traders can avoid these risks by using the *forward exchange market*. When you buy foreign currency for immediate use you buy it at the *spot rate*, but it is possible to make arrangements in advance to buy at the *forward rate*. Suppose we know that in three months' time we shall need $2 500 to pay for goods we are importing, and we fear that the spot rate at that time will be only $1.40=£1, while it is $1.50=£1 today. We could agree with a foreign exchange dealer to buy $2 500 in three months at $1.50=£1, paying a small charge for the facility. If in three months' time the spot rate has fallen to $1.40=£1, we can still obtain dollars at the old rate, and thereby save money. (The risk is transferred to the bank or foreign exchange dealer.) The dealer will meanwhile have conducted a separate contract with someone else who wanted to *sell* $2 500 dollars at $1.50=£1, so the loss he makes on one deal is balanced by the gain on the other.

In this way the trader can be protected from the risks associated with floating exchange rates at a nominal cost, and any adverse effects that they might have on trade are eliminated. This is just one example of the way in which commercial institutions adapt themselves to changing circumstances.

21.8   Questions and Exercises

(a) Short Answers

1. Distinguish between (a) the Balance of Payments, (b) the Balance of Trade, (c) the Balance of Payments on current account.
2. What are the main invisible exports of the United Kingdom?
3. Name four measures that the Government may take to improve the Balance of Payments.
4. What is the foreign exchange market?
5. What is the Exchange Equalization Account?
6. What happens when a currency appreciates in value?
7. Explain what is meant by (a) forward rate, (b) spot rate.
8. In what way does the exchange rate involve an extra risk for traders?
9. How can they overcome this risk?
10. Why does the Government worry about the Balance of Payments?

(b) **Essay Answers**
1.   What is the Balance of Payments? Show how it is made up.
2.   What is the foreign exchange rate? Explain how it operates.
3.   Show how commercial services are important in the UK Balance of Payments.
4.   What contribution is made to the Balance of Payments by *(a)* Lloyd's, *(b)* the Merchant Navy?
5.   Explain the effect on the Balance of Payments of *(a)* a British businessman flying to the USA in an American plane, *(b)* a German company running a bank account in London, *(c)* the British Government giving £1 million to the Indian Government.

(c) **Assignment**
Obtain (from the *Annual Abstract of Statistics*) figures for Britain's trade with EEC countries from 1970 to 1980. Present this information on a diagram and describe the trends revealed.

Unit Twenty-two

The Government and Commerce

22.1 Introduction

In the United Kingdom, goods and services worth over £140 000 million are
produced each year to satisfy, directly or indirectly, the wants of 56 million
consumers. About 23 million people go to work to help produce the goods and
services, and they are employed in hundreds of thousands of different businesses whose main aim is to make a profit. If the Government were to stand back
and allow all the individual units in the economy to go their own way, distortions and abuses would probably appear.

Some services would not be provided at all, others might be available only
on a more selective basis than at present, consumers would be in an impossibly
weak position in relation to producers, employees might be heavily exploited
by employers, and so on. Our purpose in this Unit is to show the need for state
intervention in commerce, and to examine some of the ways in which it
happens.

22.2 The Need for Government Intervention

There are several important reasons for the Government involving itself in the
commercial life of the country.

(a) Many services are needed by everyone, or by many people, at the same
time. There is no way of charging individual consumers according to the
amount they consume. Defence, law enforcement and street lighting are
examples of services which are more or less unmarketable. They have to be
provided directly by the state with no extra charge to the individuals who
benefit directly. They are paid for by the community as a whole by means of
taxation (see Section 22.4).

(b) Some services which could be marketed in the ordinary way would be
too expensive to be bought by a large proportion of the population. Education
and the Health Service are prime examples. It is possible to pay for private
education and private medical treatment, but it is expensive. To ensure that
everyone can use these services, education is provided free, and medical
treatment very nearly so. This is clearly to the benefit of the individuals who
would otherwise not be able to afford to use the services. It is also to the
advantage of society as a whole that its members should be well educated and
healthy.

(c) The state itself markets some goods and services, mainly through the public corporations, but also in other ways, which we examined in Unit 9. Most if not all of these could just as well be sold by private enterprise, but by establishing gigantic public corporations the Government aims to provide more comprehensive services than would be available if left to the private sector firms.

(d) The state frequently intervenes in a supervisory capacity, as we have seen on many occasions in this book. All kinds of legislation govern the economic and commercial life of the country. We shall remind ourselves of some of them in Section 22.6.

(e) Some firms and industries need assistance if they are to remain in business. It is quite normal for Governments to make grants or tax concessions to them; alternatively subsidies may be given. Sometimes an industry finds that it cannot compete with the products of overseas rivals: here the Government may impose tariffs on the competitors' products, or prohibit their import altogether. British agriculture and coal mining have often received this kind of help.

(f) Every Government has its own economic as well as political objectives, and the achievement of these may require further state interference in commerce. To take one example, the level of unemployment is usually higher in the northern parts of the country than in the south-east. To redress the balance the Government offers special incentives to firms to build new factories in the areas of high unemployment, and it may make special payments to them when they begin production.

The majority of these activities are for the benefit of the community in general and they must be paid for by the community. The Government therefore has to impose taxes to finance its expenditure. Before we consider the various taxes let us look briefly at the main items of Government expenditure.

22.3   Government Expenditure

Table 22.1 shows the main areas of Government expenditure, both central and local, in 1982.

The total of £115 000 million is equivalent to almost 50 per cent of the expenditure of the country as a whole. The largest single item was National Insurance benefits, which took over £32 000 million. Expenditure on roads and industrial services came to over £7 000 million, and this is of the greatest importance to commerce. The overall benefits to commerce from Government are much greater than this. Capital expenditure on the actual building of roads is frequently several billion pounds a year, and in addition subsidies are paid to allow the railway network to survive. Commercial life is dependent upon transport and could not function without the road and rail networks provided or subsidized by the state.

Table 22.1   Government expenditure, 1982 (current account)

		£m
Purchase of goods and services		57 877
e.g. Education	11 008	
Defence	14 323	
National Health Service	13 122	
Subsidies and grants		43 465
e.g. National Insurance benefits	31 914	
Debt interest		14 265
Balance: current surplus		196
Total		115 803

22.4   Government Income

Table 22.2 shows the Government's income in 1982, and again we include local as well as central Government.

Table 22.2   Government income, 1982 (current account)

		£m
Taxes on income		40 300
e.g. Income tax	32 304	
Corporation tax	5 861	
Taxes on expenditure		47 082
e.g. Excise duties	11 988	
VAT	14 255	
Local authority rates	12 098	
National Insurance contributions		18 069
Rent + Trading surplus		4 991
Interest and dividends		5 361
Total		115 803

(*a*) **Taxes on Income and Capital**
These are *direct* taxes, which means that they are paid directly to the Government by the person on whom they are levied.

(i) **Income tax**. This is a progressive tax, which has a levelling effect on incomes. For the 1984/5 tax year the first £2 005 of a single person's income is free of tax, while the married allowance is £3 155. After deducting any other allowances from his gross income the citizen pays tax of 30 per cent on the first £15 400, up to a maximum of 60 per cent on taxable income over £38 100.

Most people pay their income tax through the PAYE system (Pay As You Earn): their employer is given a set of tax tables by the Inland Revenue. Each person has a code number related to the rate of tax he should pay, and the employer deducts the appropriate amount of tax by reference to the code number and the level of income of the individual.

Although no one actually enjoys paying tax, most people would rather pay by this method than by a lump sum every half year, as self-employed people do.

(ii) **Corporation tax**. Limited companies have to pay corporation tax on their profits at the rate of 45 per cent. They are, however, allowed to make several deductions from their gross profits before arriving at their taxable profits, and companies whose profits do not exceed £100 000 pay at the rate of 30 per cent.

(iii) **Other direct taxes** include the capital transfer tax, levied when property over a certain value is given away or passed to a new owner at death, and the capital gains tax, levied on the profit made by selling capital assets.

(*b*) **Taxes on Expenditure**
The other taxes that we pay are related to the money we spend, and are called *indirect taxes*, since the person who effectively pays them – the consumer – does not pay the Government direct.

(i) **Excise duties** are imposed principally on tobacco, petroleum products and alcohol. These are specific taxes (so much per unit), imposed at the point of production and later included in the price paid by the final consumer.

(ii) **Value Added Tax (VAT)** is a comprehensive sales tax which applies to almost every transaction involving the sale of goods and services. It was introduced in 1973, at a rate of 10 per cent, but is now levied at a uniform rate of 15 per cent. To illustrate the operation of VAT, let us look at a simplified example, taking the rate as 10 per cent and ignoring overheads and other costs.

A forester produces timber and sells it to a carpenter for £300. The carpenter makes the wood into tables and sells them to wholesalers for £500. The wholesaler sells the tables to retailers for £550 and they are finally sold to consumers for £650. If we introduce a 10 per cent VAT, the picture changes.

As the value of the timber sold is £300, the tax payable is £30, so the forester will charge the carpenter a total of £330, remitting the £30 tax to the Government. When the carpenter sells the tables, worth £500, he adds £50 VAT to the bill. Before he remits the tax to the Government he deducts his input tax (the £30 he paid the forester). Thus he sends the Government £20 (50 − 30). The wholesalers charge £605 when they sell the tables (550 + 55) and send the Government £5 (55 − 50). Retailers sell the tables for £715 (650 + 65) and send the Government £10 (65 − 55).

In all the Government receives £65 (30 + 20 + 5 + 10), but instead of receiving it from one producer or wholesaler, as with excise duties, it receives varying amounts from different sources. But the burden of tax is all on the final consumer.

Most goods and services are subject to VAT – at present 15 per cent – but there are some that are *zero-rated* (taxed at 0 per cent) and some that are exempt from the tax altogether. The difference between these last two categories is that the seller of zero-rated goods is able to reclaim any input tax that he has paid on raw materials or components, while the seller of exempted goods cannot. Thus the VAT on components used in exempted goods is still carried forward to consumers.

(iii) Rates. Local authorities levy rates on the estimated rental value of property within their area. They are included here as expenditure taxes because the property occupier is regarded as spending money in rent to occupy the property.

(c) National Insurance Contributions

All employees and their employers contribute jointly to the National Insurance by paying National Insurance dues every week. In this way they finance unemployment benefit, sickness benefit, old age pensions and other social security payments.

(d) Trading Income

This does not contribute very much to Government income, since most of the Government's trading activities have been handed over to the public corporations. (Their income is not included in Table 22.2.) Local authorities have some income from trading when they operate local bus services, car parks and recreational facilities such as swimming pools.

The Government's raising of money through taxation affects commerce in two ways. First, all commercial organizations have to pay some tax to the Government. Limited companies pay corporation tax, and partnerships and sole proprietors pay income tax on their profits. Second, most firms have to act as unpaid tax collectors for the Government. As we have seen, they are responsible for the deduction of income tax from their employees' wages and salaries, and large firms have to employ staff specially to do this. They also have to keep detailed records, so that VAT can be properly assessed, and extra staff may be required for this too.

This problem of unpaid work on behalf of the Government is a serious one for the small firm working on a very narrow profit margin. Nor is it only a question of taxation: the Government often makes inquiries and sends requests for information concerning output. All this takes time, which the small firm can scarcely afford.

However, much of the information collected by the Government is ultimately to the benefit of the firms themselves, as we shall see in Section 22.5.

22.5   The Services of the Government

Apart from the vital services provided by the nationalized industries, which we discussed in Section 9.1, there are three main ways in which the Government helps commerce. It provides information services, it sets up co-ordinating bodies and it often gives direct financial help.

(a) Information Services

Government departments provide a wide range of information, and we have already seen some examples. The main sources from which information is currently available are as follows.

(i) The British Overseas Trade Board in conjunction with the Department of Trade provides a comprehensive intelligence service to exporters seeking opportunities overseas.

(ii) The Department of Industry publishes its weekly *Trade and Industry* which gives details of industrial developments, changes in regulations and new techniques.

(iii) The Department of Employment publishes information about employment, wages, prices, changes in the conditions of employment and new legislation which concerns employers.

(iv) On a more general basis the Government publishes its *Monthly Digest of Statistics*, *Financial Statistics* and *Economic Trends*, each containing a wealth of information which can be of use to industry and commerce.

(v) The Central Office of Information issues many publications, including reports on particular industries and areas. It also runs an intelligence service which answers individual inquiries from commerce and industry and, indeed, from private individuals.

(b) Co-ordinating Bodies

When necessary the Government can set up a body to assist industry and commerce in general or a particular branch of industry.

(i) The British Overseas Trade Board, which we mentioned above, is an obvious example of such a body (see Section 19.8).

(ii) The Export Credits Guarantee Department is another example of an organization established specially to help business people (Section 19.11).

(iii) The National Economic Development Council consists of members of Government, industry and trade unions. It meets regularly to discuss the problems of the economy and likely developments within it.

(iv) Perhaps even more useful to individual firms are the associated Economic Development Committees, which study the structure and problems of individual industries.

(v) Industrial Training Boards, financed partly by the Government, exist to promote a better trained work force in many industries. (The Boards will be reduced in number by April 1983.)

(vi) In 1975 the National Enterprise Board was set up to promote and finance improvements in efficiency. It became part of the British Technology Group in 1981.

(vii) There are in addition innumerable *ad hoc* bodies set up to study the problems of particular industries. Normally Government inspired, these bodies include representatives of both sides of industry. Some are established to solve a particular problem such as a wages dispute, while others have a more permanent existence as a kind of standing advisory body. The Committee on Invisible Exports is an example of the latter kind.

(c) Financial Assistance

There are a number of different ways in which the Government may provide financial assistance.

(i) Assistance through the Industrial and Commercial Finance Corporation for capital projects which do not justify a new issue of shares.

(ii) Tax concessions to firms investing in new machinery and factories.

(iii) Subsidies to firms creating jobs in areas of high unemployment.

(iv) A contribution towards the cost of training workers in some areas.

(v) Grants to firms for particular purposes.

(vi) Subsidies to enable essential firms to stay in business.

In all these ways the Government pursues the objectives of efficiency and a stable economy with full employment. But these objectives cannot be achieved simply by advisory and financial assistance. If businessmen are left alone to make profits and follow their own self-interest, distortions appear in the economy which may be to the disadvantage of many people. Sometimes, therefore, legislation is necessary to correct existing abuses or to prevent other abuses developing.

22.6   Legislation and Commerce

We have seen that legislation is necessary to protect consumers from exploitation, and to control the terms of hire purchase agreements. There are many other areas in which the Government has found it necessary to pass laws to safeguard the interests of the public and of the economy in general.

(a) Location of Industry

One area of commerce and industry where Government controls have proved necessary has been in the location of economic activity. The principal reason for Government action here was, and still is, to try to reduce the level of unemployment in the old industrial areas of Britain. Left to themselves firms locate new plant in the areas most profitable to them. This leads to overcrowding in prosperous areas and depopulation in poorer and less attractive areas. Since 1934 the Government has introduced a number of measures designed to attract industry to these depressed areas. The measures fall into three groups:

(i) **Financial inducements** such as those we mentioned in the last Section. The exact nature of these inducements varies, but their intention is always the same: to reduce the costs facing firms and thereby make the new location attractive to them. The Department of Industry publishes a handbook setting out the assistance available and showing some of the companies that have moved successfully to the *Development Areas*, as they are called.

(ii) **Physical controls** are imposed on industrial location. Any development of 3 000 square feet or more requires the approval of the Department of Industry in the form of an *Industrial Development Certificate*. Without this it cannot go ahead, so the Department can exercise a negative control over location. What it cannot do, however, is *force* firms to locate in a particular area. (This scheme was suspended in December 1981.)

(iii) **Local regulations** are also important. Once a firm has decided which area it wants to go to, it needs planning permission from the local authority. There are detailed regulations to ensure that residential or rural areas are not spoilt by unnecessary factory building.

Until 1965 the Government's efforts in relation to location were concentrated on industrial developments. Office location was not closely controlled. But in 1965 the Office Development Act was passed in an attempt to move offices out of London. The attractions of London have, however, proved too strong, and very little decentralization has taken place. The Government does its best to set a good example: several Government departments have been moved to the provinces, such as National Savings, Motor Vehicle Registration and Inland Revenue Centres. Private firms have been reluctant to follow, despite publicity given to the attractions of alternative sites by central Government and local authorities.

(b) Monopoly

A monopolist is the single seller of a product who has no competitors. In practice they are difficult to find, but Governments have long been on their guard against firms who dominate particular industries. Today in Britain any firm that produces 25 per cent of the output of an industry is regarded as a monopolist.

Since 1948 there has been legislation to curb the activities of monopolists and, in particular, groups of firms acting together to exploit consumers. Responsibility for implementation of the policy now rests with the Director-General of Fair Trading (see Section 7.4), and the policy itself is embodied in the Restrictive Practices Act 1956, the Fair Trading Act 1973 and the Competition Act 1980. Under the legislation the Restrictive Practices Court adjudicates upon cases where companies are suspected of combining together to act against the public interest and the Monopolies and Mergers Commission investigates individual firms suspected of acting unfairly.

(c) Labour

In recent years there has been much legislation dealing with the status and functions of trade unions, who exist to safeguard the working conditions of their members. The Industrial Relations Act of 1971 caused difficulties which many trade unions regarded as an attempt to curb their powers.

There are further examples of the way the state intervenes to control anomalies, apart from trade union legislation. Labour is affected by the *Factory Acts*, which lay down regulations about hours of work, conditions of work, safety procedures and so on. The Equal Pay Act required that women doing similar work to men should receive the same rate of pay from the end of 1975.

(d) Companies

As we saw in Unit 8, companies are closely controlled by the Companies Acts. The way in which companies are formed, their behaviour once they are formed and their rights and obligations are all carefully set out in the interests of shareholders, suppliers and customers. Company finance is so complicated and the opportunities for fraud so great that tight control is essential if people are to be persuaded to invest in, and deal with, limited companies.

There are other areas in which the state has to legislate, in our system of commerce. We have looked at some of the most important areas, but the whole scene provides scope for more detailed and specialized study. State legislation in commerce can be very much a matter of controversy, and each student will learn to form his own judgments. What is quite certain is that without certain rules being made and enforced by the state, our system of commerce could not exist and flourish at all.

22.7 Questions and Exercises

(a) Short Answers

1. Give four reasons why it is necessary for the Government to intervene in the commercial life of the community.
2. What are the main items of Government expenditure?
3. What are the main sources of Government income?
4. Name four publications produced by the Government to assist people in business.

5. What financial help can businesses expect from the Government?
6. Give two reasons why the Government seeks to control the location of industry.
7. What is a monopolist? Why does the Government control the activities of monopolists?
8. What legislation controls the activities of limited companies?
9. Why is it necessary to protect the shareholders of companies?
10. Name three Acts of Parliament which are designed to protect consumers.

(b) Essay Answers

1. Give examples to show how and why the Government intervenes in the commercial life of the country with respect to (a) transport, (b) international trade.
2. What commercial activities are undertaken by the Government? Give examples to show why these activities are necessary.
3. Explain what abuses might occur if the Government did not control the activities of (a) advertisers, (b) road haulage operators, (c) hire purchase financers. By what means do they control each of these groups?
4. Name four ways in which the Government provides assistance to people in business and explain the need for this help.

(c) Projects

1. Keep a record of legislation passed by Parliament this year affecting commercial activities.
2. Make a scrapbook of news cuttings recording Government intervention in industry and commerce.

Suggested Further Reading

General

Britain: an Official Handbook. Published annually by HMSO (London).
The Monthly Digest of Statistics. HMSO (London).

Consumer Protection

The Buyer's Right. Consumers' Association (London, 1978).
Annual Report of the Office of Fair Trading. HMSO (London).

Nationalized Industries

Annual reports of the public corporations.
Consumers and the Nationalized Industries. National Consumer Council (London, 1976).

Limited Companies

Annual reports of public companies.

Money and Banking

Cox, D.: *Success in Elements of Banking*. John Murray (London, 2nd edn. 1983).
Understanding Banking. Bank Education Service (London, 1981).

The Capital Market

Clarke, W.M.: *Inside the City*. Allen & Unwin (London, 1979).
Berman, H.D.: *The Stock Exchange*. Pitman (London, 1971).
Winfield, R.G. and Curry, S.J.: *Success in Investment*. John Murray (London, 2nd edn. 1985).

Advertising

Advertising and Public Relations in Britain. HMSO (London, 1976).
Evans, W.A.: *Advertising Today and Tomorrow*. Allen & Unwin (London, 1974).

Transport

British Industry Today: Freight Transport (Central Office of Information Reference Pamphlet R5900/79). HMSO (London, 1979).

Insurance

Diacon, S.R. and Carter, R.L.: *Success in Insurance*. John Murray (London, 1984).

International Trade

Swann, D.: *The Economics of the Common Market*. Penguin Books (Harmondsworth, 1978).
Whiting, D.P.: *International Trade and Payments*. Macdonald and Evans (Plymouth, 1978).

Index